INTERCULTURALISM:
A VIEW FROM QUEBEC

GÉRARD BOUCHARD

Translated by Howard Scott
Foreword by Charles Taylor

Accommodating ethnic diversity is a major challenge for all democratic nations and a topic that has attracted a great deal of attention in the last few decades. Within Quebec, a new approach has emerged that seeks a balance between the needs of minorities and those of the majority.

In *Interculturalism*, sociologist and historian Gérard Bouchard presents his vision of interculturalism as a model for the management of diversity. A pluralist approach which recognizes the existence of a cultural majority whose rights must also be acknowledged, interculturalism constitutes an important alternative to multiculturalism both in Canada and internationally. Written by one of Canada's leading public intellectuals and the co-chair of the Bouchard-Taylor Commission on reasonable accommodation, *Interculturalism* is the first clear and comprehensive statement in English of an approach being discussed around the world.

A translation of Bouchard's award-winning French-language work, *L'Interculturalisme: Un point de vue québécois*, this book features a new foreword by philosopher Charles Taylor and an afterword by the author written specifically for the English-language edition.

GÉRARD BOUCHARD is the Canada Research Chair in Collective Imaginaries at the Université du Québec à Chicoutimi. The author or editor of more than forty books, he was the co-chair with Charles Taylor of the Government of Quebec's Consultation Commission on Accommodation Practices Related to Cultural Differences, better known as the Bouchard-Taylor Commission.

Interculturalism

A View from Quebec

GÉRARD BOUCHARD

Translated by Howard Scott

UNIVERSITY OF TORONTO PRESS
Toronto Buffalo London

Originally published in French as *L'Interculturalisme: Un point de vue québécois*
© Éditions du Boréal 2012

English-language edition
© University of Toronto Press 2015
Toronto Buffalo London
www.utppublishing.com
Printed in the U.S.A.

ISBN 978-1-4426-4776-3 (cloth)
ISBN 978-1-4426-1584-7 (paper)

Printed on acid-free, 100% post-consumer recycled paper with vegetable-based inks.

Library and Archives Canada Cataloguing in Publication

Bouchard, Gérard, 1943–
[Interculturalisme. English]
Interculturalism : a view from Quebec / Gérard Bouchard ; translated by Howard Scott.

Translation of : L'interculturalisme. Includes bibliographical references and index.
ISBN 978-1-4426-4776-3 (bound). ISBN 978-1-4426-1584-7 (pbk.)

1. Cultural pluralism. 2. Multiculturalism. 3. Laicism. 4. Cultural pluralism – Québec
(Province). 5. Multiculturalism – Québec (Province). 6. Reasonable accommodation –
Québec (Province). I. Scott, Howard, 1952–, translator II. Title.
III. Title: Interculturalisme. English.

HM1271.B6813 2015   305.8009714   C2014-905159-X

This book has been published with the help of a grant from the Federation for
the Humanities and Social Sciences, through the Awards to Scholarly Publications
Program, using funds provided by the Social Sciences and Humanities Research Council
of Canada.

University of Toronto Press acknowledges the financial assistance to its publishing
program of the Canada Council for the Arts and the Ontario Arts Council, an agency
of the Ontario government.

Canada Council   Conseil des Arts
for the Arts   du Canada

ONTARIO ARTS COUNCIL
CONSEIL DES ARTS DE L'ONTARIO
an Ontario government agency
un organisme du gouvernement de l'Ontario

University of Toronto Press acknowledges the financial support of the Government
of Canada through the Canada Book Fund for its publishing activities.

University of Toronto Press acknowledges the financial support of the Government
of Canada through the National Translation Program for Book Publishing for its
translation activities.

Contents

Foreword

This book, by the Quebec sociologist and historian Gérard Bouchard, who was co-chair with me of the Quebec Commission on Accommodation Practices, marks an important milestone in the international discussion on how our increasingly diversified societies can become, or remain, both integrated and egalitarian.

It is a book about interculturalism, the Quebec term for the range of policies that are aimed at achieving this goal.

In the first place, cutting loose from the overheated and confused polemics around the two terms, it clarifies the distinction between interculturalism and multiculturalism, and shows why the first suits Quebec, the second the rest of Canada (chapter 3). It sees interculturalism as suitable to a situation in which there is still a historic cultural majority, which has later been joined by, and is still receiving, people of other, diverse backgrounds. This is, of course Quebec's situation today, but no longer that of Canada as a whole, or of the rest of Canada. But what makes the discussion in this book of wider relevance is that this is arguably the predicament in some Western European countries that have in recent decades become immigrant societies *malgré eux.*

The book combines in an interesting way two streams of argument: the first could be called "Quebec-directed"; the second is of more immediately evident relevance to other similar societies. But the line between the two is neither hard and fast nor immoveable. The first stream addresses the cultural fears that arose during the debate around reasonable accommodations in 2007–2008, and which are being mobilized by the present PQ government behind its "charter of secularism" (or of Quebec values, or whatever) – which Bouchard vigorously opposes.

(And this is why the line between the two directions is not fast or final, because analogous fears are arising in certain West European countries).

The main thrust of the Quebec-directed arguments can be seen in chapters 2 and 4. In the first, Bouchard raises the development of the notion of interculturalism in the Quebec context. In the second, he defends his formula against a wide array of critics.

But the main positive thrust of interculturalism could perhaps be summed up in this goal: bring it about that successive waves of immigrants come to see themselves as co-authors of the culture of the host society that will receive and integrate their successors. In this light, we can see why any widely held judgment of a minority culture as in essence alien and inassimilable will thwart this goal. As Bouchard puts it, the distinction between the majority culture and minority cultures must be "without any formal hierarchical connotation."

The crucial process is one in which the different cultures meet and fertilize each other. In this regard, anything that keeps them in separate compartments, any ghettoization, will obstruct the goal. This is the semantic force of the "inter" in interculturalism. Contact and exchange are essential. But to make this possible, both government and society have to discover and maintain a series of equilibria, and avoid extremes that would derail the process. Bouchard enumerates these in chapter 2. Discovering these equilibria is both particularly important and especially delicate in Quebec, because of its situation as "a small francophone nation, and as a minority culture on the continent." In a sense Quebec is challenged constantly to act with greater confidence and self-assurance than its people feels. That it should feel tempted to fall short of this is not surprising, but Bouchard shows that there is already an existing tradition of Quebec interculturalism that is ready to rise to the occasion.

Chapter 5 is devoted to a crucial discussion of secularism. This is most emphatically part of the argument that is of wider relevance. It is striking how throughout the Western world cultural fears in the face of immigration have tended to be coded in terms of religion. This has been exacerbated by the geopolitical situation, and the rise of Islamophobia in the West, which is in many cases fostered by think tanks and other organizations dedicated to spreading it. Bouchard offers an account in this chapter of an "inclusive secularism," which could offer a model for many Western societies. This kind of what is often called "open secularism" is not a new invention to answer the current crisis. It has roots in our past, both deep and embedded in the original situation of the Conquest, and also issuing from decisions in the last decades.

In these and in other ways, Gérard Bouchard's book not only casts a great deal of light on the Quebec situation, but will nourish an increasingly transnational debate. It will help to clarify and carry the argument further in this domain where short-sighted polemics and ugly appeals to exclusion have bulked altogether too large. Once again, our intra-Canadian debates will have opened avenues for others.

Charles Taylor
January 2014

Acknowledgments

During the writing of this book, I benefited greatly from exchanges with François Fournier, Céline Saint-Pierre, Geneviève Nootens, Pierre Bosset, Geneviève Baril, Michel Venne, François Rocher, Alain Roy, Charles Taylor, Daniel Weinstock, Will Kymlicka, Michel Seymour, Alain-G. Gagnon, Patricia Rimok, and many other colleagues. I am also hugely indebted to many researchers at the Council of Europe and the European Union with whom I had lengthy discussions on the issues dealt with here. As usual, however, I am entirely responsible for the content of the book. For my preparatory work, I received financial support from the Canada Research Chairs program of the Canadian Institute for Advanced Research (CIFAR) and the Fondation de l'Université du Québec à Chicoutimi.

INTERCULTURALISM:
A VIEW FROM QUEBEC

Introduction

Managing ethnocultural diversity is a challenge for all democratic nations.[1] This challenge can be summed up as follows: how can we arbitrate relationships between cultures in a way that ensures a future for the culture of the host society – that is, its history, its values, and its profound aspirations – and that at the same time accommodates diversity while respecting the rights of everyone, in particular the rights of immigrants and members of minorities, who, in this relationship, are usually the most vulnerable citizens? This has been, as we all know, one aspect of the enormous restructuring of modern societies that has occurred over recent decades in order to eliminate marginalization, reinvent democracy, and rebalance the power relationships between classes, genders, generations, and regions, all in a context of globalization.

Discussions in Quebec on this subject are far from new, and have often been energetic and original. As elsewhere, these discussions arise out of a desire to protect the rights and ensure the integration of all citizens. Within the majority culture (this concept is defined in chapter 2), it is also motivated by legitimate concerns about the future of that culture's identity and heritage. On the whole, Quebecers have made significant progress during the last half century in the management of diversity: the Charter of Human Rights and Freedoms, Law 101,[2] the gradual development of an original model (interculturalism), openness to immigration, the democratic nature of debates, and the denunciation of racism; these are all elements and points of reference that are characteristic of developments in Quebec and that allow us to be optimistic about the future.

But in Quebec as elsewhere, all this work of harmonizing diversity is not immune to tensions and setbacks, since it involves the encounter of identities, traditions, beliefs, and profound allegiances. This inevitably leads to reactions and debates in which emotion plays a major role along with reason, and there have always been perspectives and aspirations that have differed and even clashed. I believe there is a need for a difficult arbitration focusing on the search for a delicate balance between competing imperatives, the search for formulas of mutual adjustment that establish modus vivendi while safeguarding the capital of memory, values, and ideals that are essential to the functioning of a society.

This arbitration will also call for all the precautions and humility that must surround the quest for a general model of integration, a quest that is carried out from four perspectives: the sensitivity that must be shown towards citizens, their freedom of choice, their rights; consideration of the demands of collective life, with its own constraints and imperatives; awareness of the stake involved, as illustrated by a review of the serious abuses that marked the twentieth century; and flexibility to be observed in the conception of the model given the rapid changes most societies are currently undergoing, especially in an era of globalization.

Keeping these considerations in mind, I propose, within the framework of this essay, to first of all present my vision of interculturalism as a model for integration and the management of ethnocultural diversity in all its forms: the diversity contributed by immigrants, the diversity of minorities, and the diversity of the majority.[3] For this purpose, I will draw inspiration from the developments that have taken place in Quebec society since the 1960s and 1970s,[4] but also from discussions and experiments in Europe, where the interculturalist approach, as a formula for coexistence in a context of diversity, has deep roots.[5]

In Quebec itself, interculturalism currently enjoys broad support in the population, as shown by the public hearings of the Bouchard-Taylor Commission.[6] The vast majority of the briefs and submissions presented to the commission took a position in favour of this model as being the approach to follow for Quebec, even though the definitions they proposed for interculturalism were generally rather limited. However, a strong consensus emerged on three points: (a) the rejection of Canadian multiculturalism, (b) the rejection of assimilation,[7] and (c) the importance of integration on the basis of the fundamental values of Quebec society. Nevertheless, interculturalism is now the subject of important examinations and criticisms. There certainly remains a great deal of work to be done in the clarification, promotion, and application of this model.

It should also be remembered with respect to the management of diversity that there is no general solution that can be transferred from one society to another. Of course, any model is constructed on the basis of postulates and basic orientations that can travel more easily. But when it comes to the connections and corollaries that can be drawn from them, each nation has to design for itself a formula that is fully in accord with its heritage, institutions, constraints, sensibilities, concerns, and aspirations. The same can be said for values, and the universal ideals of equality, social justice, democracy, and pluralism. In order to avoid setting abstract, disembodied objectives without much relation to particular contexts, each society has to develop its own application, its own configuration.[8] What I present in this book is a version of interculturalism as integrative pluralism, among other possible versions.

I have already mentioned pluralism. This concept is understood here in a very general sense, as an orientation that advocates respect for diversity and the right of all citizens to cultivate, if they so desire, a more or less narrow reference to their ethnocultural (majority or minority) groups of origin, as long as this is compatible with the fundamental rules and values of a society. Pluralism therefore assumes that the cultural roots of citizens are taken into account, it condemns any form of discrimination based on the characteristics or the distinct cultural traits or orientations of a person, and it calls for great sensitivity to the rights of minorities. It can, however, be applied in various ways and be based on more than one model (multiculturalism, interculturalism, republicanism ...). Finally, pluralism should not be confused with plurality or cultural plurality, which is synonymous with diversity. Pluralism is a normative concept, while plurality is a simple state of fact. I will come back to this in chapter 3.

In Quebec, the pluralist orientation and the original application proposed by interculturalism have been subject to various criticisms, being accused of:

- establishing a civic nation regime that reduces life in society to nothing but legal rules
- accepting without distinction all values and customs (a "laissez-faire" regime of "wholesale relativism")
- sanctifying individual rights at the expense of collective imperatives
- forcing the host society to give up its fundamental values, its traditions, its identity
- rejecting the past of the francophone majority, thus sweeping aside national history
- obliging the majority to adapt to the minorities, rather than the other way around

- being a disguised form or a Trojan Horse of Canadian multiculturalism
- endangering social cohesion and national identity

These criticisms have been formulated by many authors, but a kind of compendium of them can be found in M. Bock-Côté (2007) and J. Facal (2009; 2010, chap. 3) as well as in the writings of Mario Roy, editorialist at the *La Presse* newspaper, and Christian Rioux, a columnist for the newspaper *Le Devoir*. This book will show, however, that there is no basis for any of these claims.

A second objective of this book is to meet a pressing need that is currently felt in Quebec. The recent debates around secularism, pluralism, the future of francophone identity, the protection of fundamental values, and accommodations for religious reasons have revealed in various ways the existence of significant uneasiness. In the area of the management of diversity, many citizens perceive a lack of clear references, norms, and orientations for those who are required to make day-to-day decisions in public and private institutions. Obviously, in this respect, the work of the Bouchard-Taylor Commission did not live up to everyone's expectations. This essay is intended to contribute to overcoming the atmosphere of uncertainty and to describe a possible road to the future for all Quebecers.

For a society that is going through rapid changes, it is useful to have a coherent vision of what it wants to be, of the links it wants to establish between its members, and of the representations and values it wishes to promote. From this point of view, the role played by multiculturalism in English-speaking Canada, by the tradition of the "melting pot" in the United States, by the republican regime in France, and by the discourse on cultural mixing in many countries in Latin America can provide useful examples. Finally, the reflection on approaches to collective integration finds its relevance in the fact that many nations in the world are currently coming to terms with new forms of immigration[9] and the enormous challenges they pose for democracy.

A third objective consists of challenging a certain number of misunderstandings and distortions that have created confusion in the debate on interculturalism, particularly in Quebec. I will therefore attempt to show the following:

- Collective integration is a comprehensive process that concerns all citizens and components of a society, and not only the integration of immigrants.

- Interculturalism is founded on a principle of reciprocity. Newcomers and members of the host society therefore share an important responsibility.
- Interculturalism seeks a model of coexistence that avoids both assimilation and fragmentation or segmentation.
- Interculturalism is not a disguised ("devious," some would say) form of multiculturalism.[10]
- As long as they are applied with discernment and rigour, pluralism (as an orientation advocating respect for diversity) and in particular the principle of recognition (as defined by Charles Taylor and others) do not lead to relativism and do not compromise social cohesion.[11] They are completely compatible with the imperatives of integration and the promotion of the fundamental values of the host society.
- Pluralism should be seen as a general orientation that can be applied in various ways corresponding to various models. Multiculturalism is one of these models. It would therefore be a mistake to make an exclusive link between these two concepts by presenting them as synonyms.
- The type of pluralism advocated by interculturalism can be described as integrative to the extent that (a) it takes into account the context and the future of both the majority culture and the cultural minorities, and (b) it proposes a way of linking these two components.[12]
- Accommodations (or collaborative adjustments) are not privileges, they do not lead to the creation of special rights, they are not devised solely for immigrants and members of minorities, and they should not lead to the spread of values, beliefs, or practices that are contrary to the fundamental, legitimate norms of the society. They are simply aimed at ensuring that in a spirit of equity all citizens, whatever their characteristics or cultural affiliations, enjoy the same rights.
- Interculturalism, as a pluralist model, is concerned with both the interests of the cultural majority, whose desire to survive and assert itself is completely legitimate, and the interests of minorities and immigrants. There should therefore be no opposition between, on the one hand, the defenders of the identity and traditions of the majority and, on the other hand, the defenders of the rights of minorities and immigrants. It is possible and necessary to combine in a single process of affiliation and development the identity aspirations of the majority and a pluralist orientation.
- Except in rare circumstances, rigid, radical solutions are rarely suitable to deal with the problems raised by ethnocultural diversity; hence the emphasis that interculturalism places on the search for balance and equilibrium.

A fourth objective is to present a definition of interculturalism that is distinguished from previous definitions by paying more attention to the social dimension of integration. While proposals made since the end of the 1970s have sometimes emphasized the cultural dimension and sometimes the civic dimension, my intention here is to develop a model that combines all aspects. I will therefore strive to integrate these two dimensions by combining them with the themes of inequalities, power relationships, discrimination, and racism. I will also include, out of necessity, the political dimension, given that the implementation of a policy for the management of ethnocultural diversity would require powers that are not fully within Quebec's jurisdiction.

Questions related to the management of ethnocultural diversity have been a major concern over the last three decades, and it is likely that they will continue to be so for many years to come. In Quebec, for example, the process of diversification began decades ago and will continue and even accelerate. The proportion of immigrants in the population was around 7 to 8 per cent from 1931 to 1986, from 8 to 9 per cent from 1991 to 1996, and 10 to 11 per cent from 2001 to 2006. This seems like rather a modest increase. However, according to the projections by Statistics Canada and the Institut de la statistique du Québec, this proportion will almost double during the next twenty years, rising from 11 per cent to 19 per cent in 2031. For the Montreal region, it is predicted that the proportion will increase from 21 to 30 per cent (Canada, Statistics Canada, 2010; Quebec, Institut de la statistique du Québec, 2008b). Reflections on intercultural relations will therefore remain relevant for a long time.

I note here that aboriginals will not be taken into account in this book. This decision is based on the fact that at the request of the aboriginals themselves, the Quebec government has decided that everything related to relationships with these communities should be dealt with on a "nation-to-nation" basis.[13] For their part, the populations concerned do not want to be considered a cultural minority (and even less an "ethnic group") within the Quebec nation. It is not certain either that aboriginals will accept the status of national minority in Quebec; this has been a topic of debate in their communities, the outcome of which will be up to them. For this reason, the question of the relationship between aboriginals and interculturalism should be set aside for the time being, although an important provision has now been achieved, that is, the recognition of Quebec as a plurinational state.

This essay will be based on the important contributions of Quebec authors who have already published on interculturalism.[14] I will also refer on various occasions to the European contributions to this field of research. The first chapter of the book is devoted to outlining the parameters that frame Quebec reflections on ethnocultural diversity. These parameters also constitute the conditions under which the choice of a model is made. In the same chapter I present the major paradigms that form the basis for the models for the management of diversity. In the following chapter, I outline my concept of interculturalism as the most appropriate formula for the situation, needs, and aspirations of Quebec. Chapter 3 offers a comparative reflection on Quebec interculturalism and Canadian multiculturalism. Chapter 4 examines various criticisms made of interculturalism (and especially of my idea of this model),[15] to which I attempt to respond. I will also include in this chapter justifications and observations complementary to the presentation in chapter 2. In chapter 5, I present what a secular regime for Quebec inspired by the spirit of interculturalism might be. Finally, I recall the main proposals of this book and suggest various avenues for action and reflection that it is urgent or would be useful to explore.

1
Conditions and Foundations of Quebec Interculturalism

This chapter presents the framework of a model for the management of diversity for Quebec. More specifically, it: (a) lists the conditions on which this model must be based; (b) reviews the contextual data that must be taken into account; and (c) outlines how it is constituted in terms of paradigms, that is, the area within which it is based compared to other models.

The Parameters

I will quickly list the parameters that take priority. It would be useful to keep these in mind, because each of them has its own influence on the orientation and construction of the model.

1. The background for this discussion is the Quebec nation (eight million inhabitants) as a host society for immigrants. Quebec's status as a nation is based on its distinctive characteristics: a large land base, a strong historical consciousness, a francophone identity and culture (four fifths of Quebecers have French as their mother tongue), a long Christian tradition, and specific political, educational, legal, and other institutions. This status now enjoys a substantial consensus (beyond their ideological and political differences, the vast majority of Quebecers have developed a sense of belonging to this nation) and was recognized by the Canadian Parliament itself in 2006.[1] Quebec is therefore a sociological nation with the status of a province within the Canadian Confederation.

   I will use the term "nation" in the broad sense, covering political, civic, cultural, and social aspects. There is no simple symmetry between these dimensions, but they are related in various ways.

According to this concept, which is similar to that proposed by
M. Seymour (1999, chaps. 8, 9; 2001; 2008), the last two dimensions – cultural and social – are sites of distinctive characteristics
and divisions (a majority and ethnocultural minorities, social classes,
stratifications based on gender, age, residency, etc.) while the first
two – political and civic – cut across these differences and divisions.

I will often refer to the concept of "culture," by which I mean all
the symbols that, in a given collectivity (family, community, nation,
etc.), constitute the foundation of the social bond, on the one
hand, and sustain all the components of identity, on the other hand:
perceptions of the self and others, affiliations, traditions, memory,
rituals, values, beliefs, ideals, visions of the world. I will examine
these two aspects of culture in their singularity and their fluidity,
taking into account what is constant and what is changing, generating three streams of analysis related to roots (heritage), encounter
(exchange), and project (the future).

2. The francophone majority is a minority nation within Canada and a
cultural minority on the continent. As we will see, this leads to a very
particular situation. This double condition of majority-minority has
generated contrasting collective attitudes and behaviours, marked
sometimes by confidence and boldness, sometimes by timidity and
self-doubt. As a minority, Quebec francophones have never been
able to free themselves from legitimate concerns about their future,
whether with regard to their language, their fundamental values,
their traditions, or their institutions.[2] This is a legacy of the struggles
that they have waged against attempts at assimilation across Canada
and, more generally, of their minority status.

Recently, globalization has added a significant element to these
old worries. As Jean-Claude Corbeil (2009, p. 119) points out:
"Francophone Quebecers are condemned to live dangerously."
A Quebec-wide poll in June 2009 (by Léger Marketing) echoes this
statement: close to 90 per cent of francophones questioned felt
that, for various reasons, the French language is threatened in the
Montreal region. Quebec interculturalism has to take that basic fact
into account.

The book will examine the important implications of this double
status with respect to the definition of interculturalism.

3. Reflection on the management of ethnocultural diversity in Quebec
has always had to contend with the same problem, the same tension:
how do we think jointly about the future of the francophone culture

inherited from four centuries of history and the future of all of Quebec culture? Reference to a majority-minorities relationship always implies this reflection, causing it to oscillate between two poles that, with reservations, I will qualify as extremes in the Quebec context: (a) simply identifying all of Quebec culture with francophone culture of French (or French Canadian) origin, or (b) promoting a strictly civic vision that obliterates the majority-minorities relationship. These poles each have their weaknesses. The first favours an assimilationist view of minorities; the second excludes from reflection the historical and identity heritage of the francophone majority.[3]

The spirit of interculturalism, as I envisage it, is to overcome this antinomy and propose an integrated vision of the components of Quebec culture that respects the prerogatives of everyone. But it is still both inevitable and legitimate that the francophone majority, if only because of its demographic and historical weight, be recognized as the de facto main vector for integration.

4. Since we are dealing with Quebec, it is necessary also to take into account, in one way or another, the national question. This is another lesson that emerges from recent debates. I mentioned above the double status of Quebec francophones as a cultural majority within Quebec, as the main component of a minority nation at the level of Canada, and as a cultural minority on the continent. As a minority nation within Canada, Quebec is a part of power relations that place it in a position of weakness. From the point of view of Quebec, the history of this unequal relationship, which has its roots in the British colonial regime, has been marked by tensions, disappointments, and setbacks.

Accordingly, there is in the francophone majority a very strong historical consciousness – we could say a memory under tension. It is a memory that is fueled largely by the feeling that the francophone majority still has an account to settle with its colonial past and with its present. Quebec, it should be recalled, experienced more than two centuries of domination, both from the outside (the British Empire) and from the inside (the clergy and its allies in the elites of business and the liberal professions). For many Quebecers, this historical consciousness is expressed through a desire for a restoration, by a feeling of collective emancipation that is not complete (and that can adopt avenues and options that are very diverse ideologically and politically). The fight for the language is closely associated with this national question.

In this regard, as a model intended for all Quebecers, interculturalism obviously cannot be identified with any partisan group, but neither can it ignore the aspirations related to the national question and its ramifications, or the ensuing consequences for processes of integration – for example, the fact that Quebec is not a sovereign country adds to the elements of vulnerability that I have already mentioned and imposes restrictions on the future of interculturalism as a set of policies. Like it or not, as we will see at the end of chapter 2, political factors interfere in many ways with Quebec interculturalism.

I will return to this topic, but by way of illustration, I will mention two of the many possible ways to take into account the national question without contravening the duty of reserve. One way is to promote universal citizenship values, forged in the past of this nation, namely values of affirmation, self-respect, dignity, collective mobilization and development, as well as values of equality, social justice, and solidarity. Another way is to promote the teaching of national history with emphasis on its main themes, which are that of the founding majority (see below), but with a concern for integrating the heritage of minorities by relying on shared elements and bridges between diverse themes.

5. Francophone Quebec, narrowly defined as the population of French or French Canadian origin, is characterized by another legacy from its past: a difficult relationship with the Catholic religion. This religion, for many, is associated with a negative history, with experiences of domination, of even oppression (consider the treatment of women), that bring up painful memories and are expressed today by an intense sensitivity to anything religious – a sensitivity that entails a great deal of suspicion and even hostility. This can be seen in the ongoing debate on the separation of state and religion. In many other nations, this separation is hardly more than an administrative or functional arrangement. But in Quebec it has taken on a completely different dimension, acquiring the status of a fundamental value.

6. Quebec is a society of law, of liberal tradition, that is respectful of individual freedoms and therefore of diversity. I believe that in spite of all the current misunderstandings and confusion regarding the subject, the vast majority of Quebecers believe in the principles of pluralism – with the understanding, of course, as mentioned above, that this ideal is likely to assume various definitions and applications. Similarly, as shown by empirical data, Quebec is not a racist

or xenophobic society, but, as in every society, we find stereotypes
and various forms of discrimination that go against dominant values.

7. Quebec has always been able to combine its liberal tradition with a
keen awareness of collective rights, as evidenced by its commitment
to its distinctive institutions, linguistic policies, nationalism, and
social programs and its desire for constitutional recognition. In the
same spirit, Quebecers attach equal importance to individual initiatives and collective action. On this point, they are distinguished from
Americans, British, and a few other peoples where the individual
perspective is valued above all else.[4]

8. Quebec is a francophone nation, a cultural "exception" on the continent, which has just entered an era of turbulence because of globalization. This small nation (in comparison to its close neighbours and
the main actors internationally) will therefore need all its strength
to continue to develop as a francophone entity. We can see here the
imperatives that drive the desire for integration, and especially the
danger for such a society of any form of fragmentation or divisions
that could arise from an uncompromising approach to the management of ethnocultural diversity, in particular religious diversity. That
is why, in addition to the key considerations of law and social ethics
mentioned above, Quebec has to make integration a major priority
if it wants to avoid being weakened.

9. Abstract universal values and legal rules are not a sufficient foundation for a social bond that integrates a society and maintains conditions of solidarity and mobilization. Inevitably, there will always be
a need for a symbolic cement, an identity component made up of a
sense of belonging, memory, values, and collective projects. On a societal level (this is a theme I will come back to), the universal ideals
acquire a motivating power to the extent that they are incorporated
into a common culture rooted in shared experiences, in a particular
history and context.[5] It should also be noted that, in every society,
the individual is integrated to various levels in community or collective institutions.

This statement is confirmed by the example of republican nations
officially founded on universal values, such as the United States and
France. In the case of the former, the values of liberty, progress, and
equality are rooted in powerful myths (summed up as the "American
Dream" and exceptionalism) that are sustained by the celebration
of the heroic acts of the Founding Fathers and of subsequent generations that have reproduced their model. Concretely, however,

these symbolic references are structured on WASP culture. In the case of France, Alain Dieckhoff (2000, pp. 163ff., 295) has clearly shown how this authoritarian republic, based on a principle of citizenship, has had to engage in intense acculturation and assimilation to support its endeavour (see also W.H. Sewell, 1985). Erin Tolley (2004) has given an analogous demonstration for English Canada. In reality, there are few examples of nations that have been able to dispense with culture and identity. I am thinking here of Tocqueville (*On Democracy in America*, vol. 1): "There is a society [among men] only when ... the same facts give rise among them to the same impressions."[6]

These remarks underscore the symbolic foundations of law and the sociocultural conditions of its application. They also highlight the appropriation of universal values that takes place in every society through a process of historicization, and this forces us to view the familiar particular-universal dichotomy in context. But in the opposite direction, we can also observe a movement of emancipation that evolves from specific experiences to universalization. For example, in every society, sensibilities, aspirations, and ideals forged in a particular past gradually take the form of fundamental values, both civic and universal, that are valid for all individuals and all groups beyond their cultural differences.

We can affirm, in other words, that the universalization of values results from the specific paths of nations, as recorded in national cultures.[7] But this process requires a certain amount of "pruning" and selection (the "values" forged in the history of a nation are not all commendable), and of interpretation and promotion, as I will propose for Quebec's past (see chapters 2 and 4).

An excellent example of the process of historicization in which the universal and the particular are combined is provided by the value of equality between men and women in Quebec. In fact, its growth originated with the combination of (a) a universal ideal strongly reactivated internationally starting in the middle of the twentieth century; (b) the particular experience of man-woman relationships in Quebec's past; and (c) struggles carried out by women's groups.

In summary, the so-called shared values prevalent in a given society are rarely specific in their principles since they are often found in different societies. Their distinctive nature comes from the particular process of historicization and appropriation that is associated with them. This is what gives them a particular resonance in a given society. Otherwise, there is a danger they will remain cold, disembodied references. This is why we need to acknowledge the full importance of the historical "roots" that determine the rules of life in a society.

10. Intellectuals, administrators, and politicians have to be attentive to the moods of the population. This is illustrated by the accommodations crisis in Quebec in 2005–2008. Public sentiments, especially in times of crisis, can be fueled by baseless or objectionable motivations, and we therefore need to be wary of them and fight them. But the mood of the population can also express a form of wisdom. During the (public and private) hearings of the Bouchard-Taylor Commission in 2007–2008, despite sometimes awkward and sometimes shocking presentations, Quebecers from all walks of life belonging mainly to the founding majority[8] were able to express significant messages, such as:

- the importance that should be accorded to historically constituted cultures, as symbolic capital, and to the need for continuity that is manifested in any population
- the particular situation of the francophone majority in Quebec, which is itself a minority
- the dissatisfaction that such Quebecers felt towards the elites (including intellectuals), who seemed to be insensitive to their concerns, which have been aggravated by a low birth rate, an aging population, and increasing immigration

Finally, a few populists have seized upon these messages to turn them into something that has become all too familiar, exacerbating for their own benefit feelings of insecurity and converting them into frustration and the scapegoating of immigrants. These events, in my view, have taught us two lessons: we need to keep listening to the general public and we must not abandon the management of identity to the open market of demagogues and opportunists. While it is necessary to pay attention to the feelings of insecurity of minorities, it would be a mistake to disregard these same feelings that are also manifested in the majority, on the one hand because those concerns can also be legitimate, and on the other hand because an anxious majority is never an ideal partner for minorities.

I am also grateful to the hearings of the Bouchard-Taylor Commission for making me aware in a very concrete way of the power of national myths and the strong reactions they can elicit when they come under attack or when they are not taken seriously. It should be remembered that, in any nation, the development of these powerful representations that define collective identity and goals is the result of lengthy efforts at acculturation by the government and its allies in the world of ideas, arts, and letters. Sustained by both reason and emotion, stamped with legitimacy by the government, the schools, the church, and the media, national myths have acquired an influence that makes it possible for them to be perpetuated over many generations. In Quebec, these myths have for a long time defined the nation in terms of homogeneity (this was also the case with most nations in the West), a fragile minority, loyalty to ancestors, and devotion to the threatened homeland. However, mainly during the last thirty or forty years, a new discourse has developed among part of the elites and intellectual class in Quebec, expressing quite a different message. This discourse praises diversity, warns against the tyranny of the majority, relativizes memory, tends to trivialize identity, and is somewhat critical of the nation. Why should we be surprised at the perplexed reactions to this message? Why should we be surprised that pluralism was first perceived by the general public as a problem, if not a threat, and not as a very noble value to be promoted and a solution to the problem of the encounter of cultures?

11. We would be wrong to oppose, as some do, rights and identity as if these two entities were irreconcilable, as if we had to choose between the defence of rights and the defence of identity. This view is based sometimes on a disembodied vision of law and sometimes on the erroneous postulate of the non-legitimacy of identity. A better vision of the law, more aware of its cultural foundations and social origins, as well as a recognition of identity and its attributes (language, religion, memory, and so on) as a cultural right give us a way around this false contradiction (see also G. Nootens, 1999).

Paradigms and Models

In order to clearly distinguish interculturalism from other models for dealing with ethnocultural diversity, it is useful to step back and review the five major paradigms that all such models belong to. These paradigms, which follow from collective choices, are major interpretative frameworks that situate the primary intention or defining outlook of each model. They structure the public debate in a nation, they set the parameters and the main issues, they inspire the policies and programs of the government, and, finally, they broadly fuel the perceptions that citizens have of each other.

Diversity

The first paradigm is that of diversity. Its main postulate is that the nation is made up of a set of individuals and ethnocultural groups, which are all equal and protected by the same rights; therefore no cultural majority is officially recognized (but only, one might say, minorities). In the name of diversity, raised to the rank of value and norm, all citizens affirm and express without constraint their identities and their differences, within the limitations of the law. We recognize here English Canada (or Canada outside Quebec),[9] the United States, Great Britain, and Australia,[10] to which we can add countries such as India,[11] Singapore, Sweden,[12] and a few others. I note, however, that in each of these countries the promotion of diversity produces many criticisms questioning the real level of commitment to the paradigm, which is contradicted on many counts by reality, as we will see in particular with Canada (chapter 3).

Homogeneity

A second paradigm is that of homogeneity (we could also speak of a unitary paradigm), which fundamentally affirms an ethnocultural uniformity, at least in public, and sometimes also in private life. To varying degrees, this framework establishes the existence of a single culture, assimilation being the rule. Accordingly, it gives no official recognition either to a majority or to minorities, not because each citizen is encouraged to be different, as in the previous paradigm, but because each citizen has to be the same as the others. In other words, while the diversity paradigm recognizes only minorities, we could say about the homogeneity paradigm that it recognizes only the majority.

I am thinking here of nations such as Ireland (until very recently), Iceland, Poland, Greece, Japan, the two Koreas, and a few former Soviet republics, among others. The case of France is also close to this paradigm to the extent that, in the name of an ideal of equality and universality (that many criticisms associate with a roundabout form of assimilation), this country has not shown itself to be very favourable to various expressions of diversity in public space, especially in public institutions.

Bipolarity or Multipolarity

The third paradigm is what I will call bipolarity or multipolarity. This is the case with societies made up of two or more national groups or subgroups (within a single state) taking the form of poles that are both political and ethnocultural and are supported by firmly rooted institutions, identities, and affiliations. They are sometimes recognized officially as such and granted a kind of permanence. The most familiar cases are Belgium (three communities, four linguistic regions) and Switzerland (four national languages, four linguistic areas).[13] But we could also include under this paradigm nation states such as Northern Ireland, New Zealand (Maoris and Pakehas), Malaysia (Malays, Chinese, and Indians), Bolivia, or the former Czechoslovakia.[14] In fact, all plurinational states can be grouped together under this paradigm.[15] The regime of pillars, as it existed in Holland and as it still exists in Belgium, is in keeping with the spirit of this paradigm, since it grants certain religious groups a special status accompanied by powers and privileges.

Mixité

The fourth paradigm is that of *mixité*. This is based on the idea that, through a process of exchanges and intense mixing, the ethnocultural diversity of the nation will gradually be absorbed and blend into a new culture, different from its initial components, which will then disappear. We find this paradigm in Latin America, especially in Brazil and historically in Mexico. The American "melting pot" (which aims to create a new nation or civilization from the contributions of all citizens, immigrants, and others) is also a version of this paradigm.

Duality

The fifth paradigm is that of duality. I will spend more time on this one since it forms the basis for interculturalism. It is found where diversity is thought of and managed on the basis of a relationship between minorities from recent or older immigration and a cultural majority that could be called the "founding culture." Without any formal hierarchical connotation,[16] this latter concept refers to the symbolic heritage of a population that has occupied a space for a long time (several centuries or even several millennia); that has formed a territory or habitat (what certain geographers call a "territoriality" [see C. Raffestin & M. Bresso, 1979,

1982]) in which it recognizes itself; that has forged an identity and a collective imaginary expressed through language, traditions, ideals, and institutions; that has developed solidarity and a sense of belonging; and that shares a sense of continuity based in memory. In such societies, long-established minorities can therefore also possess the status of founding cultures – in Quebec, examples include the aboriginal communities, founded long before the majority culture, and the anglophone population. I should also note that the term "founding" refers both to an initial act of settlement and a process extending over time. This process is inevitably accompanied by a structuring effect on the entire culture of a society, especially if it is carried out by the majority group.

With some exceptions, cultural majorities are founding cultures, but as always happens, they never stop incorporating over time significant contributions that blend with the existing cultural fabric and ultimately transform it. Through the effects of migrations and intercultural exchanges, the reality underlying these concepts is therefore dynamic and often varied, even though the dominant discourse tends to obscure this aspect. As we will see below, other factors ensure that the concept of cultural majority can accommodate heterogeneous and malleable content, and therefore we should use this concept with caution (as pointed out by P. Leuprecht, 2011).

Remember that, in a given society or nation, the majority-minorities relationship (and the Us-Them relationship that it usually produces) can be more or less accentuated according to regions, generations, and social groups, that it can be moved around on the pluricultural chessboard, and that the factors underlying it can vary over time.[17]

A duality relationship emerges when a majority group takes shape within a society. This phenomenon can be prompted by various causes. The members of the majority group can see themselves as homogeneous with respect to "others" defined as different; as universal as opposed to ethnic; or as fragile because they form a minority within their national, supranational, or continental environment. They can feel uncomfortable about or threatened by newcomers who apparently do not want to integrate and who have values and traditions seen as incompatible with those of the host society. The emergence of a majority can also be brought about by one or more minority groups that actually want to set themselves off from the society. Finally, the emergence of a majority can result in a split gradually created over the long history of a nation around an old founder majority culture that is not very concerned about openness.

These are cultural factors that can lead to the duality paradigm. But we also know, in the light of many studies such as those of F. Barth (1969), D. Juteau (1999), and others (in the tradition of Max Weber), that duality is very often the product of a social relationship, more specifically of a relationship of power through which certain social groups impose their culture and marginalize other groups through a process of ethnicization. In any case, duality expresses in most cases a deeply ingrained perception that there exists within the nation a gap that (a) is hard to fill, (b) cannot be filled, or even (c) should not be filled.

In most nations, and unlike the situation that prevails in Quebec, the cultural majorities are not themselves minorities, which leads to significant consequences for the definition and applications of interculturalism. Moreover, in cases where the cultural majority is also a minority in its outside environment (Quebec, Catalonia, Scotland, Wales, and others), the majority-minority relationship imposes itself all the more.

I would like to note that I have avoided using (while taking them into account) the concepts of ethnic group and cultural community. These terms assume a level of structure and homogeneity that is not frequently seen. Many authors define "ethnic group" by referring to a community of language, religion, values, lifestyle, and customs of dress, cuisine, and so on; a very strong feeling of a distant common ancestry, combined with a celebration of that representation; a desire to perpetuate the group and demonstrate it in customs and rituals; the predominance of the identity dimension over all other dimensions (class, gender, territory); strong endogamous practices; and a residential concentration. In reality, subpopulations that display these features are rather rare (I am thinking of communities such as aboriginals or Hassidic Jews in Quebec, Hutterites in Western Canada, and the Amish in the United States). Obviously, there is excessive use of the concept of ethnic group in the scholarly literature and in everyday language (see R. Brubaker, 1998, 2004).

As for the concept of cultural community, it first appeared in Quebec government documents in the early 1980s (e.g., Quebec, MCCI, 1981), and it has been widely criticized for a long time (e.g., L. Fontaine, 1993), in particular by minorities and immigrants.[18] In both cases, there is a danger of a hardening ("essentialization" or "categorization") of differences, identities, and cultural boundaries that distorts reality and can generate within the subpopulations concerned marginalization and a feeling of exclusion.[19] In Quebec, these two concepts (ethnic group and cultural community) can, however, be applied to orthodox Jews in Montreal[20] and perhaps to part of the Chinese minority. To designate other minorities, some have recently begun using the expression "Québécois d'origines diverses" [Quebecers of various origins]. But this phrase also seems inappropriate to me since, strictly speaking, it would have to include many Quebecers in the majority population. It suggests that diversity is only a trait of minorities and immigrants, which is incorrect.[21]

In this spirit, the concept of minority should be understood primarily in its statistical sense, but also in an anthropological sense. In the latter, it designates a cultural nexus or a distinct social identity that develops both in coexistence with and in relationship to the majority culture, and of which the boundaries can be very fluid (see chapter 2).

Contexts of duality can also occur in plurinational states to the extent that they encompass various cultural configurations that often include a majority-minorities relationship (I am thinking here of Canada, where Quebec and aboriginals are minority nations, and of other countries such as Spain and Great Britain that have analogous structures). I should also point out that the duality paradigm does not necessarily lead to interculturalism, but this model finds one of its most fertile breeding grounds in it. It is then designed to arbitrate a majority-minorities relationship at the societal scale.

This duality acquires the status of paradigm when, in a given nation, it begins to structure reflection and debates on diversity. It can then be manifested in the form of a more or less pronounced dichotomy or Us-Them relationship. However, the duality paradigm does not create this divide (the construction of which precedes it). It is rather its starting point, its contextual roots. If, for some reason, people wanted to challenge this paradigm in a given nation, they would therefore have to go after the factors that gave rise to and perpetuate it.

The preceding remarks require a few caveats:

- In current debates, the majority referred to is sometimes clearly defined and easily identifiable, and sometimes very vague, if not fabricated. Either way, the discussion stays within the duality paradigm with its majority-minorities dichotomy, and it remains so until the public debate itself is reoriented towards another paradigm. We should therefore be attentive to the various meanings that are ascribed to this concept. Yet, in all cases, it refers to a very broad phenomenon, that is, the existence of a majority group that is at the same time a dominant group through the control that it exercises over institutions.
- To designate the cultural majority, some authors have introduced the concept of dominant ethnic group (A.D. Smith, 1991; A.W. Doane,

1993; E. Kaufmann, 2008). This concept, however, seems to be too narrow because it limits the notion of majority culture to an ethnic reality when it can include broader content.

- As already mentioned, we have to be wary of any reductive vision that would represent the majority-minorities relationship as a conflict between a homogeneous majority and heterogeneous minorities. Beyond the most deeply rooted common language and traditions, strong elements of diversity are almost always found within the majority. Therefore, it is more accurate to talk about a relationship between two types of diversity, which the majority group tends in the first case to obscure and in the other case to amplify. It is a phenomenon that manifests itself in the current debates in Quebec and elsewhere in the West.

- Similarly, we should avoid seeing the majority-minorities duality as a fixed entity. While the dual structure is enduring, the content of its components, how they are related, and the context are constantly changing. This dynamic character does not, however, always come to light in perceptions and in debates.

- This mutability means that the concept of cultural majority should be used with caution. As the situation changes, the majority can shrink, expand, or be recomposed substantially according to the issues of the day and according to the strategies of discourse.

- In light of the above and according to the most current perceptions, we can say that in Quebec the cultural majority includes in its broadest sense all citizens who share the French language as their mother tongue (which can include a certain number of immigrants). In its narrowest sense, it is restricted to the so-called "*de souche*" [old stock] francophones, those who belong to and speak in the name of what I called the founding culture. It was mainly members of this group who expressed, during the hearings of the Bouchard-Taylor Commission in 2007–2008, a keen sense of concern for the survival of what they called "our culture" and "our values."

- The majority's feeling of threat or insecurity fueled by the presence of minorities should always be viewed with a critical eye. We have seen too many examples of majorities who treat their minorities as scapegoats because they felt themselves powerless to act against the true causes of their misfortunes. For the nations of the West, which currently feel under attack from various directions (such as the many uncertainties related to globalization, the rise of a new individualism, the erosion of the social bond, financial crises and the weakening of

governments, the aging of populations, the precariousness of jobs),
it can be tempting to make the immigrant or the minority responsible for discomfort that is often the result of major changes occurring
around the globe.

- One can see a potential risk associated with the duality paradigm. By
recognizing the existence of a majority, this paradigm can accentuate
the Us-Them relationship and open a space for the dominating ten-
dencies of majority groups, the expressions of which are very visible
in the history of the West as in other parts of the world (xenophobia,
exclusion, discrimination, etc.). It is important therefore to include
in the duality paradigm a strong pluralist orientation and corrective
mechanisms. However, this risk is not specific to the duality paradigm. Similarly, the Us-Them relationship is expressed everywhere,
but it is often kept below the surface, while it is highlighted by the
duality paradigm. In summary, interculturalism recognizes the status
of the cultural majority (its legitimacy and the right to perpetuate
its traditions, values, and heritage) while framing that status in a way
that reduces the risk of the abuses in which majorities often engage.

The majority of nations in the West currently seem to be evolving towards this paradigm.[22] In Europe, for example, many polls show that
the Muslim presence is generating great discomfort and even hostility
in many countries, and this creates the conditions for an increasingly
pronounced Us-Them relationship. On 4 January 2011 the French daily *Le Monde* published the results of a survey showing that according
to 42 per cent of the French population, Muslims represent a threat.
It also found that, according to four-fifths of the French and three-
quarters of Germans, Muslims are not integrated and are reluctant to
integrate (see also J. Sides & J. Citrin, 2007; G. Bouchard & C. Taylor,
2008, p. 189–95). In response, the British Council recently published a
document by Martin Rose (2009) that proposed a European approach
to pluralism entirely based on the duality perspective.

More generally, this Us-Them relationship is sustained by increasing
opposition to all immigration, as shown by data from the World Values
Survey (L. Barnes & P.A. Hall, 2013). It also reflects a concern regarding
fundamental values, social cohesion, and living standards; a widespread
discontent with multiculturalism; and the growth of right-wing populist
parties.[23] Finally, duality is also fueled by the feeling of alienation felt by
many immigrants and children of immigrants who criticize the host societies for not treating them equitably (C. Taylor, 2012). Cultural duality
is thus combined with social polarization.

Conclusion

These paradigms constitute the first level of analysis of ethnocultural diversity. The different models associated with them (multiculturalism, interculturalism, melting pot, hyphenation, republicanism, assimilationism, consociationalism,[24] and others)[25] represent a second level. A third level is the concrete ethnocultural structure of populations as revealed by empirical data (census statistics, monographs) on ethnic origin, language, religion, and spatialization.

The paradigms, like the models, are the result of a collective choice that is often codified in official documents. There is no geographic, demographic, or historical determinism. It is not surprising that the choice tends to align itself with historical paths, sensibilities, and social values. But there remains much room for flexibility. We know many examples of nations that have suddenly changed paradigms in recent decades. For example, in the 1960s and 1970s, Canada and Australia shifted from the homogeneity paradigm to the diversity paradigm while Quebec was abandoning homogeneity in favour of duality.[26] Similarly, England seems to be currently moving away slightly from the diversity paradigm,[27] and in Quebec there is an attempt to introduce elements of republican-style uniformization (e.g., the movement against accommodations, and against the wearing of religious symbols in government institutions and public space).

In a similar vein, given its ethnocultural composition, it would not be illogical for France to turn towards the diversity paradigm, although it seems unlikely that this will occur under current conditions. Sweden, a rather homogeneous country, has all the same defined itself officially with reference to diversity. Mexico, with its very small proportion of landed immigrants (around one per cent),[28] still rejects the homogeneity paradigm,[29] unlike Italy, where diversity has not yet strongly permeated the national imaginary. Israel remains generally tempted by assimilation in spite of the presence of deep-rooted minorities. India defines itself with reference to diversity (an abundance of languages and cultures held together mostly by political institutions) even though Hindus represent 80 per cent of the population.

There is therefore no determinism in the ethnocultural composition of a nation that would dictate the establishment of a particular paradigm. To be sure, the situation in English-speaking Canada in the 1970s facilitated the shift from duality to diversity, since people of British origin were no longer in the majority. In Australia, on the other hand, they made up about three-quarters of the total. To a large extent, changes in paradigms seem to arise from cultural and political orientations.

It should also be noted that a paradigm can inspire more than one model – and sometimes quite different models. For example, in English Canada and the United States, the diversity paradigm has led in the one case to multiculturalism and in the other to the melting pot. Similarly, duality can lead to interculturalism, but also consociationalism, just as homogeneity can be more or less pronounced, as we can see with Japan, Italy, and France. In addition, the association between a nation and a paradigm is rarely exclusive. The simplest scenario is obviously that of a nation that, on the basis of a very strong consensus, adopts a single paradigm or a broadly predominant paradigm. However, we should not dismiss the cases of nations where the public debate is more fragmented and that subscribe simultaneously to two or three competing paradigms.

The United States nowadays provides a prime example of this. On the whole, the diversity paradigm clearly dominates, with the nation being defined officially as based on a few universal ideals capable of accommodating the greatest diversity possible. However, two other paradigms are clearly present: the duality paradigm (a mainstream culture, the *American culture*, and a white race, in the face of the cultures of minorities that are perceived as hostile to integration, even threatening the English language)[30] and the assimilation paradigm (the traditional discourse of the melting pot).

The case of Brazil, a very complex one, also attracts attention to the extent that the symbolic configuration that predominates there (based on the great myth of racial democracy) is giving way to both the diversity and homogeneity paradigms. Official discourse and public debate often refer to the non-differentiation of this nation in terms of races, but at the same time this discourse and debate are very much imbued with ethnocultural diversity. Finally, we also find in many nations various amalgams of these paradigms. In other words, the theoretical clarity of the paradigms is often weakened if not compromised by mixed realities. The paradigms nevertheless remain useful tools for analysis, if only to find one's way through the proliferation of models and to highlight their basic intentions and various corollaries.

Each paradigm entails specific risks. The nations following the diversity paradigm are more vulnerable to fragmentation, those that subscribe to multipolarity are more subject to conflict, and those that adopt *mixité* can lapse into assimilation. As for nations where duality predominates, they are faced, as mentioned above, with the danger that the Us-Them relationship will harden, that it will create barriers and favour forms of domination, discrimination, and ethnic prejudice, thus entrenching a regime of unequal citizenship. The process of democratic deliberation that is central to democratic societies is thus compromised.[31] These risks are also present in the other paradigms, but they are perhaps more obvious in the case of duality because of the majority-minorities relationship that explicitly underlies it. In return, the duality paradigm feeds a critical awareness of the aforementioned risks by making them more visible.

2
Quebec Interculturalism: A Definition

In this chapter, I will briefly present my view of interculturalism, mainly from a Quebec perspective. In chapter 4, readers will also find important supplementary information (justifications, clarifications, responses to criticisms) that I have grouped separately to avoid overloading this overview.

The Origins of Quebec Interculturalism

The model that in Quebec is now called interculturalism has been gradually developed over recent decades, at least in its essential elements. This evolution grew out of an increasing awareness of cultural diversity in Quebec starting around the middle of the twentieth century (G. Bouchard, 1990) and the increasing immigration during the 1960s to 1970s. But it particularly found its source in what was perhaps the most important cultural change of the Quiet Revolution, namely a redefinition of the French Canadian nation, now centred in Quebec. As a corollary, the "French Canadians" of Quebec came to identify themselves as "Québécois" and as the cultural majority within Quebec, which then began seeing itself as a host society for immigrants.

The origins of Quebec interculturalism are summarized in G. Bouchard and C. Taylor (2008, pp. 116–18) and presented in more detail in various texts.[1] The main stages in this process were the following: creation of a ministry of immigration (1968), rejection of Canadian multiculturalism (1971), adoption of a charter of human rights and freedoms (1975), establishment of French as the official language of Quebec (1974, 1977),[2] development of a "cultural convergence" policy (1978, 1981), the Chancy report on intercultural education (1985), declaration of the government on interethnic and interracial relations (1986), enactment of a "moral contract" policy (1990–1991), Quebec-Ottawa agreement on responsibility for immigration (1991),[3] orientation focusing on citizenship (late 1990s, early 2000s),[4] a multidimensional approach that fully reintroduced the cultural dimension into government policies (2004),[5] the Bouchard-Taylor Commission (2007–2008), and struggle against racism (2008).[6]

Mention also needs to be made of the government resolutions of 1985 and 1989 recognizing the rights of aboriginals (even though the subject will not be dealt with here for the reasons given in the introduction). The resolutions were very clearly in keeping with the spirit of interculturalism to the extent that they recognized the cultural specificity and rights of these minority populations, while pointing the way to dialogue and rapprochement.

These milestones will be commented on below, but it is important to point out here the strong elements of continuity that can be identified in these initiatives, with all the inevitable trial and error. In hindsight we can observe, from one stage to another, the implementation of key components that gradually gave shape to Quebec interculturalism, for example: promotion of the French language, emphasis on rights, respect for diversity, the fight against discrimination, the special attention given to the francophone majority culture, the recognition of ethnocultural minorities in a spirit of pluralism, the protection of fundamental values (including democracy, equality between men and women, non-discrimination, and secularism), the value of integration, the quest for a middle course between assimilation and fragmentation (or the "mosaic"),[7] the need for intercommunity interactions and exchanges, the development of a shared (public) culture and a Quebec sense of identity, the participation of all citizens in civic and political life, and the principle of reciprocity in the process of integrating immigrants (and in particular in the practice of accommodations).[8]

Some authors have proposed dividing this evolution into phases. According to D. Juteau (2002), for example, government policies were first of all ethnicist, then pluralist, and finally republican. Azzeddine Marhraoui (2004, pp. 67–98) also distinguishes three major stages:

- 1968–1978: formal recognition of diversity, affirmation of the French language in the public sphere
- the 1980s: integration of immigrants and cultural minorities, affirmation of francophone culture

- starting in 1990: a "moral contract" based on the promotion of civic values and a shared public culture (see also G. Baril, 2008)

It took time to give a name to the developing process, a delay lamented in 1988 by the Conseil des communautés culturelles et de l'immigration [Council on Cultural Communities and Immigration] (CCCI, 1988, p. 6). The concept of interculturalism, in fact, made quite a late appearance in government documents,[9] and it has never been officially adopted by the Quebec government – unlike Canadian multiculturalism, which was adopted by the Canadian Parliament in 1971 and has been vigorously promoted since, and which was included in the Charter of Human Rights and Freedoms before being passed into law in 1988. In the past few years, however, government ministers in Quebec have referred on various occasions to interculturalism in official statements.

The first government text that presented a precise overview of the key elements of the Quebec policy (but without referring directly to the concept of interculturalism) dates from 1990. This was the document *Let's Build Québec Together: A Policy Statement on Immigration and Integration* (commonly referred to as the "moral contract"). This text, thanks to its clarity, cohesiveness, and concision, remained authoritative for many years, and is still often referred to today. Essentially, it put forward a definition of Quebec society based on three propositions:

- a society in which French is the common language of public life
- a democratic society that expects and encourages everyone to participate and contribute
- a pluralistic society that is open to outside contributions, within the limitations imposed by respect for basic democratic values and the need for intercommunity exchange (p. 15)

This founding text formed the basis for various programs intended to put the philosophy into practice, in particular in the fields of education (where the intercultural idea appeared at the end of the 1970s) and health services. The term "interculturalism" did not, however, appear in the document.

The 1990 text has today lost a little of its currency, for various reasons. It put a lot of emphasis on the civic dimension, thus leaving unanswered certain questions related to culture and identity, questions that have become pressing today. On the whole, it tried to gloss over the majority-minorities relationship, even though this relationship was and remains at the heart of Quebec concerns. Nor did it offer any elements that would make it possible to clearly differentiate the model being proposed from Canadian multiculturalism – another issue that constantly comes up in current debates. It allowed room for the practice of accommodations, which was innovative for the time, but without providing any detailed analysis. It had little to say on the theme of secularism, which was not really considered a problem when the document was being written. Finally, this "moral contract" allowed little room for the problem of inequalities and power relationships between the majority and minorities.

The purpose of this chapter is to review all the components developed in recent decades, while trying to organized them into an overall framework and add various elements that could provide answers to the questions raised by current concerns and controversies. The chapter will also attempt to fill a gap often lamented in the past, namely the absence of a specific definition of Quebec interculturalism (as pointed out by F. Rocher et al., 2007, in their study on the origins of the model).

In summary, my intention is to propose a concept of interculturalism as an integrative pluralism, centred on a balanced perspective on the majority-minorities relationship and conceived in a spirit of synthesis, which requires taking into account the various dimensions (cultural, civic, political, and social) inherent to the management of diversity.

The Components of Interculturalism

As a model for integration, interculturalism operates at two levels. On the macrosocial (or societal) level, it embodies a concept or a general philosophy of ethnocultural relationships that is expressed in orientations, policies, and programs for which the government and major institutions of a society or nation are responsible. On the microsocial level, interculturalism means establishing ways of living with ethnocultural diversity in the daily functioning of public and private institutions (education, health, business, and the like) and in community life in general. It is therefore possible to conceive of a practice of interculturality outside the framework of the nation, as shown by various projects carried out by the Council of Europe and the European Commission, in particular the Intercultural Cities project.[10] Thus there are, on the one hand, a set of guiding principles and programs that are defined at the societal or national level, and on the other hand, the concrete dynamics of relations between people or groups from diverse cultures.

However, in the chapters below, I will focus mainly on the first dimension, since priority is given to the definition of the principles and foundations of the model at the level of the Quebec nation. In addition, even though interculturalism can also be applied within the paradigm of bipolarity or multipolarity, I will restrict my reflections to the duality paradigm because, as I will show, this is the pattern that prevails in Quebec.

Let us begin with a short definition. Interculturalism, as a form of integrative pluralism, is a model based on a search for balance that attempts to find a middle ground between assimilation and segmentation and that, for this purpose, emphasizes integration, interactions, and promotion of a shared culture with respect for rights and diversity. This brief definition can be broken down into the seven points outlined below.

Components of Quebec Interculturalism as Integrative Pluralism

1. Respect for rights, in a spirit of democracy and pluralism, from which are derived four imperatives: (a) economic and social integration of all citizens; (b) the struggle against inequalities and relationships of domination that impinge on the rights of minorities and immigrants; (c) the rejection of all forms of discrimination and racism; (d) the need to ensure the participation of all citizens in civic and political life
2. The promotion of French as the main language of civic life and shared culture, as the official language of Quebec, as the foundation of its distinctive character, and as the vector for integration
3. Consideration of the Quebec nation in all its diversity, as made up of: (a) a francophone majority of French Canadian heritage, which has been joined by francophones of other origins; and (b) ethnocultural minorities (including Anglo-Quebecers with their status as a national minority); to which is added mutual recognition of the legitimate desire of each of these components to ensure its future in terms of identity and sense of belonging
4. An emphasis on integration, in accordance with a moral contract that binds all Quebecers and demands a principle of reciprocity in the harmonization of cultural differences
5. The promotion of interactions, rapprochement, and intercultural exchanges as means of integration and of fighting stereotypes and discrimination
6. The development of a shared culture as a meeting place for diversity, made up mainly of values and shared memory, and

---

nourished by the combined contributions of the majority and the minorities, with respect for all

7. The promotion of a Quebec identity, sense of belonging, and national culture, made up of three interwoven threads – the majority culture, the minority cultures, and the shared culture – in constant movement and broadly open to outside contributions.

More generally, interculturalism is characterized by a search for balance in the arbitration of sometimes competing beliefs, traditions, customs, and ideals, while respecting the fundamental values of Quebec.[11]

Rights

In accordance with the demands of democracy and pluralism, interculturalism respects the rights of individuals as well as diversity. It therefore favours the economic and social integration of all citizens; it fights xenophobia, discrimination, racism, and all forms of exclusion of which new arrivals as well as members of minorities are often victims; and it aims to ensure the participation of all citizens in civic and political life. In the same spirit, it seeks to reduce inequalities and relationships of domination that impinge on the rights of minorities and immigrants. In the pursuit of these objectives, it favours both corrective measures and incentives.

It also endorses the general principle of recognition. According to the current meaning of this concept, recognition relates mainly to the status or condition of minorities in a given society. It calls for the respect of cultural differences as well as of the individuals and groups that embody them, in the name of the dignity to which every person is entitled. The principle assumes, in fact, that for each individual or group, the feeling of one's own value and dignity requires that these differences are recognized by others, especially by the members of the majority culture, in a spirit of equity. Dignity requires respect both for what is unique about each individual and for what they share with others. This being said, the principle can also be extended to the majority group when it is itself a minority.[12]

In accordance with this principle, interculturalism advocates a thoughtful, responsible practice of accommodations that is compatible with the fundamental values of the society and at the same time contributes to the integration of people who are vulnerable to exclusion or prejudice by virtue of their distinctive characteristics.[13] Interculturalism also supports

the teaching of heritage languages for the benefit of immigrants, as practised in Quebec since 1978.[14]

These are essential conditions for equitable citizenship, the establishment of social relationships that respect individual differences and the
conduct of real intercultural exchanges – how indeed can we establish a
climate of exchange and a desire for integration if minorities and immigrants are victims of socioeconomic inequalities and do not have access
to the same rights as other citizens?

Among the elements mentioned above, those related to the recognition and protection of the cultures of origin of immigrants or members
of minorities often gave rise to reservations.[15] These provisions are justified not only in terms of the law (article 43 of the Quebec Charter of
Human Rights and Freedoms) but also for the sake of integration itself.
For example, many sociological studies carried out in both Europe and
North America[16] have shown that, paradoxically, immigrants (first and
second generation) integrate better when the maintenance or learning
of the languages and traditions of their countries of origin is encouraged. By mitigating the shock of immigration, these measures preserve
the sociocultural capital of the newcomers, build bridges to the host society, and speed up their adaptation. In addition, feeling more valued,
immigrants become more open to the realities of their new environment.
Finally, in this way, the children avoid a sharp break with their parents
and grandparents.[17] Furthermore, it has been demonstrated that an attachment to the culture of origin is compatible with identification with
the host society. In fact, attempts aimed at weakening or eliminating
identities of origin quite simply tend to harden them (see also D. Helly,
2002, p. 88). In other words, it is better for a society to be pluralist if it
wants to promote integration.

The usefulness for any citizen (and not only for immigrants) of culti-
vating an attachment to his or her culture of origin stems from the fact
that this link can be an indispensable resource for the development of
personality and identity. It provides psychological security, it is the source
of primary solidarity, it gives rise to a form of allegiance (loyalty to family,
to ancestors), and it creates an emotional relationship that is manifested
through memory and identity.

Finally, it is often mentioned that this link ensures the transmission of
values of the culture of origin, but this statement should be tempered in
the light of recent research. For example, Andreas Wimmer (2013), using a European database covering twenty-four countries and three hundred ethnocultural groups, were able to show that the relationship to the

group of origin was not the most appropriate way to explain the values of an individual. In other words, according to this survey, while diversity of values is partly inherited, it can be explained less by ethnocultural affiliation or identity than by social class, occupation, gender, or habitat (rural versus urban).

The French Language

As the medium for interactions, and more broadly as a support for the Quebec nation understood as a civic or political community, Quebec interculturalism is based on the recognition and promotion of French as an official language, as the common denominator of Quebec culture in the broad sense,[18] and as a vector for integration. This is a priority component. French is thus invested with a civic dimension that permits intercultural exchanges and participation by everyone in public debates. This obviously does not prevent Quebecers of all origins from adopting it to feed their identities. It can also be predicted, very legitimately, that the use of French as an official language will have the effect of developing among all Quebecers a sense of belonging and will favour the growth of a shared identity.[19]

Here, the long-term objective is to reach a point where all Quebecers share responsibility for the future of the French language as the national language, with the understanding that for many of them French is a second or third language. It is moreover acknowledged that French, even limited to its civic function, maintains other links with the cultural dimension, to the extent that, for example, it makes possible access to the media, political life, public debates, the content of school education, the national history and, more generally, the cultural life of Quebec. In other words, French has been established as the official language of public life, but it must also reflect the cultural diversity of Quebec, with each citizen being free to invest in it as he or she sees fit. The French language then becomes a multipurpose matrix open to all choices and strategies with respect to identity. It thus opens itself up to all the richness of traditions, contributions, and inventions. It is a language that is now spoken in many voices, since the multiplicity of relations to the language has become an inescapable fact.

All citizens of Quebec, immigrants or not, are therefore invited to contribute to the cause of French, in the continuation of past struggles. But beyond the provisions of the law (in this case, the Charter of the French Language, or Law 101), this commitment cannot be made a formal condition for granting the status of Quebecer. With regard more specifically to immigrants or members of minorities, it is legitimate and necessary that they be made aware of the importance of French, and that the francophone majority, in various ways, send clear messages in favour of francization. Further legal constraints can be justified when required by the situation (e.g., extending Law 101 to businesses with fewer than fifty employees or federal agencies operating in Quebec). However, this approach, while certainly legitimate and necessary, needs to be strictly governed, because it could lead to the restriction of freedoms and could compromise, for some, chances of developing a real sense of belonging to francophone Quebec.[20]

Duality: A Majority-Minorities Relationship

As a model operating at the scale of a nation, interculturalism is rooted in principle (but not exclusively) in a duality paradigm, structured by a relationship between a cultural majority and minorities. Ethnocultural diversity is therefore viewed and managed on the basis of an existing relationship between minorities from recent or not-so-recent immigration and a founding cultural majority.

Interculturalism, it is important to remember, does not create duality and does not promote it. It simply takes it into account when it has formed within a national culture, and its primary objective is to arbitrate duality, that is: (a) to right the wrongs that a majority can commit against minorities; and (b) to keep duality from becoming a source of tensions and conflicts. Interculturalism also has the objective of mitigating as much as possible duality and the Us-Them relationship that usually goes with it in a way that constantly expands the scope of an inclusive Us, without betraying diversity.

In accordance with a principle of double recognition (or mutual recognition), interculturalism therefore recognizes the de facto existence and legitimacy of a cultural majority and minorities. It grants everyone the right to secure his or her future, according to his or her choices, while promoting the closest interaction possible between these components with an objective of integration.

One can see here a significant paradox and at the same time one of the greatest challenges to interculturalism: the establishment of a balance between the imperative of pluralism and the imperative of inclusion. In other words, the desire to mitigate duality (as well as the majority-minorities relationship) in order to reduce boundaries or divisions and to create a shared culture has to be combined with the recognition of the rights of the members of the founding majority and of the minorities to remain attached to their heritage and identity.[21] The very spirit of pluralism therefore requires us to both mitigate and preserve duality.

In the case of Quebec, the model calls for an acknowledgment of the duality represented by the relationship between the francophone majority and the various ethnocultural minorities. Some commentators will perhaps see this proposition as a retreat. The course taken by Quebec over the last few decades could suggest an ongoing opening of ethnocultural boundaries and identities, the promotion of very extensive interrelationships within diversity. Significant progress has indeed been made in this direction, thanks in particular to Law 101 and the pluralist pedagogy practised in schools (it is among young people that the most striking changes have occurred). The fact remains that, on the whole, under the impact of powerful, complex mechanisms, the majority-minorities relationship survives in the reality of perceptions and behaviours. That is why it is important to take it into account in the analysis, not as an ideological or normative choice, but quite simply as an unavoidable feature of the cultural landscape (I will come back to this in chapter 4).

The concepts of majority and minority require a few clarifications. They should both be understood in a flexible manner. In Quebec, for example, the concept of cultural majority can be defined, according to context, in a very limited way (the members of the francophone culture who identify closely with the heritage of New France – those who formerly defined themselves as "Canadiens" and then "French Canadians") or in a very broad way. According to contexts and issues, the concept can among other things refer to all those who speak French (as a first, second, or other language), to the members of the host society, to the citizens who share certain so-called fundamental values, or to those who define themselves as being of Christian or European heritage. In other words, its meaning can sometimes be almost ethnic, sometimes ethnocultural, and sometimes cultural in a very broad sense (e.g., a majority agreement on the so-called universal values such as equality between men and women, non-violence, and the like).

As mentioned above, from one situation to another the majority can thus contract or expand according to issues and discursive strategies. In the pages below I will unless otherwise indicated use the term to refer to the members of the founding francophone culture, which currently represents 70 to 75 per cent of the Quebec population. This being said, it is clear that many of these maintain a rather distant connection with that founding culture, that some do not experience duality as an Us-Them relationship, and that others (young people especially) do not even perceive that duality. In other words, many members of the majority culture, without in any way denying their origins, identify first and foremost as Quebecers. We are therefore not dealing with a uniform block, frozen in time. Ideally, we would be able to refer to detailed statistical data, but currently such information is not available.

As for the concept of minority, as I indicated in the previous chapter, it should be understood primarily in its general statistical meaning, in this case a subpopulation characterized by the existence of a cultural nexus or of a distinct social life that develops in coexistence or in relationship to the majority culture, and of which the boundaries can be very porous. This last qualification is essential: the degree of sense of belonging to or affiliation with a group varies a great deal. For example, in Montreal, indications are that orthodox Jews and the Chinese population have stronger community ties than Quebecers of Arab origin or of the Muslim faith. The concept of minority should thus be understood in a way that leaves room for the flexibility that results from the freedom of choice of citizens and the complexity of identity dynamics, which is always fueled by interactions. It is important also to recall that duality, far from creating an impenetrable barrier between the majority and the minorities, leaves open the entire field of citizenship and shared culture (see the section below entitled "A Shared Culture").

I will therefore discuss all Quebec minorities in their relationship with the majority by making the necessary distinctions, but still without going into the nuances related to their specificity (history and patterns of settlement, interrelations, strength of feeling of belonging and solidarity, and so on).

The anglophone minority deserves special mention given the status that distinguishes it from other minorities. This minority can, in fact, be qualified as national because of its long history, because of the rights that are recognized for it under the British North America Act of 1867 (reaffirmed in the Canadian Constitution of 1982), and because it is an extension in Quebec of a neighbouring majority nation. Accordingly, the Quebec anglophone minority enjoys rights that are not recognized for other minorities (school boards, separate education and health care systems, elements of bilingualism in civic life, etc.).

Finally, I do not consider it necessary to restrict the concept of minority to immigrants of the first, second, or third generation, as suggested in a document from the Conseil des relations interculturelles [Intercultural Relations Council] (CRI, 2009, p. 2, n. 1). Once again, certain groups that settled earlier clearly show a desire to preserve their identities and their traditions separately from the majority culture (understood in the broad sense), even if they share many elements. They therefore constitute themselves as minorities; for this reason, they have less power in society and are more subject to various forms of discrimination.

From a perspective of duality, Quebec interculturalism must therefore arbitrate a majority-minorities relationship. In one way or another, since the 1960s, reflections on diversity in Quebec have almost always been based on this framework. One could even say that most of the initiatives intended to move these reflections forward (culture of convergence, shared public culture, "moral contract," focus on citizens at the end of the 1990s, etc.) were attempts either to deepen our understanding of the majority-minorities relationship or to conceive of a future for the francophone majority. With some exceptions, concern for minority rights has always been a major factor, as a call for caution, given the unequal power relationship that is inherent in contexts of duality.

Any relationship of duality places the majority in a dominant position. Experience shows that majority cultures, unconsciously or not, naturally tend to legislate according to their traditions, customs, and interests, mainly at the expense of minorities. From this point of view, interculturalism has an advantage over other models (multiculturalism or the republican model, for example) since the duality paradigm gives high visibility to a fundamental power relationship and consequently focuses attention on its possible abuses.[22]

This is precisely the basis for and the logic behind practices of accommodation and adjustment, practices intended to correct imbalances that infringe on the rights of certain people because of their characteristics or their cultural choices (see chapter 4).

One can see here the importance of mediation, the goal of which is to resolve situations of tension or conflict that arise at the community level or in the daily life of institutions. Like the practice of accommodation, cultural mediation is the art of smoothing over the difficulties of integration by arbitrating the encounter of values and traditions. A lot of tact, however, as well as special training are required to build bridges across ethnocultural differences and devise often temporary compromises and transitional processes that permit new arrivals to overcome the shock of immigration. One of the main problems is designing adjustments while avoiding either concealed assimilation or relativism of values; hence the need to practise mediation by referring constantly to major orientations established at the macrosocial level.

Cultural mediation is well established in many countries in the West.[23] In Quebec itself, it already has a long history,[24] and the number of practitioners is growing, although needs exceed the resources currently available.

This being said, interculturalism extends to all citizens responsibility for intercultural relations and unofficial mediations in daily life, especially the management of situations of incompatibility that inevitably occur in the life of institutions or within the community framework. It is therefore up to every citizen who is placed in a situation of interculturality to contribute to mutual adjustments and accommodations. The courts obviously maintain their indispensable function, but as a last resort only, when citizen action has failed to resolve disagreements. It also follows that beyond government policies, interculturalism encourages at the microsocial level the creative initiatives of individuals and groups. The importance of these interventions at the microsocial level in favour of integration has often been demonstrated.[25] On the whole, we can therefore identify four avenues for action corresponding to as many categories of actors: (a) the judiciary; (b) the government and its branches; (c) civil institutions and organizations; (d) and individuals and groups in their living and working environments.

One last question needs to be asked: Can we imagine in Quebec a way out of duality? There is no simple answer to this question, and it leads to a great deal of speculation. For Quebec to move to another paradigm, one of the following scenarios would have to come about, including some that are highly unlikely:

• The members of the founding culture will abandon their heritage and their identity (diversity paradigm).
• The members of minorities will choose to assimilate to the majority culture (homogeneity paradigm).
• The expanding shared culture will reach the point of including most of the Quebec ethnocultural space (*mixité* paradigm).
• Interculturalism fails, identities harden, the ethnocultural space fragments (bipolarity or multipolarity).
• The dual structure remains, but it abates substantially, which makes possible the shift to a form of diversity paradigm. (Recall here that

the paradigms are choices that can ignore and even contradict the ethnocultural make-up of a society.) The vision that young Quebecers (especially in Montreal) have of intercultural relationships seems to suggest a shift in this direction. On the other hand, the concern many members of the francophone majority feel about the future of their culture pushes in the opposite direction, as does the vitality of identities and affiliations within various minorities. Furthermore, the demographic structure of Quebec, in which the founding majority weighs heavily, plays in favour of the maintenance of duality.

Whatever the outcome of these hypotheses, what matters is that the exchanges and interactions advocated by interculturalism engage the majority and the minorities in a dynamics of openness and rapprochement rather than one of entrenchment and tension.

Integration

Interculturalism places a great emphasis on integration. To avoid any misunderstanding, I emphasize that I am not at all talking about assimilation. In accordance with North American sociological tradition, the concept of integration designates the set of mechanisms and processes of socialization through which social bonds, along with their symbolic and functional foundations, are constituted. These mechanisms and processes engage all citizens (old and new) and operate at various levels (individual, community, institutional, governmental) and in many spheres (economic, social, political, cultural, and so on). It should also be pointed out that integration is never finished, that it is an ongoing, open-ended process.[26]

With respect to immigration, integration requires a willingness and mutual effort on the part of both the members of the host society and new arrivals. I borrow here the definition used in the Bouchard-Taylor report (pp. 114–15), which is based on concepts of participation, reciprocity, interaction, equality, respect for rights, and socioeconomic integration. Once again, according to this concept, and contrary to how the term is frequently used in Europe, the concept of integration is therefore devoid of any assimilationist connotation.[27] For more clarity, we could speak of "integrationism" to designate forms of integration that do not respect diversity.[28]

I also want to emphasize the concept of reciprocity, since integration is not a one-way process. The host society, in various ways, should facilitate the integration and adaptation of immigrants. In return, immigrants agree to comply with the fundamental values and rules that govern the host society, and to adapt to its institutions.

The importance accorded to integration is in keeping with the requirements of social cohesion and especially with the reality of Quebec society as a francophone nation. This expression requires qualification. All inhabitants of Quebec – including those who do not speak French – are part of this nation, and on an equal footing. The fact remains that, sociologically, this nation can be qualified as francophone (a) because of the founding majority culture; (b) because French is the official language of Quebec; and (c) because the majority of Quebecers of non-francophone origin are capable of communicating in French. It should also be recalled that it is mainly the francophone character of Quebec that is the basis for its distinct status on the entire North American continent and that earned it recognition as a nation by the Canadian parliament in November 2006.

Francophone Quebec faces constraints that are a source of vulnerability and that fuel a feeling of insecurity. Concern about integration and unity is in a way a constant in the history of this nation. It is no surprise that the language of public debate reflects this concern; people talk a great deal about solidarity, collective projects, unifying solutions, inclusive policies, quest for consensus, consultation, shared values, and the like.

This emphasis on integration is also in keeping with legal requirements. A democratic society needs to be concerned about the economic and social integration of its citizens, especially the most disadvantaged, many of whom are immigrants. It also needs to foster participation in civic and political life for everyone. But integration, although a high priority, must not become a straitjacket. It is necessary to recognize the right of certain citizens to live on the margins of the predominant model of society (within the limitations permitted by law) or to opt for various ways of integrating. Here also, flexibility is essential.

Rapprochements and Interactions

In a spirit of integrative pluralism, interculturalism favours interactions, rapprochements, exchanges, and joint initiatives. It is especially important to ensure that these exchanges not only bring the minorities closer to each other, but also bring together members of the majority and minorities. At its core, the argument is simple: these interactions serve a general objective of integration, they are intended to bring together or harmonize values and norms that are different or even divergent (see A. Wimmer, 2013; J.S. Coleman, 1990, chap. 11), they help to reduce the stereotypes and false categorizations that fuel discrimination and exclusion, they are an essential precondition for participation in public debates, and they create fertile ground for the arbitration of conflicts.

Another argument in favour of interactions concerns the benefits to be gained from ethnocultural diversity. A society can benefit from its diversity if the individuals and groups that primarily make it up each live according to their own ways. Finally, we can expect these interactions and these shared initiatives to generate a memory that transcends the identity of each of the participating groups, thus contributing to solidifying bonds and developing solidarity at the societal level. In other words, while identity is often the mother of joint action, it can also be its child.

It is important, however, that these interactions not be limited to intercultural dialogue. This kind of exercise can peter out if it is not extended to joint initiatives and concrete projects focusing on needs that emerge at the community, institutional, or national level, and from which all the actors will be able to benefit. This is an effective means of putting diversity into action and realizing its potential. It is also a way of creating a sense of belonging based on an experience of collaboration that favours, in the long run, the memory of what the actors will have done together.

In another direction, the best means to counteract the discomfort that some can feel when faced with a stranger is not to keep their distance, but to come together to destroy false perceptions and facilitate the stranger's integration into the host society. Exclusion is objectionable not only in moral or legal terms, but also from a strictly sociological perspective.

This philosophy is based in large part on "contact theory" (or "contact hypothesis"),[29] which postulates the positive effects of rapprochements. The theory has been verified in many studies,[30] but it has also sometimes failed, when old conflicts and powerful relationships of domination blocked rapprochements (see, among others, R.D. Putnam, 2007, pp. 142–3). One of the most interesting experiments to have been carried out recently was a British government initiative following interethnic riots that occurred in 2001 in a few working-class cities in northern England (in particular Liverpool and Birmingham). An important project was also launched in Northern Ireland in 1994 (M. Hewstone, N. Tausch, J. Hughes, & E. Cairns, 2007). In Quebec, various polls conducted over the last five years show that negative perceptions, apprehensions, and tensions are reduced substantially with increased contacts.[31]

It goes without saying that the effectiveness of intercultural dialogue is limited by power relationships, practices of discrimination, exclusionary measures, and social inequalities. This is an important constraint, and it is why this dimension must be included in interculturalism, coupled with a call for social change.

A Shared Culture

In the same spirit, interculturalism also advocates the development of a shared culture with two major components. The first is made up of prescriptive elements. First there is French as the language of civic and public life. There are also the values or norms included in the charter and in laws, which are therefore imposed on all citizens; we are thinking here, in particular, of equality, justice, liberty, democracy, respect for human life, non-violence, and separation of state and religion. The requirements of pluralism and the policy of recognition end where these values are called into question. It should be noted that I do not consider these shared values the sole foundation of life in society, but they certainly constitute a very important component (under certain conditions that will be presented below). It is also essential, if we want to remain faithful to pluralism, that these values maintain a fundamental character, with a civic orientation (as pointed out by F. Rocher, 2008, p. 162).[32] The second component is made up of norms or models corresponding to broadly shared but uncodified values (solidarity, personal autonomy, mutual respect, respect for the past, civic-mindedness, etc.).

Some of these values were forged through the history of Quebec (see below), and they can have a civic orientation to the extent that they possess a universalizing potential. They are therefore likely to be shared freely by all citizens, like certain values brought by immigrants or coming from the pasts of cultural minorities. All this, once again, is subject to debates, negotiations, and collective choices, against the background of divergences of view, divisions, and conflicts, with the understanding that democratic debate on disagreements is itself part of the dynamics of the shared culture.

In other words, the shared culture is constructed through the combined work of all heritages, including, of course, that of the founding majority, which occupies a crucial position.[33] Again, one sees how the cultural capital contributed by that majority, far from being sacrificed (as some claim), can invest or reinvest itself massively, and continue to develop in the shared culture, in permanent contact with diversity. This statement is also based on the idea that a symbolic capital that isolates itself and refuses change is condemned to grow poorer.

The second component includes everything related to affiliation (or identity-based dynamics) and national history. It also draws from the rituals of government, from the experiences of public life, from the dynamics of exchanges and interactions, in the intermingling of traditions, beliefs, and visions of the world and in what could be called the culture of everyday life (the specific characteristics of language, current symbols disseminated by the media, and so on). The shared culture is therefore made up of strictly civic content, prescriptive in nature, and cultural content, which is more sociological (or, in the current terms of the debate, "negotiable" elements and "non-negotiable" elements).[34]

The state has the duty to intervene directly in the first component, as the promoter and guardian of fundamental citizenship values. However, with respect to the second component, its initiatives – although desirable and legitimate – should be compatible with the principle of citizens' freedom of choice and action. For example, at the level of microsocial life (that of the neighbourhood, recreation, intercommunity relationships), it is important to give free rein to the initiatives and creativity of the actors. It is mainly at this level that the bridges and social bonds are created that open people up to other forms of rapprochements and understanding.[35]

One expects that, broadly open to all the contributions of diversity, the shared culture would be a focal point for inventions and changes. It is precisely one of the objectives of interculturalism to open up new avenues, "clear new horizons of meaning."[36] And it is because this shared culture is in constant movement in response to public debates and intercultural life that its contents do not lend themselves to any specific definition or inventory, apart from what is included in laws and the charter.

With respect to national history, it is completely legitimate and even necessary that it be based broadly on the memory of the founding culture,[37] but in a way that makes it significant and accessible to all citizens by emphasizing its universal content, and including the experiences of minorities. Unlike what is stated by J.-Y. Thériault (2010, pp. 147–8) and a few others, this does not lead to sanitizing that history to the point that it becomes a disembodied narrative. Quite the contrary, the idea is to bring out the universal at the heart of its singularity: through its specific characteristics, show the threads that transcend them and can connect with other threads, a process that necessarily requires the application of a perspective based on comparisons.[38] Here, the path has been laid out by Gaston Miron, who formulated very relevant reflections on the relationship between universal and particular.[39]

The main objective is to highlight and dialogue on the fundamental values that have emerged in the course of the historical experiences of the majority and the minorities and that provide roots for identities. Approached in this way, the national history can be a significant nexus for encounters and intercultural fermentation, while ensuring a future and an expansion for the memory of the founding culture. An immigrant or a member of a minority will never be able to entirely adopt the historical consciousness of Quebec and the identity references that are associated with it in the same way as members of the founding culture, who have deeply internalized these very early in their lives and have integrated them into a strong identity. But immigrants and members of minorities will be able to subscribe to the values that come out of that history, appropriate them in their own ways, understand them, and share the challenges.[40] The national memory is therefore fully part of the shared culture, of which it is a key component.[41]

Defined in this way, the shared culture fulfils five related functions: (1) it promotes integration, in that it guarantees for minorities and new arrivals the assurance of full citizenship and protects them from exclusion; (2) it reduces duality and the Us-Them relationship that duality creates; (3) it builds bridges for the members of the majority as well as ethnocultural minorities that want to renegotiate their identities of origin and fear being closed up in a "straitjacket" or an "ethnic ghetto";[42] (4) it is a place for the encounter, expression, and promotion of diversity;[43] and (5) it gradually creates a sense of belonging, which is necessary to any society since this is the primary element that supports the social bond. In broad terms, interculturalism opens two major avenues for definitions of identity and for integration: that of filiation, for those who wish to maintain an allegiance to their culture of origin, and that of affiliation, for those who wish to distance themselves from it to integrate into the shared culture.

This argument in favour of a shared culture is not valid only for small nations. For example, one basic concern throughout the entire history of political thought in the United States has been how to overcome diversity and divisions of all kinds to create unity and establish consensuses.[44]

A National Culture

According to the above, interculturalism encourages a broad, dynamic vision of the Quebec national culture as a composite that emerges from three closely intertwined threads, in constant movement and largely opened to outside contributions: the majority culture, the minority cultures, and the shared culture. However, I am proposing this position while surrounding it with all necessary qualifications and reservations. First of all, these threads intersect in many ways and, according to the logic of interculturalism, it is expected that this characteristic will become more and more pronounced. Second, this culture is fueled in part by its own movement, but more and more it also integrates contributions of globalization. As T. Cantle (2011) points out, opening up to globalization represents both a challenge and a means to enrich interculturalism. This is an avenue of reflection to be pursued further, especially for a minority culture such as francophone Quebec. Third, these threads definitely contain hard cores, but we also find a great deal of fluidity, interrelationships, and shades of identity. This suggests that we should use the concept of culture carefully, since it often evokes realities that are deceptively assumed to be static and compartmentalized.[45] Interculturalism also advocates a very flexible view of identity dynamics, which are always in movement. Otherwise there is a risk of building largely imaginary boundaries. In recent decades, many studies have indeed demonstrated the unstable, negotiated dimension of identities,[46] in parallel with their mechanisms of rootedness and continuity.

These remarks call for a balanced concept of culture that takes into consideration both (a) roots and continuities (language, memory, founding myths, territoriality, etc.)[47] and (b) fluidities – what is always being renewed or negotiated.

Under these conditions, it is clear that the definition of the Quebec nation must incorporate the contents of the founding culture, but it must also be open to other symbolic references forged in the past of minorities or brought by immigrants (by virtue of what I have called the process of historicization). Finally, this culture must be based as much as possible on the shared language and values that emerge from the intercultural dynamic. This way, all citizens are assured of being able to contribute to the development of the national culture on the basis of their own backgrounds. Interculturalism is therefore built on a gamble: one expects in the long run that a dynamic of exchange will shape an original Quebec culture marked with the seal of the French language. In other words, it takes up the familiar challenge of creating an identity within diversity.[48]

We can conclude that there exists in Quebec a national culture, an official language, a majority culture, and cultural minorities – including a national minority made up of Anglo-Quebecers. It is on the basis of these components that a new *Us* is currently being constructed that incorporates all the diversity and gives a new face to Quebec as a "francophonie nord-américaine" (North American French-speaking nation) – an expression used by G. Rocher (1973, part 1, chap. 1) a long time ago.

Complementary Remarks

This reflection on the definition of interculturalism needs to be extended in four directions.

Duality

How can we mitigate duality while respecting the right of people (whether members of the majority or minorities) to remain loyal or maintain some attachment to their first culture and to their identity of origin, which constitutes precisely an important source of Quebec duality? As indicated above, we need to navigate here between, on the one hand, the sociological imperatives of cohesiveness and unity and, on the other hand, the demands of pluralism.

For the sake of brevity, I will only remark that identity dynamics, although crucial, are the product of a history that is still developing, and that they therefore have to remain open to change. It is also important to point out that, in a context of increasing diversity, they have to be maintained in osmosis with each other, so as to avoid the hardening of intercultural relations. Similarly, it is useful for each ethnocultural group to become aware of its own diversity, thus avoiding fetishizing its roots as if its members' sense of belonging and solidarity were based only on homogeneity resulting from a long history. A society should also be concerned about promoting as much as possible the consolidation of a shared culture as a decompartmentalization measure.

Moreover, it should make efforts to bring out the strengths that unite citizens beyond their differences – I am thinking of the defence of rights and citizenship values, the reduction of discrimination or, in the context of Quebec, the struggle for the French language, which is of vital interest to both francophone immigrants (North Africans and others) and members of the founding majority. Finally, the fight against stereotypes, and all forms of intercultural rapprochements, are moves towards a mitigated duality, free from tensions. This being said, it is obvious that all these measures are likely to be futile if the ethnocultural grid is structured by sharp socioeconomic divisions. Once again, as already mentioned, it is clear that interculturalism has to mobilize both the social and the cultural.

Secularism

The spirit of interculturalism, as it has just been characterized, favours the promotion of a secular regime based on two major principles. The first involves a search for balance between the five components of any secular regime: (a) the mutual autonomy of religion (and more generally, convictions of conscience or visions of the world) and the state; (b) neutrality of the state in the area of religion; (c) freedom of conscience; (d) equality of religions; and (e) the protection of religious symbols with heritage value.[49] Second, interculturalism invites us to design a type of management of religious diversity (and convictions of conscience) that avoids as much as possible exclusion and respects basic rights, while remaining in accordance with interculturalism's objective of pluralist integration. I see religious diversity as one of the crucial elements of cultural diversity; that is why I am including in these pages a description of a secular regime conceived in the spirit of interculturalism (see chapter 5).

Insecurity within the Cultural Majority

As we have seen, there are insecurities among many members of the Quebec cultural majority, because it is itself a minority. Accordingly, many feel a need for protections, particularly with respect to language, traditions, and values. It should be recalled that the main criticism levelled at the report of the Bouchard-Taylor Commission was that it paid almost all its attention to the situation of immigrants and minorities while neglecting the fate of the founding majority, which also feels a need for long-term protections to guarantee its future. Opinions may differ on this subject, but the question has been posed and it is a complex one: how can we satisfy this aspiration of the founding majority without infringing on the fundamental rights of other Quebecers, without creating in Quebec two classes of citizens?

With regard to this question, it should be pointed out that the cultural majority now possesses significant means to ensure its future. Simply through its demographic and sociological weight, it is assured of exercising decisive influence on the development of the shared culture, which exercise is completely legitimate. This shared culture is not being constructed from scratch; the Quebec cultural space is structured by a collective life that is part of a long history (aboriginal, francophone, anglophone, and allophone). On the basis of its numbers, the francophone majority has affirmed itself as a principal component. As much as it has a duty to share and redefine the symbolic territory that it has developed, it would be unreasonable to think that it should withdraw from it.

I also recall that this majority controls the majority of public and private institutions, including the government and the media. In addition, francophones are in the majority in sixty-six of the seventy-five federal electoral districts in Quebec.[50] All this should inspire a minimal sense of security. What could be added?

One thinks first of all of the political route, that is, the possibility of Quebec obtaining additional powers within Canada or a radical change to its constitutional status; this will be commented on below. As for the legal route, I have already indicated that it is important to proceed with caution. In accordance with the wishes of its citizens, Quebec has always been and should remain a society of law. Nevertheless, two significant elements legitimately favour the majority. First of all, it can happen that the courts themselves agree that certain rights be limited or even suspended for higher reasons. This is what happened in Quebec with Law 101, of which the Supreme Court of Canada recognized the legitimacy (even though it reduced in various ways the initial version of the law). Similarly, it is usually recognized that the Quebec government has the right to select immigrants on the basis of their knowledge of French by making it an important criterion when evaluating candidates. It is also acknowledged that Quebec can give priority to cultural expressions in the French language in its cultural development programs (in arts, literature, etc.)[51]

Moreover, as all the democratic nation states do (including the most "civic" ones such as Canada, the United States, and Switzerland), francophone Quebec can allow itself some latitude with respect to the ideal (often professed but achieved nowhere) of the cultural neutrality of the state. This radical principle, which forbids government from intervening in the definition and promotion of a public morality or a concept of the good ("the good life"), has its roots in the liberal philosophy of John Locke, John Stuart Mill, and Immanuel Kant; during the 1970s and 1980s, authors such as John Rawls (1971), Ronald Dworkin (1978, 1985), and Bruce Ackerman (1980) were among its main proponents. According to the principle, it is solely up to (free, autonomous) individuals to cultivate the values of their choices, protected from the interference of the state or its substitutes.[52]

Once again, I do not know of any governments, even among the most democratic, that conform fully to that philosophy; all practise some form of cultural interventionism in favour of the majority.[53] Quebec can therefore legitimately practise cultural interventionism and demand an appropriate amount of flexibility that permits it to provide itself with certain protections in the name of historical continuity and collective cohesiveness, when these measures do not conflict with fundamental rights. In conformity once again with other nation states known for their liberalism or their profession of "civic" faith, Quebec does not have to feel obliged to respect a position of strict neutrality or abstentionism in the area of culture when it comes to protecting its national language, promoting citizenship values, or safeguarding its traditions. For example, for Jocelyn Maclure and Charles Taylor (2010, p. 86), "it is only natural that certain public norms should be rooted in the attributes and interests of the majority."[54] Similarly, the "civic pact" advocated by M. Labelle (2008a, p. 42) from a republican perspective is presented as being "neither neutral nor abstract." I should mention that this cultural interventionism can also play in favour of certain long-established minorities, which therefore contribute to the continuity of a society. It should be noted, finally, that I do not include this interventionism among the components of interculturalism, quite simply because it is not specific to it; on the contrary, it is found everywhere (see chapter 4 for more extensive comments on this subject).

The above remarks bring out clearly the nature of Quebec interculturalism as a search for balance. This dimension is particularly evident here. It is a matter of arbitrating the tension between two sometimes divergent imperatives: to respect ethnocultural diversity and to ensure the continuity of the symbolic foundation that has sustained the social link in the long term. Interculturalism builds on a logic of weights and counterweights, in accordance with a process that cannot be reduced to simple geometry. This is due in large part to its rejection of binary or dichotomous thought, which has the effect of polarizing and radicalizing when, most often, reality calls for a constant and difficult effort of conciliation, synthesis, and balance between various competing imperatives.

The Constitutional Arena

The fourth direction leads to the Canadian constitutional arena. As everyone knows, Quebec is faced with a competition and even a contradiction between two linguistic policies,[55] two regimes of integration, citizenship, affiliation, and identity, one controlled at the Quebec level, the other at the Canadian level. For example, immigrants settling in Quebec can content themselves with the English language by virtue of federal legislation. Similarly, the staff of Canadian government agencies working in the territory of Quebec are not subject to Law 101, which established

French as the language of work. Such a double system has many other implications for political, economic, social, and cultural life – in particular in the teaching of national history (F. Ouellet, 1995).[56]

In the area of the management of ethnocultural diversity, the only model that is prevalent under Canadian law is multiculturalism, and the Supreme Court of Canada, which takes precedence over the courts of the provinces, has to take this into account in its judgments.[57] Similarly, the Canadian charter takes precedence over the Quebec charter. It is therefore accurate to say that the provisions of Quebec interculturalism can be invalidated by federal institutions on the basis of a philosophy and legal culture that are different from the Quebec tradition. This has been demonstrated by cases in which judgments of Quebec courts involving requests for accommodations were overturned by the Supreme Court of Canada (see S. Grammond, 2009; L.-P. Lampron, 2009). At a broader level, it is also true that with the current state of affairs within Canada, Quebec does not possess a status or powers that would permit it to fully position itself as a host society.

Quebec is therefore a nation within another nation that wishes to affirm its predominance. Its policies are subject to Canadian policies, and its development is inevitably restricted by that dependence. Furthermore, the Canadian government often imposes on Quebec policies the latter does not want – the latest examples of which are abolition of the firearms registry law, the new punitive policy in the area of youth crime (Bill C-10), the promotion of monarchist symbols, and increased militarization.

These constraints have an indisputably negative effect on Quebec's ability to effectively manage its ethnocultural reality. In practice, however, it can be asserted that:

- Canadian multiculturalism is already subject to varied applications in the anglophone provinces, which shows it has some flexibility;
- the model has changed a lot since 1971 and it continues to evolve – recent changes are even bringing it oddly close to Quebec interculturalism (see chapter 3), which significantly expands the scope for interpretation of section 27 of the Canadian charter;
- these two models can be seen as two different applications of the pluralist orientation, which both forms the basis for the distinctive nature of interculturalism and ensures its legitimacy from the Canadian perspective;
- the term "multicultural" can be interpreted in more than one way, so that section 27, for example, could be understood as a simple reminder of plurality and a general obligation to respect diversity.

While these considerations seem to shield interculturalism from any political intervention from the federal government, the fact remains that Quebec policies based on interculturalism can still be contested before the Supreme Court. Here again, there is a solution for this eventuality. If it came to the point where, through its judgments, the Supreme Court repeatedly contradicted and imperilled the fundamental values of Quebecers, they would then be fully justified in resisting these judgments, either by using the notwithstanding clause of the Canadian constitution or by resorting to other legal and political means.

In short, Quebec has a certain amount of flexibility,[58] but it is narrow. It is obvious that any progress in the political and constitutional arenas would be welcome. For example, we often hear discussion of the possibility of Quebec obtaining new legislative powers, the adoption of a Quebec citizenship and a Quebec constitution recognized by the federal government, the redefinition of Canada as multinational, the recognition of the collective rights of Quebec, and access to political sovereignty.[59] These measures, obviously, would strengthen the status of Quebec as a host society and as a nexus for the management of ethnocultural diversity. They would also help to better ensure the future of Quebec as a French-speaking entity in North America.

However, for various reasons (mainly the inflexibility shown by the Canadian government and the political divisions that prevail in Quebec), we will perhaps have to wait for a long time before significant progress can be achieved in this area. Should we, however, as Raffaele Iacovino (2009, pp. 209–10, 213), Daniel Salée (2001, p. 163), and a few others seem to think, declare a moratorium on discussions of a Quebec model for the management of diversity?

Such a scenario does not seem feasible. First of all, the problems related to intercultural life in Quebec call for the development of policies and the implementation of solutions in the very short term. In addition, Quebec already has powers that it has used in the past (among them the charter of rights, Law 101, integration policies, selection of immigrants, policies to fight discrimination, and school curriculum) and that have made significant progress possible. Finally, the establishment of a broad consensus on interculturalism and the adoption of appropriate policies will reveal areas of friction and give shape to necessary demands. It is necessary, obviously, to work at both levels.

Finally, according to some, the recognition of the ethnocultural duality of Quebec would weaken neonationalism and lead to the failure of the sovereignist movement. This position does not seem well founded. Taking into account the majority-minorities relationship is only a reflection of the deep structure of the ethnocultural reality of Quebec, and doing so will further understanding of that reality, which can only be useful whether one considers the future of Quebec inside or outside the Canadian framework. Changing perceptions without changing the reality is not a good principle of governance. However, if the analyses that I am presenting in this book are accurate, this duality structure will remain for a long time, like it or not. In itself, duality opens up all constitutional options; it neither favours nor prejudices any.

Conclusion

The conception of interculturalism that I have just presented is based on a few key ideas that it will be useful to review to better highlight the goals and originality of this model.

Principles, General Orientations, Specific Contexts

The conception of a model for the democratic management of diversity takes as its starting point universal ideals that must be applied in a given context. The result is always a remarkable combination of universal principles and distinctive characteristics. The same is true of Quebec interculturalism, which, being based on democracy, the rule of law, and pluralism, combines these major orientations with the (a) traditions, (b) demographic, social, and cultural characteristics, (c) collective priorities, and (d) sensibilities of Quebec society. Accordingly, certain attributes of interculturalism are common to many models, while others are specific or exclusive to it. Among the specific ones, we can mention duality, the emphasis on integration, the practice of interactions, and the promotion of a shared culture. Among the others, one finds in particular the principle of recognition and the practice of accommodations, which are both inherent to pluralism.

But even here, interculturalism advocates specific features. In Quebec, for example, it is recommended that the criterion of integration be given a lot of weight in the examination of requests for accommodations. In the same spirit, the principle of recognition should not be an obstacle to the expansion of the shared culture. As for pluralism, it reaches its limit when it comes to fundamental, civic, and universal values, such as equality between men and women and non-violence.

The definition that I have presented proposes an approach to managing ethnocultural reality that is aligned with the duality paradigm. But it goes without saying that the arrangements set forth do not necessarily suit other nations where the reflections are also taking place from a perspective of duality. Duality, like interculturalism, remains open to a wide variety of configurations according to specific contexts. It is predictable, for example, that certain nations will want to emphasize economic and social integration or the struggle against discrimination, while others will give priority to the development of the shared culture or to the harmonization of cultural differences. Therefore I have focused this reflection mainly on the Quebec reality, in which the majority-minorities relationship is deep rooted. But it is different in other societies – European ones in particular – where duality has emerged more recently and under very different conditions. The majority culture can therefore deal with it according to various features and resonances inherited from its history, with its own specific provisions and adjustments.

Arbitrations and Negotiations

As I have pointed out, interculturalism calls for constant negotiations and mediations to smooth over the divergences inherent in the encounter of cultures. Here, the primary actors are the citizens, who are daily engaged in the management of diversity. At another level we find the policy-makers within public and private institutions. But all this raises the question of the arbitration of these exchanges: who resolves persistent disputes? In a democratic society, we should rely first of all on public debate, then on political authorities and, as a last resort, the courts. The ideal, obviously, is that the citizens themselves are able to take responsibility and bring this arbitration to a successful conclusion. That is why it is important to inform them, to raise their awareness and make them more responsible. Furthermore, it is obvious that Quebec society, like any society, is the site of structural power relationships, which are sources of various inequalities. Interculturalism is necessarily interested in this key dimension; hence the emphasis put on the fight against discrimination and racism.

An Expanded Concept of Citizenship

Interculturalism is intended as a comprehensive model that takes into account, as is fitting, all aspects of the management of diversity, by virtue of a broad conception of citizenship defined with reference to five dimensions:

- a cultural dimension: the harmonization of differences, in particular religious ones
- a legal dimension: respect for and arbitration of individual and collective rights, including cultural rights
- a social dimension: socioeconomic integration and the fight against inequalities, relationships of domination, discrimination, and racism
- a specifically civic dimension: participation in political life
- a political dimension: on the one hand, the management role of the government, and on the other hand, in the context of Quebec, its role as mediator between Quebec and Ottawa[60]

Being mainly based on respect for rights and diversity, interculturalism needs to encompass all these dimensions. We know that ethnocultural differences are often the cause not only of stereotypes and prejudices, but also of discrimination, economic and social exclusion, and inequalities. Racism, for example, hides behind stereotypes or false representations. It is therefore necessary to target these to show that they are groundless.

The Quest for Balance

Interculturalism is the model that is best suited to the parameters listed at the beginning of chapter 1. It proposes a way of living together that is in continuity with the Quebec past and is the one best suited to the challenges of the present, namely the double objective of unity and respect for differences, in keeping with a broad concept of citizenship. It is aimed not only at avoiding the segmentation of Quebec society, but at strengthening it culturally and socially. It is a model that calls for democratic debate, as well as a mixture of firmness and flexibility: firmness on principles and fundamental values, and flexibility on how they are applied. All this is in the service of a common objective: to learn to live together in a spirit of respect for our differences and, to this end, cultivate the essential virtues of openness, prudence, and moderation.

Finally, more than any other model, interculturalism works to find balance. This is the case especially in Quebec, where it is necessary to arbitrate, while respecting differences and rights, the relationships between minorities and a majority that is itself a minority. Furthermore, it is best to defuse as much as possible the Us-Them relationship by reducing duality, while also recognizing that this means another imperative emerges, namely the right of citizens to remain attached to their culture of origin.

As I have indicated, the result is that, in the same spirit of pluralism, both the cultural majority and the minorities can legitimately ensure their survival. Here again there is a narrow path to be followed that consists of promoting the expansion of the shared culture and strengthening the national culture of Quebec, but without imperilling the diversity of cultures that sustain them.

More generally, the quest for balance arises out of the ultimate goal of interculturalism, which is to develop a middle-ground approach, a third way between fragmentation and assimilation.[61] We therefore need to apply a particular conception of pluralism and of the cultural foundations of a society.

Coming back to the Quebec context, this general orientation is expressed more specifically in many ways, such as the following:

- combining within Quebec culture the elements of continuity (identified with the founding majority) with the new elements of diversity introduced by immigration and embodied in the minorities
- in the conception of the intercultural dynamic, taking into consideration both roots and fluidities
- promoting a view and a practice of the law that take into account the legitimacy of identities and the associated aspirations
- ensuring the future and development of the French language while encouraging the growth of multilingualism
- implementing policies that reconcile individual rights and collective rights
- managing diversity so as to decide equitably, within various traditions, visions of the world and aspirations – those that can be established as fundamental values; those that, while legitimate, are based on individual choices; and finally, those that should simply be rejected (I am thinking here among other things of extreme concepts of honour that incite violent crimes)
- recognizing affiliations, traditions, and identities while avoiding hardening them or creating artificial boundaries that impinge on individual rights
- teaching a national memory that is structured around the past of the founding majority as the main theme and reflects it fully, but includes the trajectories of minorities, especially the values and ideals of which these trajectories are vehicles, all in keeping with the development of a shared culture

- managing religious diversity in a spirit of respect for rights, with the twofold concern of avoiding exclusion and safeguarding the founding principles of secularism
- in the area of accommodations, establishing a functional balance between the formulation of specific norms and the room for cultural interventionism by decision-makers in institutions

Quebec, as a small francophone nation and as a minority culture on the continent, has always been a society under tension, and the negotiation of equilibrium has always been a key to its survival and its development. Its history has always been a collective balancing act. In the area of management of diversity, it should be recalled, for example, that just when Quebec was making attendance at French school mandatory for immigrants (under Law 101) it was also introducing a program for the teaching of heritage languages in public schools. In the same spirit, the intercultural policies promoted over the last few decades have provided protection for a francophone culture, but at the same time promoted rights and citizenship. In so doing, they reconciled the affirmation of a strong identity, support for neonationalism, with the promotion of liberal values. The "moral contract" of 1990 is very representative in this regard, as well as the concepts of shared public culture, integrative pluralism, or inclusive secularism.

All this makes Quebec interculturalism a complex model, shaped with prudence and nuance and developing around a few guiding principles bound together by the search for balance. On the basis of the majority-minorities relationship, it tries to unite, in the spirit of liberalism, the civic and the cultural, the individual and the collective. We could certainly wish for a simpler formula, but as we can see with the assimilationist models, simplicity in the area of ethnocultural diversity is not the right formula. Interculturalism is an approach conceived around bridges, relationships, and arbitrations; it is the opposite of a polarizing perspective that is characterized by the creation and hardening of antagonisms (see G. Bouchard, 2001a).

Quebec Interculturalism: A Tradition of Thought

In conclusion, I would like to point out the significant elements of consensus that currently exist around the conception of interculturalism in Quebec. The purpose of these reminders is not to conceal the areas of disagreement. They are aimed at showing the existence of a tradition of coherent thought on the subject. They also provide me with the opportunity to express my indebtedness to those who have preceded me. In short, we find within the Quebec intellectual and scientific communities a continuity similar to what I have identified in government documents of recent decades.

Generally, first of all, intellectuals who have studied and promoted interculturalism have all positioned their reflections within the framework of Quebec as a nation. They have also all emphasized the key role of francophone culture (mainly the French language), and all have stressed the protection of the rights of all citizens, especially of members of ethnocultural minorities, which includes recognition of the diversity of Quebec society and the fight against discrimination, racism, and exclusion. There is therefore a broad consensus on the pluralist orientation, as well as the priority to be given to integration, exchanges, rapprochements, and interactions.

Concern for preserving the fundamental values of the host society is also very prevalent in these discussions, as well as the search for balance, in particular with respect to the need to combine the future of francophone, majority culture, and that of the minorities.[62] Accordingly, most authors in one way or another make room for the majority-minorities relationship. Furthermore, they largely agree in recognizing the legitimacy of the historical consciousness of the francophone majority and on making it an important dimension of Quebec culture. As I also mentioned, the idea of defining interculturalism as a middle road between multiculturalism and republicanism is quite broadly shared.[63]

Finally, the project of a shared (public) culture is supported by many authors, although this element remains controversial.[64] Likewise, there are differences of opinion on the importance to be given to what belongs respectively to culture and citizenship, these two terms being frequently – and wrongly – seen as mutually exclusive.

3

Interculturalism and Multiculturalism

In the Quebec context, it is not possible to talk about interculturalism without broaching the subject of multiculturalism. I will therefore digress a bit to situate Quebec interculturalism in relationship to Canadian multiculturalism. I recall first of all that, for political reasons, all Quebec governments (federalist or not) have rejected multiculturalism since its adoption by the federal government in 1971.[1] This decision was in keeping with a tradition of thought that had been firmly established in Quebec's political culture. Since the middle of the nineteenth century, Quebec francophones have fought for acceptance of a definition of Canada as being made up of two nations (anglophone and francophone) sharing the same rights. This vision of the country was, however, undermined by the introduction of multiculturalism (on the initiative of Prime Minister Trudeau), who denied Quebec's status as a political community and made Quebec francophones just one ethnic group among many others at the Canadian level. In this sense, multiculturalism had the effect of weakening Quebec and, for this reason, it has always been vehemently opposed within the francophone population.[2] For the same reason, Prime Minister Trudeau came to be reviled by many Quebecers (see K. McRoberts, 1997, A.I. Silver, 1997; S. Paquin, 1999; D. Forbes, 2007).

From a sociological point of view, it is also obvious that multiculturalism had been designed for anglophone Canada. Concern for national language is absent and, except for a few authors, the questions related to the status of the national minority have received little attention. It therefore closes the door on a binational or multinational conception of Canada. Finally, I recall that this model does not recognize any national or majority culture.

How Does Interculturalism Differ from Multiculturalism?

The idea of interculturalism is born of the rejection of multiculturalism and the desire to develop a model that is more suited to the needs of Quebec society, in particular the need to better protect the characteristics of francophone Quebec. Accordingly, the members of the cultural majority have always paid a great deal of attention to the definition of interculturalism, specifically to ensure that the Canadian model is not reproduced in Quebec. In the same spirit, Quebec researchers are regularly called upon to explain the differences between these two models. However, for various reasons, there are no simple answers to this question.

One of these reasons, as we will see, is the fact that Canadian multiculturalism has evolved considerably since its introduction in 1971 (this is an important fact that is not always taken into account, particularly in Quebec). Another reason concerns the highly polysemic nature of this concept, which assumes different meanings from one author, one school of thought, or one country to another (see N. Meer & T. Modood, 2011). We need therefore to carefully select the standard of comparison.

First, I will refer to the most widespread perception of multiculturalism currently in the West, which commonly defines it (and criticizes it) with reference to five main features:

- a definition of the nation as a collection of individuals and groups, which does not recognize the existence of a national or majority culture
- an openness to diversity that can jeopardize integration, going as far as to expose a society to the danger of fragmentation
- a practice of pluralism that tends towards relativism, to the detriment of fundamental, universal values
- a promotion of ethnocultural minorities that constrains those of its members who would like to distance themselves from it
- little concern for the establishment of a shared culture that would ensure for the nation or society an essential symbolic foundation, a rallying point that is a source of cohesiveness and solidarity

It is obvious that interculturalism, as I presented it above, is very clearly distinct from this version of multiculturalism. It could even be said that, on all these points, it advocates orientations that are diametrically opposed.

But is it appropriate to identify Canadian multiculturalism with the configuration that I have just outlined? The answer to this question has to be "no" because of the changes that it has gone through in the course of its history (see, e.g., W. Kymlicka, 1998; D. Helly, 2000; Y. Abu-Laban & C. Gabriel, 2002) and because of the characteristics that it has come to exhibit (W. Kymlicka, 2010, 2012). In the 1970s, for example, the preservation and promotion of the diversity of languages and cultures were key elements of the Canadian model. Starting in the 1980s, the social dimension (the fight against inequalities and exclusion) became salient, along with the legal dimension, expressed, among other things, in the fight against racist discrimination. At the same time, the programs aimed at perpetuating the folk traditions of minorities were gradually abandoned.

With the 1990s and the beginning of the 2000s there emerged an increasing concern for collective cohesiveness, for integration and shared values, for the formation (or consolidation) of a Canadian sense of belonging and identity. An analysis of polls taken since 1983 shows an increase in support for a policy aimed at the integration of immigrants into a strong Canadian culture. This statement was endorsed by 26 per cent of respondents in 1995 and 32 per cent in 2005 (see www.crop.ca/en/blog/2011/55).

Among intellectuals, we also see a few pleas for a redefinition of multiculturalism, which, concretely, was moving towards interculturalism (e.g., J. Tully, 1995). Even more recently, the model provided more room for concepts of interactions ("interactive pluralism"), exchanges, Canadian values and participation.[3] It should be noted that the idea of exchanges between ethnocultural groups was already mentioned in the text of the motion of 1971, but it was barely applied and did not get much attention. According to N. Meer and T. Modood (2011), this dimension is, however, at the very heart of multiculturalism – but this is a statement that goes against the current perception.[4]

Other recent calls for increased "connections," harmonious relations, and intercultural dialogue demonstrate the need for a shared culture.[5] According to Minister Jason Kenney, it is time for Canada to build bridges rather than silos (statement reported in *Le Devoir*, 11 February 2009, p. A3). It is also hoped that all the components of the Canadian mosaic will become part of a whole. Finally, the Canadian government has recently launched a new program (Inter-Action) intended to promote intercultural exchanges (Canada, 2011).[6] It appears that this evolution is far from over. According to W. Kymlicka (2011), after having overcome the challenges of ethnicity and discrimination, Canadian multiculturalism now has to face the problem of secularism, which, again according to this author, will require a redefinition of the model.

From the above, readers may be interested to note that in recent years Canadian multiculturalism has seemed to depart somewhat from the diversity paradigm and to draw closer to duality. At the same time, it also drew closer to Quebec interculturalism. If we add to all this the persistent feeling in anglophone Canada that "Canadian" culture is constantly under threat from the expansion of American culture, then the Canadian situation is getting even closer to the one that prevails in Quebec. I will refrain, however, from making any judgment on the strength or intensity of these movements, and I will not venture to speculate on their future (polls conducted over the last ten or fifteen years show that multiculturalism still enjoys strong support outside Quebec). But they are worth mentioning, and Canadians will definitely have to be attentive to them in the years to come.

Continuing in the same vein, we note that the duality paradigm is also manifested in the Official Languages Act (which established the rule of bilingualism in the public service) or when all francophones are considered as a minority within Canada. These elements are not peripheral; according to W. Kymlicka (2011), the duality created by bilingualism policy constitutes the only possible basis for the survival of Canada as a country. From another perspective, Canada also belongs to the paradigm of bipolarity or multipolarity; think of the status of aboriginal peoples or Quebec's status as a nation that the Canadian Parliament recognized in 2006. Canadian multiculturalism is thus presented as a hybrid, unsettled system. Once again, this makes it clear that, as indicated in the previous chapter, the paradigms are really a matter of choice – and, in this case, of political choices that can contradict each other and that do not always mirror ethnocultural reality.

The recent evolution of Canadian multiculturalism in the direction of both duality and interculturalism is the origin of ongoing confusion in Quebec. In fact, a certain number of participants in public debates assert the similarity of the two models, but for opposing reasons. Some, associated with the conservative vein of Quebec nationalism, seek to discredit Quebec interculturalism by identifying it with Canadian multiculturalism and attributing to it failings that are usually associated with the latter (fragmentation, relativism, etc.), while in reality it is pluralism that they are going against. Others, usually from a Canadian or federalist perspective, deny the significant differences that continue to exist between the two models by maintaining that interculturalism is only a variant of Canadian multiculturalism.[7]

However, the two models are still very different, for the following
reasons.

1. The most decisive and most obvious element is that interculturalism
    is concerned with the Quebec nation as a whole, as a host society,
    a nation whose historical, sociological, and institutional roots are
    deep and whose existence is the subject of a very broad consensus.
    Interculturalism also assumes the development of a sense of belong-
    ing (as a priority or not) to this nation. For its part, multiculturalism
    recognizes Quebecers of French Canadian origin only as forming
    an ethnic group (or a "community") among all the others that make
    up the Canadian mosaic; more generally, it rejects a plurinational
    concept of Canada (see the 1988 law).[8]
2. The two models belong to opposing paradigms. The federal gov-
    ernment still endorses the idea that there is no majority culture
    in Canada, that it is diversity that fundamentally characterizes this
    country, and that this concept should determine all reflections on
    the ethnocultural reality. Accordingly, the perception of an Us-Them
    relationship is not prevalent in anglophone Canada.[9] As for Quebec,
    the reflection on diversity was traditionally structured, as we have
    seen, by the duality paradigm, placing in the forefront the majority-
    minorities relationship. This choice echoes the minority status of
    francophones on the North American continent and the anxieties
    that it inevitably entails. The result is a specific vision of nationhood,
    identity, and a national sense of belonging.

    It follows from this that the main challenges are not the same
    for the two sides. In one case, the existence of a majority culture is
    recognized and the development of a shared and national culture is
    emphasized. Therefore what matters here is to manage in a pluralist
    spirit the relationship between the majority culture and the minor-
    ity cultures. In the other case, this relationship is not formalized
    since the existence of a majority culture is not recognized. In addi-
    tion, the concept of national culture is problematic. The challenge
    consists then of implementing a common symbolic denominator
    to form the foundation of the social bond.

    A clarification is necessary, however, with respect to the affirma-
    tion according to which there is no majority or national culture
    in Canada. Without going into an extended critique of this postu-
    late, I will point out that, in various regions of Canada, significant
    segments of the anglophone population (if the media are to be
    believed) maintain a feeling that there is a real *Canadian* culture

inherited from the past and that this culture is not sufficiently expressed within the framework of multiculturalism. According to many, it is threatened by the diversification brought about by immigration. The commonplace opposition, sometimes explicit, between "real" Canadian values and the "others" follows the same lines (E. Tolley, 2004). Finally, the concerns regularly expressed with respect to the growing influence of American culture highlight the feeling that there is a national culture to preserve.[10]

From a different perspective, it has also been shown that English Canada, like any other society, is not exempt from the dynamics of power that inevitably operates between a cultural majority, which is supposed to embody continuity and symbolic "normality," and minorities (E. Winter, 2011).

3. Because they themselves constitute a minority, Quebec franco-phones instinctively fear forms of sociocultural fragmentation, marginalization, and ghettoization; hence the particular emphasis that interculturalism places on integration and more especially on interactions, rapprochement between cultures, the development of a sense of belonging, and the emergence of a shared culture along with respect for minorities. Traditionally, Canadian multicultural-ism does not cultivate this concern to the same degree. Remember that the idea of multiculturalism was put forward in the 1960s at the initiative and in the interest mainly of minorities coming from Eastern Europe, for a long time established in Western Canada and completely integrated, but looking for official recognition beside anglophones and francophones. The model can thus put more em-phasis on valuing difference and "ethnic" groups.

4. Further to the above, it can be seen that a strong collective dimen-sion permeates interculturalism. This characteristic separates it from multiculturalism, which is often criticized because it is very suscep-tible to centrifugal forces.[11]

5. Another distinctive trait arises from the fact that Canadian multi-culturalism pays little attention to the protection of a national lan-guage. This is because inevitably, for reasons of survival, immigrants who settle in anglophone Canada will always want, sooner or later, to learn the language of the continent. It is very different with French in Quebec, which is always struggling to ensure its survival. This concern is obviously rooted in a cultural motivation, but also in the fact that the language plays a key role in social integration, collective cohesiveness, and civic life.

6. More generally, everything that is recognized for immigrants or minorities in terms of rights and accommodations in the nations of the West is accompanied by a concern for values and even for the cultural future of the host society (or, where applicable, of the majority culture). This kind of antinomy is felt more intensely in minority nations worried about their future, in which respect for diversity acquires an entirely different dimension. In other words, the issues arising from the practice of pluralism are far reaching and give rise to tensions that are not known by more powerful nations that are firmly established culturally and politically. This is a constraint that inevitably permeates Quebec interculturalism much more than Canadian multiculturalism.

7. Another element of differentiation is related to collective memory. Because of the struggles that the Quebec francophones have had to carry out in the course of their history, an intense memory as a small, fragile, combative nation has naturally developed. For many francophones, this memory carries a strong message that inspired a feeling of loyalty if not a duty for present and future generations. Reference to this past lie at the heart of the imaginary of the founding majority, which can be another source of tension: in a context marked by the growing presence of immigrants and minorities, how can this memory of the majority be transmitted without diluting its symbolic content, without stripping it of its psychological resiliency, all the while making room for minority narratives?[12] These kinds of challenging questions do not have the same resonance from a multiculturalism perspective, where the issue of a majority culture is simply absent.

8. The specific elements that have just been mentioned are expressed concretely in various ways, in particular in how the principle of recognition and the management of accommodations are applied. In the latter case, as I have indicated, requests for accommodations in Quebec will have more chance of being accepted if they favour integration. For example, allowing the wearing of the hijab (headscarf) in the classroom encourages Muslim students to continue attending public schools and to be more open to the values of Quebec society. The same is true for the offering of special menus in school cafeterias, a reasonable adaptation of exam schedules in accordance with the dates of religious activities, a flexible policy for certain educational activities where this does not violate the Education Act, and the like.

9. In the opposite direction, Quebec interculturalism also has to acknowledge the particular relationship to religion that has been built up in the course of Quebec history. Abuses of power committed by the Catholic clergy have resulted in suspicion towards churches and clergy that is expressed today by a great sensitivity to the separation of state and religion that we find no equivalent to in either anglophone Canada or Canadian multiculturalism.

10. More than multiculturalism, interculturalism promotes a dynamic perspective in its vision of relationships between cultures and its vision of their evolution within the shared culture or in coexistence with it. As we have seen, concern for the practice of interactions and for the existence of a shared symbolic foundation has come rather recently to Canadian multiculturalism.

On the whole, as we have seen, interculturalism has proven to be very sensitive to the problems and needs of the majority culture, because, in the context of Quebec at least, that majority is itself a minority. Multiculturalism does not show this concern, once again because it does not recognize the existence of such a culture. For the same reason, the search for balance becomes more imperative in the Quebec context (see also A.-G. Gagnon, 2010, esp. pp. 258–9, 261; A.-G. Gagnon & R. Iacovino, 2007, chap. 4).

Other authors will likely be tempted to see another difference in the fact that Canadian multiculturalism, unlike Quebec interculturalism, is characterized by its commitment to the cultural neutrality of the state. But as I noted in the previous chapter, that claim is baseless, since no state practises such a hands-off approach. Likewise, I do not agree with an analysis by W. Kymlicka (2003) according to which the two models are distinguished by the fact that multiculturalism operates at the macrosocial level, in particular as a government policy, while interculturalism works at the microsocial level (interpersonal relations). This is a reductive vision of interculturalism, which operates fully at these two levels.

The above remarks bring out a contrasting vision of the two models. Nevertheless, if we compare the policies actually implemented over the last few decades by the Canadian and Quebec governments in the area of intercultural relations, significant similarities can be observed (see M. McAndrew, 1995, 2005; D. Juteau, 1994; L. Pietrantonio, D. Juteau, & M. McAndrew, 1996; D. Juteau, M. McAndrew, & L. Pietrantonio, 1998; A. Nugent, 2006). How can we explain this paradox? Apart from the evolution already mentioned of multiculturalism in the direction of interculturalism, I believe that these similarities are due in part to the fact that the two models fundamentally share the same pluralist orientation as well as the major objectives that define it (equality, respect for diversity, non-discrimination, civic and political participation, rejection of assimilation and exclusion, etc.), an orientation of which, however, they propose different versions, suited to their realities.[13]

But the similarities also result from the fact that successive governments in Quebec have not sufficiently aligned their policies with the interculturalist model. A gap has developed between the official philosophy and the policies actually in place. This is a deficiency that has been criticized for a long time, and a strong effort needs to be made to remedy it in Quebec. It is urgent to design projects and policies that will give real substance to the spirit and distinctive goals of interculturalism.

Canadian Multiculturalism: A Hybrid, Shifting Model

I return, in conclusion, to the hybrid, shifting nature of Canadian multiculturalism to point out an interesting paradox. W. Kymlicka (2007a) presents this model as being made up of three silos. This claim refers to an interplay of relationships between the majority host society and (a) immigrants and ethnic groups; (b) national minorities ("substate national groups"); and (c) the aboriginal populations. He also asserts that each of these subsets or silos has followed its own course in the past and is subject to different policies belonging to specific processes. The paradox comes from the fact that the 1971 motion that introduced multiculturalism actually contained a formal warning against this kind of tripartite definition of Canada ("there cannot be one cultural policy for Canadians of British and French origin, another for the original peoples and yet a third for all others" [House of Commons Debates, 8 October 1971, pp. 8545–8]). From this perspective, the vision of multiculturalism put forward by W. Kymlicka is in direct contradiction with the founding vision of the model.

This contradiction also leads to an ambivalence that can be summarized as follows:

• According to a broad representation of Canadian multiculturalism, all three silos must be considered. But then this is a break with the most common representation (in Europe in particular), which is centred on a single silo, namely relations between individuals and ethnic groups.

- If we endorse this limited vision, Canada can no longer be identified only with multiculturalism, since two main components are excluded.

In summary, from the perspective of the limited definition, Canadian multiculturalism appears as different but slowly evolving towards Quebec interculturalism. In the hypothesis of the broad vision, that of the three silos, the model becomes at best hybrid and at worst contradictory. From one conception to another, what is gained in scope is lost in consistency. This being said, the model has definitely experienced significant failures, especially in terms of the struggle against discrimination, the aboriginal question, and the relationship with Quebec. Nevertheless, it is fair to say that, all things considered, within the framework of anglophone Canada, the model works. One only has to compare the situation of interethnic relationships in anglophone Canada with those in other Western countries (W. Kymlicka, 2012). Beyond that, it is a model that is based more on pragmatism than on any intrinsic cohesiveness. In addition, it is a model that has been constantly evolving since its introduction and that is perhaps about to undergo many other changes.

Finally, the heterogeneous, ambivalent character of Canadian multiculturalism is not limited to the elements that have just been mentioned. Analysing the content of the *Globe and Mail* and the *Toronto Star* during the 1990s, E. Winter (2011, pp. 184–5 and passim) was able to identify three competing visions of the model, which she calls "republicanism," "liberal-pluralism," and "liberal-multiculturalism." We can also see another important ambivalence in the fact that, according to many authors, multiculturalism defines the Canadian nation as being made up of a set of ethnic groups of which the distinctive natures need to be protected and promoted, while for others this model emphasizes individuals and their rights, in accordance with liberalism. From this last perspective, ethnic groups are only involved indirectly, to the extent that citizens can feel a legitimate need to cultivate a more or less close affiliation or identification with their cultures of origin, hence the need to protect them; this is the very foundation of the policy of recognition. Thus these two competing visions (communitarian and individualist) of Canadian multiculturalism are the source of another point of confusion.

In summary, multiculturalism is the site of four types of ambiguity:

- confusion between the stereotype that has been established at the international level, especially in Europe, and the Canadian model

- the original, unitary definition of Canadian multiculturalism (1971) and the thesis of the three silos
- a perception of the model centred on the protection of the rights either of individuals (in the spirit of liberalism) or of ethnic groups (in the spirit of *communitarianism*)
- a static vision of the model as opposed to a dynamic vision that takes into account various elements that it has borrowed since 1971

4

Criticism and Defence of Interculturalism

Until the beginning of the 2000s, the reflection on interculturalism remained mainly the prerogative of experts, academics, and other intellectuals. But over the last decade, the theme has caught the attention of the media and the general public. Discontent over the practice of accommodations, which was accused of disregarding the fundamental values of Quebec, had a lot to do with this. But because of a few unpopular judgments made by the Supreme Court of Canada,[1] it is multiculturalism that has received the most criticism, so that interculturalism appears more than ever to be the alternative model for Quebec. The individuals and groups who gave their opinions at the hearings of the Bouchard-Taylor Commission were almost unanimous on this point.

However, interculturalism has recently received criticisms from various scholarly, ideological, and political communities. The purpose of this chapter is to review those criticisms and offer some necessary clarifications. I have divided the criticisms into two subsets: those (cultural) based on a concern for the future of the majority culture and those (civic) that express concern for the respect of rights.

The Cultural Criticisms

This first type of criticism rejects interculturalism on the pretext that it will result in the weakening of the majority culture, forcing it to "renounce itself" (according to a common expression) and even to practise "self-hatred" (J. Quérin, 2011, p. 249). These criticisms draw a great deal of their strength from the fact that they rely on – and stir up – concerns and profound aspirations of the cultural majority, namely: (a) the fragility as a minority in North America and the need to continue the

historical struggle for the francophone nation; and (b) the duty of affirmation and correction that arises from a long past of domination and
humiliation ("we have to stand up for ourselves," "we have to show our
pride," etc.). It should also be noted that in both cases the appeal is to
loyalty to ancestors.[2]

As one might suspect, there are few members of the cultural majority
who remained unmoved by these two themes: they lie at the very heart of
its symbolic heritage and they have motivated key episodes in its history
(including the Patriote movement of 1800–1838, the long resistance to
linguistic assimilation, and the Quiet Revolution). The question is whether these themes are well served by certain attacks on interculturalism.

Essentially, in its version that I classify as radical, and with sometimes
significant variants from one author to another, the argument can be
summarized as follows:

1. Interculturalism is a faithful, though disguised, version of Canadian
   multiculturalism. This is a model that continues the efforts of Prime
   Minister Trudeau to weaken the Quebec nation.
2. The pluralism that it calls for compromises francophone Quebec by
   directly undermining its culture (values, identity, memory, language),
   by promoting fragmentation – at the expense of integration – and by
   establishing the reign of cultural relativism ("all values are accepted"
   or, worse, "only the minorities can assert their values").
3. The principle of recognition and the practice of accommodations
   are especially harmful mechanisms of interculturalism.
4. Because of the emphasis on rights, interculturalism mostly serves
   minorities. It has little to offer to the founding majority.
5. We should instead implement a model establishing within Quebec
   society a formal hierarchy that recognizes officially, in legal terms,
   a privileged status for the majority culture.
6. Quebec should apply a policy of long-term assimilation aimed at
   blending immigrants and minorities into the majority culture.
7. Pluralism leads to a cultural and even spatial fragmentation of
   Quebec society.
8. The proponents of pluralism have constructed a veritable myth
   around the economic and demographic impact of immigration.
9. The promotion of the shared culture will smother the founding
   culture.

I will examine each of these propositions, showing what is erroneous,
excessive, and unacceptable about them. The objective is not to present
a detailed review of the literature concerned,[3] but to bring out key aspects on the basis of various particularly representative texts.[4]

Argument 1: Quebec interculturalism is only a facsimile of Canadian multiculturalism

This is one of the widespread affirmations among the adversaries of interculturalism. But we need not examine this statement here, since it was adequately discussed in the previous chapter. I will note, however, that, with rare exceptions, no evidence is provided to support the argument. People simply affirm that the two models are identical – and therefore equally harmful – due to the fact that they are both based on pluralism and therefore have all its negative aspects.

In reality, pluralism is a philosophy or a fundamental orientation that, since the end of the Second World War and in various forms, has spread throughout the West and other countries. Various factors have contributed to this; the horrors of war, the excesses of totalitarian regimes, criticism of colonialism, the rejection of Eurocentrism, the internationalization of migratory movements after the Second World War, vigorous denunciation of racism, and the activism of disadvantaged groups and minorities. It is this general orientation, adopted by powerful international organizations, which has inspired the emancipation of all forms of minorities (racial, religious, sexual, etc.) as well as galvanizing the feminist movement. Canadian multiculturalism and Quebec interculturalism both offer a version of that pluralist orientation, each being governed by different situations, traditions, and sensibilities. The same can be said for the republican model in its American and Swiss versions.

Behind this gratuitous association of interculturalism and multiculturalism, we might suspect there is sometimes an opposition to pluralism and, when all is said and done, assimilationist sympathies that people do not always dare to admit.

Argument 2: In the long term, interculturalism, like pluralism, undermines francophone culture and hinders the political liberation of Quebec

Interculturalism is said to be conceived mainly to serve the rights of minorities and immigrants and to contribute nothing to the majority culture. In addition, it is thought to undermine francophone Quebec, to endanger its values, language, identity, and memory, and to "strip it of its distinctive historical characteristics"; we must therefore conceive a Quebec "free of pluralism" (M. Bock-Côté, 2006, 2009a). Interculturalism is also accused of stripping the majority culture of its legitimacy (for example, J. Beauchemin, 2010a, 2010b). Finally, it is seen as a continuation of the destructive work of Pierre Trudeau. Let us take a closer look at these assertions.

The idea that interculturalism pays little attention to the majority culture does not correspond to my definition of it, which is based precisely on the majority-minorities relationship and the perspectives of development of the majority culture in and through duality. In addition this definition constantly highlights the fact that the francophone majority is also a minority, which calls for specific provisions. More specifically, with respect to values, many criticisms maintain that the tolerance given to immigrants and members of minorities makes it possible for them to promote their values at the expense of the most basic Quebec values (these are understood mainly as separation of church and state, equality between men and women, and protection for the French language).[5]

In fact, this general perception, which is founded mostly on particular isolated cases of accommodations brought to the attention of the public, has never been shown to be based in fact. It also postulates that the values brought by immigration are on the whole incompatible with Quebec values. Empirical data on this subject are unfortunately very incomplete. We can, however, refer to a Canada-wide survey commissioned by the Trudeau Foundation and Dalhousie University in November 2011,[6] which shows that in Quebec as well as the other provinces the majority of immigrants believed in the same fundamental values as the members of the host society, and with equal intensity. Similarly, in a cross-Canada survey, A. Bilodeau (2011) showed that immigrants coming from undemocratic or weakly democratic countries show strong support for democratic values.[7] What we can take from this is that many immigrants have chosen to immigrate to Quebec precisely for the values and rights promoted in that province. Of course, this is not the case with all immigrants, but should this then be seen as a serious threat to the foundations of civil society?[8]

There is no disputing that certain immigrants display values that are not compatible with those prevalent in Quebec. But interculturalism, by promoting integration and interactions, tends to create conditions favourable to adaptation in the long run. This is attested by a survey carried out in 2009, which shows that acceptance of homosexuality, for example, is much higher among the children of immigrants (71 per cent) than among their parents (44 per cent).[9]

What must be firmly pointed out is that interculturalism, far from lapsing into relativism, establishes respect for fundamental values as a principle. In the past, a few administrators of public institutions have accepted requests for accommodations that contradicted this principle, departing from the spirit and letter of the model. These cases need to be seen as either simple errors or differing views that have to be fought.

Many are also concerned that the constitutive values of francophone heritage will no longer be expressed because of interculturalism, which is accused of trivializing these values because of its pluralist allegiance. I think I have shown on the contrary how important it is that this symbolic heritage survive and continue to develop within the shared culture. But there is one condition to be respected. In order for these values to be promoted with all Quebecers and be expressed in legislation and in the courts, it is necessary that they have a broader scope – in other words, that they are suited to being shared freely by all citizens and to serve as the social bond. This is clearly the case with the values that I have already identified as arising out of the history of the cultural majority (equality, social justice, solidarity, survival of French, collective affirmation, etc.).[10]

Does it then follow that the shared culture should be sustained only by those values? That would be contrary to the spirit of balance and equity that underlies interculturalism. Other values are contributed by immigrants and members of minorities, who should also have access to the shared culture, under the same conditions.

The idea of compatibility or convergence of values seems to find favourable conditions in Quebec. As I have pointed out, the experience of a colonial regime has left in the francophone majority a specific heritage of values that is also found among immigrants who have experienced colonial dependence in their countries of origin or who have fled despotic regimes.[11] Values such as liberty and equality can still emerge from different paths or heritages, which makes them all the more compatible with a shared sensibility (see G. Bouchard & C. Taylor, 2008, p. 134–5). Paths vary and always will. It is on the resulting convergences that we need to rely. In summary: disparity in the past, unity in the future.

With respect to equality between men and women, a few glaring blunders, which received a lot of media coverage, quite rightly led to strong protests among the Quebec population in recent years.[12] But it should be recalled that corrective measures were quickly taken, and the administrators of public institutions seem, for the most part, to have learned the lesson well. One might think that, in this regard, the great vigilance exerted by various organizations and groups provides a guarantee against possible abuses and excesses.

It should also be remembered that the law offers a substantial remedy. In fact, certain jurists go as far as to favour giving equality between men and women precedence over other rights (especially freedom of religion), given that this value is rooted in the general and fundamental right to equality. This is what justified the inclusion of interpretative clauses in the Quebec (section 50.1) and Canadian (section 28) charters. This is also what permitted us, in the report of the commission that I co-chaired with Charles Taylor, to write that any request for accommodations that could infringe on equality between men and women should normally be rejected (p. 178). A similar orientation can be found in the jurisprudence of the European Court of Human Rights (E. Bribosia & I. Rorive, 2010) and in various international treaties (L.-P. Lampron, 2009, pp. 254ff.).

Other commentators have noted that equality between men and women is already protected by the Quebec (section 10) and Canadian (section 15) charters. It has also been pointed out that it would be ill-advised to establish a rigid, a priori hierarchy in favour of this right, since certain situations call for flexibility. For example, in residences for senior citizens, it is agreed that intimate care be provided by staff of the same sex. It is also understood that women who are victims of rape are assigned female police officers. The same goes for security searches and inspections in airports. However, in the eyes of many jurists, any hierarchy goes against the principle of the interdependence and balance of rights.[13] In addition, for P. Bosset (2009) for example, the legal definition of reasonable accommodation already contains a provision (undue hardship) that should make it possible to reject requests that infringe on the rule of equality between men and women (no request can encroach on the rights of others).

With respect to religion, for the time being attention seems to be focused on the question of the separation of state and religion. This is mainly concerned with manifestations of religious beliefs among the staff of public institutions, which are said to compromise both the principle of secularism and equality between men and women. This argument is, however, far from being proven, as we will see in chapter 5. This is the topic of an ongoing debate, but the idea of a formal hierarchy that entrenches the precedence of equality between men and women over freedom of religion, although asserted by many, does not seem to have much of a future because of the challenges it raises.

The fate of the French language, which is also said to be compromised by pluralism, is presented differently. Here, progress has been made. For example, improvements have been observed with respect to the francization of allophones, and the proportion of immigrants stating that they know French on their arrival is increasing – which does not, of course, negate the fact that there remain significant reasons for concern, related not to pluralism but to the insufficient resources devoted to francization.

I will make one last remark on values. On this subject as with others, a priori statements, based on common sense or intuitive assumptions, often replace empirical knowledge, and this can lead to erroneous perceptions. This might be the case when concerns are expressed about traditional or "reactionary" values brought by certain immigrants. According to one of the results of a study by A. Wimmer (2013), this distance or this incompatibility of values seems to exist especially where immigrants are victims of exclusion. They are thus pushed to the margins where they develop a ghetto culture. In other circumstances, we do not observe this cultural marginalization. For example, the authors show that individuals of the Muslim faith, in the twenty-four European countries studied, do not stand out any more than Catholics from the national majority cultures. The familiar divide between Islam and European culture is therefore fueled above all by superficial differences in customs.

With respect to identity, it is legitimate and necessary that the majority culture preserve the essential elements that define it and that it has inherited from its past. This is a cultural capital that is essential to the symbolic and institutional foundations of society. Interculturalism recognizes this legitimacy, which is in keeping with the flexibility required for the application of pluralism, but we need to be wary of projecting a disembodied vision of it. In the case of Quebec, this means that we have to take into account the fact, already mentioned, that this cultural majority is also a minority.

It has also been stated (J. Beauchemin, 2004, 2005) that, under the influence of pluralism and other factors, Quebec became a very fragmented society, to the extent that the political "subject" is itself splintered – Beauchemin speaks of "the decline of the representation of a unitary national political subject" (2002a, p. 33; 2005), and suggests that it then becomes very difficult to build consensuses around major collective projects, for example, the political sovereignty of Quebec.

This pessimistic argument can be criticized in various ways. First of all, it underestimates the importance of the divisions that have always characterized traditional Quebec: economic and social hierarchies, owner-workers conflicts, cultural inequalities (in education in particular), the urban-rural divide, the regions-metropolis opposition, political allegiances (Blues against the Reds), the laity and the clergy, and ethnic and religious divisions, among others. From a contemporary perspective, this kind of society can hardly be qualified as homogeneous (and "unitary"). It is true that with the francophone majority nationalism was very strong, but isn't that also a characteristic of the contemporary period? In other words, the divisions within Quebec society are not a recent phenomenon, and we have to beware of a nostalgic perspective that portrays past societies as more integrated than they actually were.

Second, isn't the multiplicity of actors and social movements a positive factor for democracy? We can see this as a sign of a vital civic life, which is a source of social change and offers protection against the monopolistic temptations of the state. Third, it would be wrong to postulate that these social actors do not possess a societal vision beyond their immediate interests and do not cultivate affiliations outside their own networks. This would be a very simplistic perception of social movements, integration processes, and the dynamics of identity. Finally, if we look at the values conveyed by these movements, we realize that they are inspired by progressive ideals such as equality, social justice, democracy, and non-discrimination. Why would it be so difficult to develop on the basis of these ideals strong coalitions or major collective projects?

The Quebec of recent decades could, in fact, be cited as an example of the advancement of the status of women, the democratization of education, the growth of ecological awareness, adjustments to ethnocultural diversity, and spectacular struggles against poverty and socioeconomic inequalities (G. Bouchard, 2013a). We can also observe that this society, beyond its attachment to the French language, shows a sensitivity – perhaps unprecedented in its history – to fundamental values: democracy, equality, social justice, non-violence, respect for rights, secularism, and respect for diversity. The argument regarding fragmentation of the political subject and the impossibility of major collective projects betrays a nostalgic, idealized vision of consensus and ignores the sociological conditions of its construction. It can be an attractive idea, but it has certainly not been substantiated.[14]

Many fear that the respect for diversity inherent in pluralism forces the cultural majority to give up its memory ("its profound intentionality") or at least to dilute it on the pretext that it cannot be imposed on other Quebecers. I believe I have shown in the preceding chapters that this is not at all the case. In fact, the reality is quite the opposite. The view that I advocate portrays the past as essentially the struggle of a cultural minority to ensure its survival and its development in a difficult environment. It also highlights the struggles of a society to free itself from the systems of domination that affected its development as a nation. On the basis of these two examples (and there are many others), we can see the universal dimensions that emerge from this history, dimensions that are primarily accessible and significant in the eyes of all Quebecers, old and new.

These remarks show the need for the continuity of the majority culture but also for its openness. The position that I am attempting to refute here instead intensifies the dangers of isolation and withdrawal. In short, interculturalism and the concept of pluralism that it implements protect against a double marginalization: that of the majority culture and that of the minority cultures. It is Quebec culture as a whole that would suffer from this.

Argument 3: The principle of recognition and the practice of accommodations are harmful

This criticism, frequently expressed, needs to be examined in two stages. It maintains first of all that the principle of recognition is an obstacle to the integration of immigrants because it encourages them to perpetuate their traditions and their identities of origin. This statement, which seems to be based on common sense, is contradicted by observation. As I have indicated, many empirical studies conducted in various countries have shown that giving immigrants the possibility of maintaining a continuity with their cultures helps them to overcome feelings of insecurity that inevitably come with the transition from one society to another (some authors talk about the "shock of immigration"; see chapter 2).

Programs aimed at teaching the languages of immigrants to their children (while the latter are being acculturated to the language and customs of the host society) favour the integration of everyone by strengthening or restoring the connections children have with their parents and their grandparents. Validation of the identities and languages of immigrants also convinces them that they are contributing something to the host society, which disposes them favourably towards their new fellow citizens. This kind of program, by contributing to the maintenance of family stability, plays a role in providing a bridge for integration into the new environment. The exceptions seem almost always to involve the existence of external structural factors, for example, entrenched practices of discrimination towards certain immigrant groups that are thus confined to enclaves (M. Kalbach & W. Kalbach, 2000). In her study on a Montreal borough with a strong Asian presence, A.M. Fiore (2010) was able to verify that maintenance of the social and cultural capital of immigrants works in favour of their integration and not the reverse.

Another argument in favour of the maintenance of languages of origin also emphasizes the cultural and socioeconomic benefits associated with multilingualism in a context of globalization. Moreover, it has been demonstrated that, among Quebec students from immigrant backgrounds, mastery of French and the mastery of other languages go hand in hand (Québec, MELS, 2009; M. McAndrew, 2011a, 2011b; J. Erfurt, 2010).

Finally, it should be noted that in Quebec assistance to ethnocultural minorities and recognition of identities has in no way called into question policies of social redistribution. It is even remarkable that this issue, which has been so intensely discussed in various Western societies (do diversity and pluralism compromise solidarity and social cohesion?), is practically absent from public debate in Quebec.[15] Moreover, as V. Armony (2010, p. 77) has observed, there is no evidence that there is a correlation in Quebec between the number of immigrants and the state of the social fabric as reflected by the usual indicators of collective pathology (mainly crime statistics). It is instead in the area of culture that the Quebec debate has its roots.

According to the second element of this criticism, the practice of accommodations is said to be reprehensible because it infringes on the rule of equality, endangers the fundamental values of Quebec (mainly secularism and equality between men and women), favours cultural fragmentation, and creates privileges by allowing certain people to circumvent the law or by granting them special rights.

With regard to respect for equality, it is precisely the purpose of accommodations (or adjustments) to correct the forms of discrimination that result from an overly formal concept of equality, which tends to treat all citizens as if they were the same.[16] We now know that this results in various forms of inequality. A prime example is the old Quebec law that established Sunday as the religious day of rest. This provision obviously suited most Quebecers since they belonged to a Christian religion, but it violated the rights of other believers for whom Saturday was the day reserved for religious duties. Another example concerns menus in public cafeterias, traditionally designed for the tastes and dietary customs of the majority. Accordingly, jurisprudence is more and more putting aside the abstract conception of equality in favour of a more concrete ("substantial") approach that takes into account the differences protected by the charters – a change in direction that, once again, does not benefit only immigrants and members of minorities.[17] In the cultural domain, this is the case, precisely, with the freedom to practise the religion of one's choice.

Accommodations therefore do not result from frivolous requests; they are imposed by the obligation to respect the fundamental rights of all citizens, as inscribed in the charter. And, contrary to widespread opinion, they do not create special rights for those requesting them and they do not exempt them from application of the law; they instead provide everyone with the means to enjoy the same fundamental rights. Hence, far from infringing on the rule of equality by establishing privileges, accommodations function to restore equality where it is lacking. The title of a book by Y. Geadah (2007) sums up this principle well: the right to difference and not difference of rights.

Contrary to another common perception, the practice of accommodations has the effect (and, in part at least, the objective) of favouring the integration of those making the requests. In the education system, for example, a systematic refusal to accommodate can lead to parents withdrawing their children from public school to register them in an ethno-religious private school, which results in a higher risk of marginalization and fragmentation since these children could then be partly excluded from the cultural life of the host society. This is why the integrative nature is an important criterion in the processing of requests. For the same reason, it is also important to facilitate the task of immigrants who, often, come from a society very different from the host society and are suddenly plunged into a world in which they are unaware of the codes and rules.

With regard to the supposed privileges that are said to be created by the practice of accommodations, it is enough to recall that respect for the law is one of the primary conditions to be met; a request should be rejected when it violates a law, unless it can be shown that that law is unjust and should be amended.

A final argument in favour of accommodations is based on the principle of reciprocity. If we acknowledge that liberal states have no obligation to strict cultural neutrality and that majorities have a right to certain advantages, in particular according to the principle of interventionism (chapter 2 and below) we have to, in return, recognize for minorities the right to a corrective mechanism to protect themselves against potential abuses by majorities. This argument is particularly well founded in the case of Quebec because of the principle of double recognition, which is a linchpin of interculturalism.

In summary, the function of these accommodations – or collaborative adjustments – is to permit certain citizens who are victims of discrimination or disadvantages (because they are different) to exercise their fundamental rights, unless there are compelling reasons to restrict them. In this sense, accommodations indeed derive from a legal obligation. It should be recalled, however, that requests are admissible only if they (a) respect the rights of others; (b) comply with the law; (c) are in keeping with the fundamental values of the host society; (d) do not disrupt the normal operations of an organization or institution; (e) do not result in excessive costs; and (f) favour the integration of those making the requests.

I will dwell for a moment on another criticism that is often expressed according to which the practice of accommodations will always be arbitrary because they are decided on a case-by-case basis and are not subject to strict procedures. The examination of requests is subject to the criteria listed above (and others can be added), taking into account all the contextual data. However, situations are rarely identical, and sometimes a few details are enough to make a difference (see chapter 5). That is why requests need to be dealt with individually, while referring to guidelines that are as precise as possible. But the degree of precision possible is limited. Most of the requests oppose two rights that need to be reconciled or decided between. In the absence of a formal hierarchy among rights, it is impossible to decide in advance on which side to take. Here again, what is sought is a balance: overly precise guidelines impose a straitjacket on the administrator, and guidelines that are too broad leave things too vague. However, this problem is not specific to accommodations. In fact, it underlies the entire practice of the courts.

In light of the above, one can see that what needs to be condemned is not the principle of accommodations itself, but the clumsy or ill-conceived way with which accommodations have sometimes been administered in the past by certain politicians and administrators in public institutions. Consider, for example, the directive issued in November 2011 (by a Canadian senior civil servant) prohibiting Christmas decorations in federal buildings located in Quebec. What was forgotten was that these symbols have long since become secularized and that a very big part of the population, far beyond Christian communities, has adopted them. A similar example was a decision made in December 2011 in a preschool in the Saint-Michel neighbourhood of Montreal. A Muslim student was authorized to wear a soundproof helmet intended to prevent her from hearing the music and songs that were part of the instructional activities. The request was motivated by the parents' conviction that Western music and songs contravene the beliefs of the Muslim religion. The minister responsible felt the request had to be approved in the name of integration and the interests of the child. Obviously, for these same reasons, the request should have been rejected.

This kind of unreasonable decision is precisely what tends to discredit the practice of accommodations, as well as very unjustly favouring a backlash against Muslims, immigrants, and minorities. In my view, the population should exercise vigilance in demanding a rigorous and disciplined practice of adjustments rather than rejecting outright this indispensable mechanism for the protection of the fundamental rights of citizens (see also G. Bouchard & C. Taylor, 2008, pp. 277–84).

In itself, the practice of accommodations (for religious or other reasons) seems inevitable. It falls fundamentally within the rights of citizens as well as the counsels of common sense, courtesy, and basic goodwill. This explains why accommodations have come to be practised by institutions in many countries where they do not even have legal recognition. I am thinking here of most countries in Europe, and especially France, even though the republican regime there views them with hostility. We nevertheless find practices of accommodations in the education system, the operations of the courts, municipal governments, health-care institutions, prisons, the military, public and private enterprises, the calendar of public holidays, cemeteries, and so on.

Argument 4: Interculturalism serves mostly the interests of minorities

It is true that interculturalism puts a strong emphasis on rights, especially where they are the most threatened, that is, among people and groups that exhibit some sort of difference. Immigrants and members of minorities, which are universally vulnerable subpopulations, are obviously closely concerned, but the members of the majority are as well. More generally, a sensitivity to rights will serve all citizens without distinction. Moreover, beyond the legal dimension, the definition that I have presented of interculturalism gives a central role to the majority culture as the vector of integration, but in a spirit of balance and without causing any prejudice or discrimination to the minorities, whose fundamental rights are respected. I have also pointed out that exceptional circumstances could justify legal protections provided that they pass the test of the courts, as illustrated by the example of Law 101. Finally, with regard to the protection of heritage and what I called the ad hoc principle of interventionism, I have shown that the majority possess appreciable tools to ensure its future as the pillar of the societal culture.

Argument 5: We should formally establish the precedence of the cultural majority over minorities

I argued above for a principle of interventionism and flexibility and I have already spoken elsewhere of elements of ad hoc precedence (to clearly distinguish it from an a priori legal precedence) (G. Bouchard, 2011). Note that, in my view, this kind of provision should be applied only in certain contexts, be based on overriding reasons, and pass the test of law. Like the argument regarding the preservation of heritage, its use should therefore be strictly controlled so as not to unduly extend its scope. However, there are some who would like, through a law or a section in the Quebec charter, to establish a formal, a priori precedence in favour of the cultural majority. This would officially establish that the members of minorities do not have the same rights as the founding majority.

This demand is sometimes expressed in radical ways (recognition of a structural hierarchy, affirmation of the pre-eminence or official predominance of the majority culture). It also takes softer forms that declare, for example, that the francophone majority should be clearly identified as the heart of the nation, which is an ambiguous expression open to many interpretations.[18]

It is acknowledged that pluralism and respect for minorities have to be combined with protections for the future of the francophone majority in Quebec. This is a societal priority. But the path of a formal hierarchy should be excluded because it would create excessive advantages or privileges that minorities and immigrants would be deprived of. It would create in a way two classes of citizens, which is unacceptable first of all for legal reasons, in the name of equality and equity (Quebec is a liberal democracy), and because it would be an obstacle to the objective of integration that is central to interculturalism.

Argument 6: In the long term, minorities and immigrants should blend into the majority culture

This assimilationist position was expressed by various participants at the public hearings of the Bouchard-Taylor Commission, with some even declaring that this was the main idea of interculturalism. Polls conducted from 2000 to 2009 show that it enjoys significant support (more than 50 per cent) among the population (see M. Girard, 2008, pp. 69–71). There are, however, few policy-makers, researchers, or intellectuals who have endorsed it very explicitly.[19] The model that is quite often contrasted with interculturalism is that of cultural convergence, which, in its various formulations, is presented as a form of assimilationism. The idea was first put forward in two government documents (Quebec, Ministry of State for Cultural Development, 1978; Quebec, MCCI, 1981); it was then found more assertively in the writings of F. Dumont (1995, chap. 3), who was one of the authors of two government texts.

According to Dumont, "if there is a culture of convergence one day, it will not be a laboratory compound or convention; it will be the French culture," which was becoming in this way "the rallying place of all the others" (p. 67). And, in the same spirit, French in Quebec was supposed to be "a language in its fullness, that is, a culture" (p. 67), by which we necessarily understand the French or French Canadian culture. But what then becomes of those who belong to other cultures who have learned French thanks to Law 101? This reminder is important because Fernand Dumont is used as a reference for most of the proponents of this model today, who argue that immigrants should blend into the majority culture.[20]

There are a few variations from one author to another, but the essential framework of the argument is the same, and it has varied little during the last thirty years: the intercultural dynamics of Quebec should be systematically oriented according to the francophone majority, which is its integrative nucleus and with which members of minorities and immigrants should therefore assimilate. For G. Gagnon (1988), for example, "Francophone Quebec culture must always remain their unique nexus of convergence" (p. 41).[21] According to J. Beauchemin (2003, p. 36), minorities should be expected to "assimilate to the majority." Similarly, according to M. Bock-Côté (2010), "those who join a country are sooner or later called upon to blend into it" (p. 75).

The model of cultural convergence, as it has been formulated, must be rejected. But we should first of all eliminate possible misunderstandings. There is certainly no denying the sociological fact of the weight of the majority culture and the dominant influence that, inevitably and quite legitimately, it is normally called upon to exert in intercultural life and in the evolution of Quebec culture. The problem is the normative dimension that proponents of convergence introduce and the corollaries that can be associated with it. There are three main reasons for this.

First of all, in the name of the principle of a formal precedence in favour of the majority, it would be necessary to establish an a priori hierarchy among Quebecers, between those who belong to the francophone "old stock" and those who do not, thus creating two classes of citizens (I am referring to the criticisms I outlined previously on this subject). Second, the institution of this legal (or a priori) precedence gives excessive latitude to the cultural majority, by opening the way to measures that can lead to ethnic discrimination. Third, the convergence model offers immigrants and members of minorities two rather radical options: either assimilate to the founding majority, or experience a form of exclusion, on the margins of the national culture, even if they have learned the French language. These two avenues are contrary to the spirit of interculturalism, which aims at integration and recognizes for all citizens the right to cultivate an attachment to their culture of origin without suffering discrimination.

Gérard Godin himself, the minister who had sponsored and endorsed the first formulation of the convergence model in 1978, wrote in 1987 that it "had the defect of not taking into account the Other" (quoted by M. Labelle, 2008a, p. 26). Similarly, the Jesuit Julien Harvey, at first sympathetic to the culture of convergence, later criticized it for "giving practically all the space to the majority" (also quoted by M. Labelle, 2008a, p. 30).[22]

Argument 7: Pluralism fragments Quebec society

There is no empirical data to support the idea that immigrants do not integrate or are resistant to integration. The most serious failure of integration is the inability of Quebec society to reduce underemployment among new arrivals, a factor that exacerbates social marginalization. However, this is not the effect of pluralism, but rather of a lack of pluralism. Many are also concerned about initiatives taken by the government to help immigrants preserve their languages and elements of their cultures of origin. In reality, as I have mentioned on a few occasions, these measures have a positive effect on integration. Finally, with respect to the ghettoization argument, it is contradicted by very solid surveys comparing Montreal and other Canadian metropolises (P. Apparicio & A.-M. Séguin, 2008; X. Leloup & P. Apparicio, 2010; X. Leloup, 2011; see also G. Nootens, 2010a).

Note also that interculturalism offers guarantees against the potential segmentation of Quebec society. I am thinking of the promotion of the shared culture (with its various components, such as language, values, and national memory), all the rights enjoyed by all citizens, and the civic life that everyone is invited to participate in.

Argument 8: Pluralism has constructed a veritable myth around the economic and demographic benefits of immigration

This argument was presented recently in Quebec by B. Dubreuil and G. Marois (2011), and it prompted many favourable reactions in the media. However, their book has some significant weaknesses, of which I will briefly mention a few. The first problem concerns the contradictory presentation of the argument. On the one hand, the authors formulate very radical statements, for example:

- One can be favourable to immigration, but for reasons "that have nothing to do with economics or demography" (p. 301); on this Dubreuil and Marois talk about a "misconception," a "myth" (pp. 10, 12, 27, 302).
- The idea that immigration can mitigate the negative effects of the aging of the population "has no empirical basis" (pp. 14, 16); immigration "offers no remedy against aging" (p. 15).
- Immigration does not make it possible to mitigate the negative effects the aging of the population has on public finances (p. 10).
- Immigration has a marginal impact on the Quebec economy (pp. 13–14): it has "no real effect on prosperity" (p. 14); "it changes nothing about economic prosperity in general" (p. 302).
- "Economically and demographically, Quebec does not need immigration"; it is "an imaginary remedy" (*La Presse*, 26 February 2011, section "Plus," p. 7).

In terms of economics, the reasoning of the authors can be summed up as follows: (a) since it is very difficult to integrate immigrants occupationally, their economic impact is null or insignificant; (b) to better integrate them, it would be necessary to be more selective; (c) but tightening the selection criteria would result in a reduction in the number of immigrants, and therefore, once again, a null or insignificant impact (p. 206).

Elsewhere, however, the discourse is much more conciliatory and suggests that immigration has a positive impact: more modest expectations need to be cultivated (p. 16 and conclusion); by reforming the programs and tools (e.g., the selection grid), by improving support measures for integration, and by decreasing the number of entries, we can obtain beneficial effects, of which the authors give various examples (pp. 298–300, 302). What they are against is an "inordinately optimistic vision" (p. 11), the "myth of miracle immigration" (p. 303), and the illusion "of magic solutions" (p. 306). Their objective "is to bring everyone back to more realistic expectations" (p. 306), by which the reader understands that immigration is useful, but not as much as is commonly thought.

The exercise could be extended, but these few excerpts very clearly reveal what is no doubt the main weakness of the book. Few people would disagree with the second series of statements: who would want to encourage unrealistic expectations, overly optimistic visions, magic solutions, or indulgence in myths? But in other parts of the book, the authors contradict this statement. And it is not clear whether the book is a welcome word of warning against dangerous illusions or an attack on immigration from the economic and demographic perspective. To no one's surprise, it was the latter version that caught the attention of commentators and won over a section of the public.

The real argument of the book is that Quebec society could very well (or should?) do without immigration and reconcile itself with the consequent economic and demographic decline and the cultural and political effects. This explains, at least in part, the rather dismissive way in which the authors receive predictions for labour requirements (1.3 million jobs to be filled between now and 2018) and the significant share that would have to be filled by immigration (17 per cent).[23] But this argument is not made explicitly, which adds to the book's lack of clarity. In summary, Dubreuil and Marois have conceived the project, useful certainly, of demystifying the issues of immigration; but in so doing they have given substance to another myth. To really be of service to the public, they would have had to provide a more credible overview: to show, with the necessary qualifications, all the dimensions of the complex questions discussed and all the points of view on these highly controversial questions.

The debate on this subject, to which Dubreuil and Marois do contribute some insights, therefore remains open. Until I have information to the contrary, I remain loyal to the position expressed in 2008 in the report of the Bouchard-Taylor Commission (pp. 222–3). This position, which does justice to the complexity of the question, can be summed up in the four following points:

- Immigration will not solve the problem of the aging of the Quebec population (it "is not, of course, a miracle cure," p. 223), but it can contribute to mitigating and delaying its impact.
- Economic analysts are very divided on the overall effects in the long term, but few experts dispute that immigration is a positive factor in the short term, in particular in view of pressing labour requirements.
- The economic contribution of immigrants has been decreasing in the last few years because of adverse economic conditions.
- The economic and social integration of immigrants depends more on the willingness of a host society (the extent of resources and measures put in place) than on what is called the "capacity for reception," which is a vague concept that is very difficult to measure.

Argument 9: The shared culture is growing at the expense of the founding culture

Remember first of all that nothing suggests that the majority culture or the minority cultures should deny themselves and blend completely into the shared culture; simply, that culture is formed spontaneously from the preceding ones while contributing to transforming them, according to and at the rate of individual choices. Similarly, it would be a mistake to believe that intercultural exchanges inevitably lead to a confusion of identities (see T.H. Eriksen, 2007).

To the extent that the shared culture in Quebec is expressed mainly in French and nourished by all the ethnocultural diversity, its development represents an avenue to the future for the founding majority given that the population numbers on which it is based are declining[24] and that, in the context of globalization, it should open itself up more than ever to diversity. It therefore should not be seen as a concession and even less an alienation or renunciation for the majority group, but an opportunity for enrichment, renewal, and expansion. In addition, insofar as the shared culture is the product of intercultural exchanges in daily life, it is predictable that in the long run the founding majority will leave a very strong imprint on it. This scenario is favoured by Law 101, which established French as the official language of Quebec. Beyond that, it simply reflects the demographic, sociological, and historical weight of the francophone majority.

The idea that interaction with immigrants and minority cultures inevitably leads to changes in the majority culture sometimes gives rise to reservations within that majority culture. And yet there is solid data from the social and historical sciences and from contemporary observation indicating that healthy cultures, precisely in order to adapt and survive, are constantly evolving, mainly through the impact of the contacts they have with each other or with other cultures and through the impact of the challenges and constraints they have to overcome.

The history of francophone Quebec itself provides an excellent example of this. Suffice it to refer to the changes that this nation has undergone since the beginning of the nineteenth century: it was first open to all ethnic groups (according to the program of the Patriote movement), then limited to French Canadians and defined at the level of Canada (the period of "Survival"), then politically organized around Quebec and gradually opened up to all Quebec citizens (during and after the Quiet Revolution), substantially redefining along the way the components of its identity, in particular by removing religious references from it.

Conclusion

Interculturalism avoids the main pitfalls of the convergence model by opening up to other avenues that are much more realistic and more acceptable, to reach similar objectives. It has, in fact, the advantage of respect for the rights of all citizens while avoiding creating a hierarchy. In addition, it safeguards what is considered essential from the perspective of the culture of convergence, namely the survival and development of French-speaking Quebec. It does this in three ways: first, by fully recognizing the majority culture and its right to perpetuate itself through the entirety of its language, traditions, and fundamental values forged from its history, identity, and memory; then by giving the majority culture the possibility of investing its full weight in the shared culture and affirming itself in it; and finally, by favouring the use of an ad hoc cultural interventionism. Beyond these provisions, we have to agree that the future of the francophone majority in Quebec is based on its collective dynamism and the motivation of its members.

Concerning the various measures (political, legal, etc.) to be implemented to ensure the survival and development of French-speaking Quebec, the remarks above highlight the importance of distinguishing among four levels corresponding to as many possible spheres of intervention: language, values, identity (sense of belonging, memory), and culture in the anthropological sense of the term (traditions, customs, lifestyles). The different levels can allow and call for specific measures. For example, because of its civic nature, language can be subject to extensive legal protections, as can fundamental values, and aspects that belong to identity can in certain circumstances also benefit from legal support (I am thinking of national history and heritage). But it is different with traditions and customs, which belong to a particularist logic.

Civic or Legal Criticisms

I will examine here another series of objections based on the liberal legal tradition and the imperatives of citizenship, and sometimes also conceived from a republican perspective. During and in relationship to the International Symposium on Interculturalism held in Montreal in May 2011, a few participants criticized Quebec interculturalism, making the following assertions:

1. There is no cultural majority in Quebec; the idea of a duality is therefore without foundation. Moreover, it is necessary to deal

with individuals and not with pseudo-groups, categories, cultures, communities, minorities, or "boxes." It is preferable to rely on citizenship (which unites) rather than on identity or culture (which divides). Many studies have shown the unstable and even artificial nature of concepts of ethnocultural and identity boundaries; rather than clearly defined demarcations, we observe mostly exchanges, osmoses, in-betweens, transitions, all governed by individual strategies and negotiations oriented towards the construction of "à la carte" identities.

2. There is, in fact, a cultural majority in Quebec, but to make the majority-minorities relationship a significant element in the analysis is ill advised because it means creating a duality artificially, giving it a consistency that it does not have in reality.

3. Recognition of a majority/minority relationship is inappropriate and even dangerous, since it leads to the creation of an Us-Them relationship, which becomes more rigid and opens the way to various forms of discrimination by the majority, which, like all majorities, has a monopoly on power. There is also a risk of "re-ethnicizing" intercultural relationships in Quebec. Finally, interculturalism confirms the existence of a hierarchy among Quebecers and stigmatizes minorities, especially immigrants.

4. In addition, putting emphasis on the majority and the minorities and accepting their identity projects means promoting the irrational when the realm of reason should be encouraged.

5. The francophone majority is not threatened; the insecurity it expresses is not founded, but is just strategic rhetoric. In any case, any measure aimed at reducing the feeling of vulnerability will only maintain the level of anxiety and stimulate that majority's appetite for power.

6. We need to confine ourselves to a strictly civic (or citizen) concept of ethnocultural reality by focusing solely on rights and individuals, in keeping with traditional (so-called procedural) liberalism and republican philosophy. Accordingly, the majority-minorities relationship as well as the identity dynamics of which it is the vehicle should be excluded from the analysis or at most appear in the background.

7. Only a strictly civic approach makes it possible to effectively counteract discrimination and racism. Interculturalism is a "culturalism," and it gives too much importance to the cultural dimension of diversity, thus neglecting more fundamental issues such as power relationships, inequalities, discrimination, and racism.

8. The idea of the ad hoc principle of interventionism should be
   rejected, because it formally establishes unequal status between the
   majority and the minorities.

   On the whole, we are therefore faced with another option (with a
liberal variant and a republican variant), another model of management
of diversity, another possible avenue in the pursuit of pluralism and the
consolidation of an equitable society, and another way to deal with intercultural relations. I believe that this avenue, which is strictly civic and
legal, and which overlooks the majority culture, is very ill advised in the
Quebec context and should be rejected. Below I give the reasons that
interculturalism, as a model focusing on a search for balance and open
to all the dimensions of collective life, seems preferable to me. I will
present them in the form of a response to the criticisms listed immediately above (continuing the numerical listing of arguments throughout
this chapter).

Argument 10: There is no cultural majority in Quebec and the idea of a duality is without foundation

It is certainly difficult to precisely define Quebec's cultural majority or
express it quantitatively since its scope is variable, just like the degree of
intensity demonstrated by those who claim to belong to it. Its existence,
nevertheless, is manifested in various ways. First of all, following a very
simple logic, if we do not recognize the existence of a majority, how can
we talk about minorities? Here we are faced with a major challenge because in Quebec, the perception of minorities or ethnocultural groups
("communities") is deeply rooted (I am thinking of the representation
of Anglo-Quebecers, Jews, Chinese, Italians, Greeks, Arabs, Muslims,
etc.). Moreover, if we refrain from thinking about the majority and the
minorities, we are agreeing indirectly with the definition of multiculturalism, which represents the nation as a set of individuals more or less
attached to their groups of origin, without reference to a majority culture, a national culture, or a shared culture. I have already explained
why this concept does not suit Quebec.

Second, as in any society, there is in Quebec a dominant cultural elite
(this is one of the features of the cultural majority) that controls the
major institutions. This elite tends to establish its values and to govern
according to its vision of the world and its traditions. This has the effect
of marginalizing other values, visions of the world, and traditions, and
therefore often results in forms of direct or indirect exclusion and discrimination. It is precisely the purpose of charters and practices of accommodations to contribute measures that correct these excesses.

Third, and more specifically, the members of the founding franco-phone culture form in Quebec a majority group that recognizes itself in an identity and in a memory that are rooted in what I call master myths. One of these myths is sustained by an experience of domination under-gone for more than two centuries, from both the outside (the colonial regime) and the inside (domination by the clergy and a large part of the elites). Another master myth grows out of the constant struggles to en-sure a future for the French language and for francophone culture. The first myth has led to a desire for collective affirmation (of "re-conquest") that fuels the national question, and the second has generated a more or less keen feeling of fragility and insecurity that feeds on a minority con-sciousness as well as a great sensitivity to everything related to the fate of the language. Together, these myths have given substance to a national-ism that conveys strong values (such as equality, social justice, solidarity). Its expressions and its avenues (sometimes conservative, sometimes lib-eral) have changed with the time periods, but this nationalism has always been driven by the same fundamental motives and, in quasi-totality, by the same majority group (except for recent years).

This cultural majority has been heard throughout the history of Quebec: in, for example, the many episodes of the struggle for French and (until the 1950s) for the Catholic religion, the countless patriotic campaigns, the promotion of the settlement of the regions and life on the land as a guarantee of French Canadian culture, anti-Americanism, the promotion of friendship with France and international francophonie, and the autonomist and then the sovereignist movement. More recently, it has been from within the cultural majority that most of the concerns were raised that led to the accommodations crisis. Similarly, appeals for the promotion of fundamental values such as secularism and equality between men and women are rooted in large part in the memory of the Quiet Revolution, celebrated as a great episode of renewal for the fran-cophone (formerly French Canadian) majority. Finally, the recent con-troversy surrounding the former Parti Québécois government's project of a charter of values pitted members of the majority against members of minorities. Fortunately, the defeat of the government in the April 2014 general election has put an end to this project, which has been rejected by the new Liberal government. However, the debate on this issue is undoubtedly far from over.

In the face of this, one must unreservedly acknowledge the important contribution of postcolonial and postmodern studies, which have dem-onstrated the constructed, contradictory, and often arbitrary nature of identities ("negotiated," "cobbled together," "à la carte") as well as the strategies governing the construction of collective memories (overestimation of continuity, underestimation of the diversity of the majority group, etc.). The fact remains that identities are usually perceived, internalized, and experienced as authentic by the actors, and they play a significant role in the formation and evolution of individual consciousness as well as motivations for behaviours.[25]

In other words, while many analyses show convincingly that identities are not "primordialist" or "substantialist" (to use the accepted vocabulary), we can observe nevertheless that they are commonly experienced as such by a large number of people for whom they are the foundation of profound allegiances and loyalties. This is the case in all nations, especially in small nations such as Quebec, which are former colonies and cultural minorities in their continental environment, and which for a long time have mobilized around powerful master myths focusing on survival and collective re-conquest.

Likewise, it is certainly necessary to guard against the danger of an artificial hardening (or "essentialization") of cultures and the relativization of the concepts of group and ethnocultural affiliation, and to allow for the elements of fluidity (e.g., multiple identities) mentioned above. But once again, there are indisputably hard cores that survive the test of time. Interculturalism, like any analysis of culture, has to take into account these two dimensions: what belongs to fluidity and what belongs to rootedness.

That is why, while recognizing the existence of the majority and minority cultures, the model also has to acknowledge the principle of identity choices (which allows individuals to define themselves freely) and promote a shared culture as a place of encounters, exchanges, cross-fertilization, inventions, and changes. It also accepts that the roots themselves are sites of constant changes under cover of continuity, as shown by many studies on this subject. Finally, it recalls that, to function and be transformed, every society needs a symbolic foundation largely inherited – with some exceptions – from the past of the cultural majority. Again, the quest for balance is the rule.

In light of all these elements (shared language, identity, memory, master myths, affiliation), it seems very difficult to deny that what we have here is a majority ethnocultural group, with the understanding once again, of course, that its substance is variable and that its boundaries are sometimes porous. Similarly, for all the reasons that have just been mentioned (in summary: because it exists and it profoundly structures perceptions), I believe that this group, which is both a majority and a minority, has a right like any other to a form of recognition. It seems difficult to dispute that its identity, traditions, memory, and the values they embody are just as legitimate as those of ethnocultural minorities.

Argument 11: There is a cultural majority in Quebec, but it is ill advised to give recognition to that reality and distinguish it from (or oppose it to?) minorities, as the duality paradigm calls for

Like it or not, duality is a structural fact in Quebec. It is in a way a corollary of the previous argument. The counterpart of the existence of a cultural majority is obviously the existence of minorities. It is understood that this corollary can be the result of practices of exclusion by a dominant elite that pushes to the margins citizens who exhibit differences (of language, religion, customs, etc.). This difference can even be created or amplified by the majority, which thereby creates a pretext for dismissing or excluding those citizens. In these cases, the minorities take on a forced, artificially constructed character.[26]

But minorities are not always created by exclusionary strategies. They can also result from a specific pluralist integration policy and sometimes even from a desire for self-marginalization on the part of certain groups that want to create a distance from the surrounding culture – I have already mentioned in this regard the cases of the Hassidic Jews in Montreal, the Hutterites in the Canadian West, and the Amish in the United States. Once again, interculturalism considers these two possibilities: in the first case, to bring an end to exclusion; in the second, to give each minority the possibility of a different model of integration (within the limitations of current law).

According to one interpretation of pluralism, the majority-minorities relationship must be criticized and rejected because it grows out of a tension artificially maintained by false perceptions. According to another concept – the one being defended here – this relationship can and should be criticized because it certainly includes a potential for tension and domination, and because it inevitably involves a share of stereotypes and distortions. But, as I have already mentioned, it can also result in large part from the legitimate desire of many citizens to remain very close to their culture of origin (or maintain some kind of a link with it), and that desire should be respected in the very name of pluralism.

The majority-minorities relationship in Quebec seems to be unavoidable. It is largely fueled by the linguistic and cultural insecurities that have always been evident in the founding majority, it has been a key aspect of government discussion on diversity since the 1960s,[27] and it pervades the vocabulary of public debate, among both non-experts and experts.[28] It is also present in the language of novels, essays, the media, and polls – especially since issues related to political allegiances and the national question are regularly touched on – and it is employed by both liberal and conservative intellectuals. Commentators and experts on cultural mediation in businesses or institutions are constantly confronted by it.[29] For the last few years, it has structured in large part the opposition to accommodations (which supposedly threaten "our" values, "our" culture) as well as the debate on secularism ("we have banished religion from public life, the immigrants have brought it back to us"). And for forty years, it has fueled opposition to Canadian multiculturalism, which is commonly criticized for weakening the founding francophone culture by putting it on the same footing as other cultures (or "ethnic groups") living in Canada. Finally, the members of ethnocultural minorities experience this relationship on a daily basis, constantly being called upon to position themselves with respect to the majority in their process of integration.

How deeply rooted duality is in the Quebec imaginary is attested by its longevity and its hold on perceptions. We can see another sign in the fact that the government has twice attempted unsuccessfully to relegate it to the background: the first time in 1990 with the "moral contract" and a second time at the end of the 1990s with the "offensive on citizenship."[30]

The majority-minorities relationship is expressed with more or less intensity depending on the period. For example, if we restrict ourselves to recent years, an Us-Them relationship was strongly manifested during the 1995 referendum, culminating in the statement by Premier Parizeau on the "ethnic vote" and the affirmation of a francophone Us in opposition to the minorities. We also know that this divide was particularly strong during the accommodations crisis, which reached its peak in 2007–2008. If we exclude the role of certain media that attempted to enflame passions, we inevitably find an important cause of that crisis in a concern or discomfort mainly found in the majority cultural group (or more precisely, a very substantial fringe element of this group). And it should be recalled that the very mandate of the commission that I co-chaired with Charles Taylor talked about the balance to be protected "between the rights of the majority and the rights of minorities" (G. Bouchard & C. Taylor, 2008).

At another level, the language of philosophy and political science in the West makes extensive use of the majority-minorities relationship (it can be seen, for example, in the debate on the cultural neutrality or non-neutrality of nation states and in the controversy between egalitarian liberalism and communitarian liberalism [see D. Helly, 2002]). In Canada, constitutional and political debates commonly refer to Quebec as a minority nation. Yet who is involved here if not, primarily, members of the francophone majority? This reference in itself clearly assumes the existence in Canada of a national majority. We therefore also find at this level a majority-minorities relationship, even though, as we have seen in chapter 3, multiculturalism denies the existence of a majority culture in Canada.

Finally, recall that duality is not limited to Quebec. In various nations of Europe, we can see a majority-minorities relationship emerging; this is the case in England, the Netherlands, France, Denmark, Germany, Italy, and other countries. However, this change is more evident in perceptions, as shown in the media and public debate, than in official discourse. It is remarkable that, in certain cases, this duality leads not to interculturalism, as is happening in Quebec, but to forms of assimilation. The evolution of the debate on diversity in the United States also shows elements of a more and more marked duality. The well-known book by Samuel P. Huntington (1996), with his theory of eight conflicting civilizations, is very representative of this dualist vision. The change in the United States is above all fueled by Latin American immigrants and, more generally, by the rapid demographic growth of minorities. According to the most recent statistics, they currently represent 37 per cent of the total population of the country and close to half of the population eighteen years of age and less.

It is therefore wrong to claim that interculturalism artificially creates the majority-minorities relationship. Once again, it does not create it and does not promote it, but it has to acknowledge it, simply because that relationship exists, because it has a strong influence on intercultural life, and because it structures in a very large way thinking on Quebec diversity. That is why it is suitable as an analytical category. Interculturalism seeks to arbitrate this relationship in a way that keeps it from evolving towards a deep Us-Them chasm and towards tensions that are likely to lead to forms of discrimination and exclusion. It is also aimed at mitigating it in various ways, for example, by imbuing the school curriculum with pluralism (this is one of the most remarkable achievements of Quebec interculturalism); advocating rapprochements and interactions; relying on shared values and symbols; promoting a shared culture sustained by both the majority culture and minority cultures; preventing the hardening of identities, affiliations, and ethnocultural divisions; strengthening

the civil foundations that unite all Quebecers; encouraging political participation; intensifying efforts at economic and social inclusion; fighting inequalities and discrimination; and mitigating power relationships
that negatively affect minorities.

On the subject of the majority-minorities relationship, I will add a remark on an argument recently formulated by E. Winter (2010, 2011),
who suggests that we have to bring into this relationship a third entity and
reject binary logic. The definition of the relationship between a majority
and minorities will always involve a reference to a real or widely imagined
society that, playing the role of foil, convinces the majority to agree to
concessions to the minorities. According to Winter, the majority is motivated to make these concessions for various reasons, in particular because
it wants to avoid alienating the minorities by pushing them closer to the
"enemy." The expanded model therefore involves a trio: Us, Them, and
the Other. The author suggests that, according to this logic, the third
entity indirectly helps to articulate the relationship between the first two
and even brings them closer together by reducing the perception of their
differences and by uniting them in rejection of the Other.

From this perspective, for English Canada for example, the third entity is sometimes Quebec (characterized as intolerant and ethnocentric)
and sometimes the United States (perceived as assimilationist, ultra-
individualistic, violent). According to Winter's reasoning, one can imagine that in Quebec it is multicultural Canada that plays the role of the
Other.

Argument 12: The duality paradigm reintroduces ethnicity, stigmatizes minorities, and leads to discrimination

On the contrary, I maintain that taking the majority-minorities relationship into account is useful in preventing ethnic prejudice and discrimination. Six arguments can be mentioned here. First of all, I do not see how
taking duality into account would lead to a re-ethnicization of intercultural relationships more than pluralism itself, which leads to the recognition of cultural and identity dynamics. Second, and as I have just pointed
out, duality is an important key to analysis. The report of the Bouchard-
Taylor Commission referred to the majority culture and to minorities
more than thirty times; these references were a major part of the highlights reported in the media in May 2008. This key to analysis is indispensable for understanding and possibly putting into perspective the
immediate source of duality (most often a feeling of discomfort, a worry
aroused by the immigrant). While culture and identity contribute to

generating divisions in society, I do not see how an approach that ignores this by focusing strictly on individual rights and citizenship would make things better. It is necessary instead to combine these two dimensions in a single process, to implement a citizenship regime that fully integrates the cultural aspect.

Third, as various authors have pointed out (including G. Rocher, 2000; E. Winter, 2011; D. Juteau, 1999; L. Pietrantonio, 2000; G. Nootens, 2010a, pp. 65–7), duality is the site of a specific power relationship – in this case, a very unequal relationship – which it is therefore important to expose and which must be dealt with in order to remove or assuage the systemic obstacles to integration and equity. Like all majorities, the francophone cultural group, as a dominant group, tends to favour a kind of governance that does not always do justice to diversity (including the diversity that exists within the group[31]). As in any society, we therefore have to exercise vigilance and take corrective measures as required (which is the purpose of accommodations, measures to ensure access to equality and to fight exclusion and discrimination, etc.).

Moreover, this domination relationship particularly affects women, who are doubly disadvantaged since they have already been relegated to a position of inferiority by the structure of gender relations in society.[32]

One of the merits of interculturalism is that it brings to the fore this power relationship and the excesses it is prone to. In this area, models based on the diversity paradigm are vulnerable to the extent that they tend to gloss over the existence of the majority culture and the relationship of dominance that it generates (readers will recall that this is a criticism often made of Canadian multiculturalism).

Making full use in the analysis of the majority culture and the majority-minorities relationship does not create a space for discrimination but, quite the contrary, blocks that space by seeking the most equitable formulas to democratically arbitrate this basic relationship and to fully implement the pluralist orientation while always taking into account the fact that in Quebec the founding majority is also a minority.

Fourth, the duality paradigm has the advantage of drawing attention to the majority as also being of an ethnocultural nature, and therefore arising from a specific history and sustained by distinctive characteristics. It thus impedes the common tendency of majorities to position themselves as universal (or "civic") while the minorities are labelled as ethnic.

Fifth, the analysis of the majority-minorities relationship helps in conceiving and implementing more appropriate policies and more effective management of diversity, for example, by promoting: (a) various forms of rapprochements and interactions between majority and minorities; (b) knowledge and mutual understanding between these groups in order to fight stereotypes and exclusion; (c) consciousness-raising among the founding majority regarding diversity and the profound changes that it brings to society; and (d) participation in civic life as a site for encounters and mobilization. Fear of a "re-ethnicization" of intercultural life seems to me all the less founded given that interculturalism, at least as I have defined it, emphasizes many provisions that go in the opposite direction (while recognizing the inevitable and legitimate role of rootedness): intercommunity exchanges and actions, free choice of affiliations, fluidity of identities, promotion of a shared culture, protection of rights, and the fight against stereotypes.

Finally, it is necessary to emphasize that majorities do not all or always behave badly. Given the many precedents in Europe and elsewhere, one must obviously be sensitive to the risks of abuse by majorities that become ambitious, aggressive, and vengeful. But if we search the earlier and more recent history of Quebec for events that would provide foundations for such a concern, we will find fewer than in most Western societies. Francophone Quebec is a former colony that was itself dominated by an arrogant power convinced of its superiority. On various occasions, French Canada has had to resist attempts at assimilation and various forms of discrimination. And when, starting in the 1960s, francophone Quebecers really resolved to emancipate themselves and affirm themselves collectively through a neonationalist fervour, what did they do? They distinguished themselves by a series of progressive, liberal, and pluralist policies unprecedented in their history, sustained by a democratic ideal focusing on social equality (G. Bouchard, 2013a).

In the broader context, it can be asserted that certain nations have shown openness and generosity towards minorities; others, in spite of difficult circumstances, have been able to develop and maintain a liberal orientation. It also happens that dominant cultures are the right path to advance democracy and human rights (see D. Brown, 2008). It would be a sociological error to underestimate the weight or deny the legitimacy of traditions and collective identities. Largely governed by emotion, they do not appeal to overly rationalist minds. And yet, like the myths[33] that sustain them, they belong to a universal mechanism that runs through the history of all societies and weighs heavily on the orientation of their destiny. Unpredictable, irrepressible, they can invest themselves in the most noble causes as well as the basest; responsibility falls to the social actors, who have a great responsibility in this regard.

Argument 13: The majority-minorities relationship exacerbates the dynamics of identity and its irrational aspects

Does making room for the majority-minorities relationship, and for the identities and myths that sustain them, mean carelessly promoting the irrational? It certainly never enters my mind to question the need to extend as much as possible, in these highly inflammatory matters, the prerogatives of reason. But it is also useful to recall the existence of powerful symbolic mechanisms, the functioning of which will always largely elude rationality. Let us first of all give the lie to an illusory claim according to which, after three centuries of Enlightenment, the irrational has been subjugated by reason as the driving force of the evolution of our societies. This is a statement that is clearly and constantly refuted by countless counterexamples, as demonstrated by international current events as well as the evolution of sciences, arts, and literature.

Second, what exactly does this harmful "irrationality" that should be expunged from collective life consist in? It no doubt includes many erroneous perceptions, distortions, and extremist notions that should be condemned and fought. But it also includes affiliations and loyalties founded on values – humanist, moral, or religious convictions – basic aspirations, traditions, heritages, sensibilities, allegiances, and solidarities: in short, a whole symbolic baggage that does not belong primarily to reason and that nevertheless forms the basis for social life, that gives it meaning, that knits it together and moves it forward. Finally, there will be general agreement, I imagine, on the fact that not everything irrational is necessarily unreasonable.

As history, both early and recent, teaches us, the irrational can lend itself to the worst excesses. The remedy for that, if there is one, is certainly not to claim to banish it, since this would mean lapsing into dangerous utopianism, and would lead to the eradication of religion, identity, and everything that is based on emotion and affectivity, in particular literary and artistic creation. We should instead try to better understand the irrational in social life (its roots, its mechanisms, its expressions), to contain it if necessary and to orient it if possible by working to promote democracy, awakening the consciousness of citizens, giving them a sense of responsibility from a very young age through education, campaigning for more just, more equal, more inclusive societies, promoting open and equitable public debate, and finally, encouraging the formation of many organizations devoted to civic reflection and to the advancement of public ethics and awareness. However, as we know all too well, nothing can ever be taken for granted; it is up to each generation to ensure the moral order of societies and to rebalance reason and emotion.

On this subject, there is perhaps an important lesson to be learned from the evolution of Russia after the end of the USSR. As we know, new elites took power in 1991 and, sure of their success, immediately began to make energetic efforts to establish a liberal regime on the model of the West, based on democracy, a market economy, individualism, and human rights. This initiative quickly met with failure. An appealing explanation has been proposed by political scientist Y. Brudny (2013). According to this author, the failure was due in large part to the fact that the new elite neglected to relate its new program of governance (and the new national imaginary associated with it) to the old Russian national myths and the traditions that perpetuated them. This omission then permitted a non-liberal elite to successfully establish a reactionary regime that was able to exploit the old symbolic undercurrents of the Russian people to gain their support, with the results we all know about.[34]

The history of England in the nineteenth century offers an analogous example. Trevor-Roper (1992, pp. 19–20) has shown that the growth of liberalism was slowed down there by a desire for radical change at the expense of traditions and social connections that were already established and considered reactionary. "Voids" were thus created that conservatives were quick to fill by encouraging, to their advantage, old customs and related symbols. M.J. Sandel (2010, p. 249) has proposed an analysis of the same kind regarding the American Democrats who, in the 1970s to the 1980s, left the field of moral values, anxieties, and collective ideals open to the right, which contributed to the rise of religious conservatism and the triumph of Reaganism.

In my view, episodes of this kind show the need to consider carefully, in their legitimacy as well as in their complexity, the identity dynamics of majorities and the manifestations of insecurity or concern that often arise in them. Failing that, pluralism can experience significant setbacks. And isn't this precisely what we are currently observing in many Western societies? It could well be that the type of misunderstanding illustrated by these three examples is related to this failure. Obviously, we have to reject in Quebec a dangerous polarization that the current debate tends to harden by artificially opposing, on the one side, the interests of the majority culture (its identity, language, memory, etc.) and, on the other, the promotion of rights.

Argument 14: The recognition of the founding culture on the basis of its fragility and its double status (majority and minority) belongs in reality to the realm of strategic rhetoric and the thirst for power

I maintain that the founding majority in Quebec, which is also a minority, likewise deserves recognition and protection. First of all, that majority has the same legitimacy as the minority cultures. In addition, in terms of heritage, it ensures a substantial contribution to the symbolic foundation of Quebec society (see below).

The sources and intensity of concerns manifested within the founding culture have certainly varied with time, but it is a constant and an important parameter to consider with respect to the development of francophone Quebec; these concerns cannot simply be attributed to erroneous or manipulated perceptions. Polls conducted during the 1990s show that Quebec francophones were very concerned about the situation and future of their language (E. Gidengil, A. Blais, R. Nadeau, & N. Nevitte, 2003) and some data predict an increase in the feeling of insecurity in coming years, with as a possible consequence a growth of an intensified Us-Them relationship and the attendant tensions. As I mentioned in the introduction to this book, it is predicted that the proportion of Quebecers from immigrant backgrounds will reach 19 per cent in 2031 (it was 11 per cent in 2006) and will rise to 30 per cent in the Montreal region. We also know that Quebecers whose mother language is French are now in a slight minority on the island of Montreal, which feeds a growing sense of discomfort.

Other demographic trends are moving in the same direction, in particular low fertility rates and the aging of the population (Quebecers younger than twenty years old represented 40 per cent of the population in 1971, 26 per cent in 1991, and 22 per cent in 2011 [M. Pagé, 2011]). To this should be added the impact of globalization, which, whatever people say, is expressed mostly in English (at least in the West and on a few other continents). We can also see this in Quebec where francophone multinational companies are increasingly using English in their international and even internal communications. At the same time, because of its low fertility, the founding majority will probably continue to shrink (at least in proportion to the total population). This shows, from another perspective, the importance of the shared culture. For the cultural majority in demographic decline, it offers a positive outlook for the future, and a potential for redefinition and expansion in a broader perspective of continuity.

Young Quebecers are also known to be attracted by American-type cultural practices. In addition, there are certain signs to suggest that the passion there has always been for the French language in Quebec is cooling a bit among the younger generation, those who are deeply integrated with globalization and very open to culture that is expressed in English. In this context, it is not alarmist to nurture a concern for French and for French-speaking Quebec. It is therefore completely legitimate to grant the latter, as necessary, specific protections, as was the case with Law 101.

Is the foregoing an ill-conceived desire to reassure the majority, which will only increase their insecurity by legitimizing it and whetting their appetite to the detriment of minorities? As an answer to this, we can cite the example of Law 101 and the effects it has had not only for the cultural majority but for Quebec society as a whole. The majority group was reassured to the point that, twenty-five years later, it has been accused of dropping its guard regarding new perils threatening French. Moreover, Law 101 has established in civic life a linguistic peace at the end of fifteen years of conflict in addition to contributing substantially to a redefinition of Quebec identity, henceforth open to all citizens. This law, controversial in the beginning, is now the object of a strong consensus. Finally, by soothing the concerns of the majority, it has encouraged the adoption of liberal policies in the area of diversity.

It is therefore likely that the majority-minorities relationship has been established for a long time to come as a central feature of the ethnocultural reality in Quebec. But this does not prevent the growth of a shared culture, and Quebec society as a whole will always be able to remain united in terms of citizenship through a set of rights and mutual commitments.

Argument 15: It is necessary to focus the reflection on individuals, rights, and citizenship, and relegate to the background the cultural and identity aspects

According to various analysts, the rule of law that governs civic life and the rationality that forms the basis for it are enough for social life.[35] As I said in chapter 1, I believe that this position comes from a disembodied, unrealistic concept of life in society. In its classical liberal version, it assumes that citizens are self-sufficient, self-made, and governed only by reason. They must therefore be protected from the intrusions (the "contaminations"?) of collective institutions, identity, and the like. This is a goal that certain people perhaps achieve but that, sociologically, remains a creation of the mind.

Following the most common path, individuals are formed in the environment in which they are born and raised, with a complex heritage of feelings, emotions, roots, and loyalties, and it is on the basis of this baggage that they can gradually acquire a grasp of more abstract and more rational categories, more universal aims and principles. It is in this way too that they can construct their personalities and identities. But these categories and these principles always remain connected in a way to the reservoir of values, aspirations, memory, and identity from which they emanate and from which individuals continue to draw sustenance to varying degrees throughout their lives. Similarly, a society can only perpetuate itself and develop on the basis of a symbolic foundation made up of shared ideals and references.

For these reasons, interculturalism, as a search for balance, tries to combine rights and identity, reason and emotion. It therefore argues for mediation, interrelationships, bridges, syntheses, in accordance with the fabric and movement of social life. Here again, the model proves resistant to dichotomous thought. Basically, the type of liberalism that advocates radical individualism leads to a kind of marginalization and impoverishment of citizens, who are asked to put aside what, in any society, is the primary source and sustenance of ideals, what structures identities, and what gives meaning to life and even establishes rights.

If Western democracies had limited themselves to this ultraliberal credo celebrating the autonomy of individuals, how would they have been able to adopt policies aimed at counteracting structural inequalities or fighting racism and other factors of discrimination? How could equality between men and women have made progress and come to be confirmed in charters? Individuals exist only in configurations of meaning and affiliation, in power relationships and structures of inequality.

In a different way and to a lesser degree, the same comment applies to the republican model, which, on the pretext of equality and universality, aims to assimilate immigrants and minorities to a culture, and even to an ethnicity, that refuses to acknowledge itself. This can be clearly seen in France where, as many studies have shown, a strongly ethnicized national culture has taken shape on the basis of what was presented as solely universal values.[36] This cultural aspect is, however, officially denied, like duality, which is manifested currently in the form of the cultural majority (very "French") and the Muslim minority (associated with "diversity"). The example of this republican model thus provides a powerful argument against any regime that claims to confine itself to the civic dimension by cloaking itself in the most noble universal values. But why should the aspirations of a nation to universal values lead it to deny its distinctive characteristics?

In Quebec, M. Labelle and X. Dionne (2011) argue for a civic-style approach that does not reject taking into account the cultural aspect but relegates it to a secondary position ("the fertile ground for dialogue should therefore be political before being cultural," p. 42). This process intended to establish "a citizenship without domination" (p. 47) is certainly very attractive, but one might wonder how to deal with crucial questions such as the majority-minorities relationship, all the problems of ethnocultural roots and identity dynamics, the simultaneous protection of the attributes of the founding majority and the rights of minorities, the multiplicity of memories, the management of the policy of recognition and pluralist measures (including the practice of accommodations), and the definition of the shared culture to be promoted. More generally, how will pluralism, which leads to respect for distinctiveness in culture and identity, be combined with the universalist orientation of the civic approach?[37]

Argument 16: Interculturalism is concerned only with culture

Contrary to a criticism that is sometimes heard, the scope of interculturalism is not limited to the cultural, with all aspects of shared life and integration supposedly reduced to it. In other words, interculturalism is not a form of "culturalism." It seeks to destroy the cultural roots of discrimination and dissipate the unfounded fears that can also motivate behaviours of rejection or withdrawal. It also strives to promote certain civic values, to relax rigid identities and combine collective memories. The fight for rights therefore also takes place through culture. But it is clearly understood that interculturalism cannot be limited to this. As already indicated, the denunciation of the power relationships and economic structures that generate inequality and exclusion is also among its priorities. These structural factors should command attention for two reasons: they contribute to creating intercultural divisions and hinder efforts at rapprochement and exchange that could mitigate those divisions. In short, interculturalism is concerned with all the inequities that arise out of cultural diversity and the mechanisms that produce and perpetuate them.

But in itself, the model is not and is not intended to be a general theory of inequalities, of the structure of power relations and class relationships in a society, although it proposes effective means to mitigate them. I have also pointed out that an opposing process, centred on the political and social factors that structure relationships of domination and contribute to marginalization,[38] would not be exempt from dealing with specific problems that emerge inevitably from diversity and intercultural encounters, independently of the structural mechanisms that ultimately produce them.

Argument 17: Cultural interventionism, and the ad hoc political leverage that makes it possible, go against the spirit of pluralism

Experience teaches that the practice of cultural interventionism is universal and inevitable. Many intellectuals, liberals, and others have in fact demonstrated or recognized that the ethnocultural neutrality of nation states (or, more precisely, of the majorities that control them), often desired or proclaimed in principle, does not exist in reality. All nation states choose one or more official languages, impose the values considered fundamental and inscribed in charters, define the relationship between state and religion, strongly orient the construction of memory and collective identity, determine an educational curriculum, select immigrants, determine the rituals of civic life, and protect heritage and works of scholarly culture against the mechanisms of the market. They also adopt policies of assistance to certain disadvantaged individuals or groups. Inevitably, the government's management approach still calls on specific cultural choices, which is equally true of liberal societies that need to base themselves on a unique system of values, produced by a history (autonomy of the individual, liberty, rationality of the citizen, equality of rights, meaning of human dignity, tolerance, popular sovereignty, etc.).[39]

Many authors have also pointed out that the position of abstentionists is fundamentally contradictory: they argue for the cultural neutrality of the government in the name of liberty and autonomy of individuals, while at the same time they expect the government to protect these fundamental values of liberal society.

Some authors therefore acknowledge non-neutrality as a kind of inevitability, but others see it as useful and even necessary in order to avoid harmful consequences. It has been shown that an officially abstentionist state unofficially serves the interests of the majority, reproducing that group's values and visions of the world, and favours inequalities by giving advantage to men and by closing its eyes to the social harm of laissez-faire policies (see also G. Bouchard, 2011, p. 414, n. 26). A bias in favour of neutrality is contrary to pluralism since it leads to the rejection of the principle of recognition and the practice of accommodations in favour of disadvantaged citizens. It is also an obstacle to the contextual ("substantial") approach of the law, which is more and more inclined, out of a concern for equity, to take into account the cultural roots of the people (chapter 4).

A sociological argument can be added to the above. All societies need a symbolic foundation[40] (identity, memory, traditions, values, ideals, founding myths, etc.) to ensure their balance, their reproduction, and their development, and the law in itself is not enough to fulfil those functions. Especially in a context of tensions, change, or crisis, only the existence of broadly shared references – that is, a specific culture and national identity – make possible the elements of affiliations and solidarity that provide the basis of any form of collective mobilization for the pursuit of the common good (reduction of social inequalities, improvement of health care, environmental policies, etc.). These are the conditions that make democracy, civic participation, social justice, and the meaning of mutual responsibility possible, and they should never be taken for granted. It is therefore desirable for liberal states to support – as all of them do – the symbolic foundation in which institutions and, more generally, the social bond are rooted.

It is apparent that, in any society, the maintenance of a symbolic foundation requires a continuity that is provided in very large part by the majority culture and the values forged in its history. For a society to have control over its present and its future, it needs to adopt orientations and ideals that are based on both heritage and goals for the future. While the latter aspect is indisputably the responsibility of all citizens, the former belongs mainly to the path of the founding culture.[41] These remarks highlight the particular situation of the majority culture as the support for the entire societal or national culture. In this sense, interventionism is therefore not a tool of both the majority and minorities. The remarks also highlight the always ambiguous status of the majority culture: on the one hand, it has to be restrained because of the relationship of domination that it tends to establish with minorities; on the other hand, it has to be preserved in the interest of the symbolic foundation or the national culture.

In a sense, the objection could be made that, through these measures, the majority is unjustifiably appropriating the public space for itself. Part of the answer to this criticism lies in the principle of double recognition, already mentioned, and the reciprocity that it entails: cultural interventionism, as long as it is limited by the law, can be seen as an accommodation, this time in favour of the majority rather than minorities. This arrangement is justified by the fact that the maintenance of the majority culture also ensures the reproduction of the symbolic foundation, and therefore also serves the minorities. We are very much here in the spirit of interculturalism, which advocates a logic of harmonization through mutual adjustments.

In this regard, an important lesson emerges from recent Quebec experience. The main criticism formulated against the report of the Bouchard-Taylor Commission came from the founding majority. In the minds of many, the report gave a lot to minorities and immigrants but very little to the majority; it was forcefully recalled that since French-speaking Quebec is itself a minority, it also needs protections, and hence the need for balance. However, the principle of interventionism and the political leverage that it justifies precisely address this concern.

Another argument is based on the diversity of cultures and identities at the international level, celebrated by UNESCO as a source of innovation and creativity, just like biodiversity. UNESCO made this a major priority in November 2001, with its initiative receiving the support of 185 states.[42] But while there was agreement on the need to preserve cultural plurality on that level, could the majority groups in nation states, as the main supports for national cultures, not see themselves as invested with a legitimacy, if not a particular responsibility in the fight against the powerful currents of standardization brought about by globalization?

One last argument, a pragmatic one, argues in favour of cultural interventionism. Early and more recent history has taught us to fear minorities when they become fanatical and turn to terrorism. But it has also taught us to fear just as much (and maybe more) cultural majorities, which are prone to adopt aggressive behaviours when they feel humiliated, unjustly treated, or victimized. It is prudent to take this fact into account. The principle of interventionism can, in fact, mitigate in certain majorities feelings of anxiety that can easily develop into hostility, especially when exploited by social or political actors. However, this principle will no doubt displease proponents of legalism or absolute liberalism. It should be recalled that attempts to create a perfect society can sometimes have the opposite effect.

To be sure, the principle of interventionism departs to some extent from the ideal and very abstract vision of society as being formed of an entirely neutral government and a set of completely autonomous, rational, and self-reliant citizens; but it comes closer to the complex, shifting, omnipresent, and unpredictable reality of identity dynamics and the uncertainties of social and political life. In other words, this approach proceeds from a more sociological and more realistic vision of liberal philosophy.

However, the use of this political leverage should be carefully circumscribed. Otherwise, it may simply jeopardize the practice of accommodations, of which one of the goals, as mentioned above, is to protect minorities against the abuses (often unintended or unconscious) of the majority.[43] It is also important to see that it does not become a pretext for discriminatory actions by authoritarian majorities. Here too, there is a delicate balance to be negotiated with caution and moderation. In this regard, all majority groups have important responsibilities given that they largely control the institutions of the host society.

Interventionism must therefore operate within the limits of fundamental rights. Otherwise there is a danger of falling into ethnic discrimination.[44] Some will perhaps argue that exceptional situations can occur. But the danger to the cultural majority would have to be very great, and how could this be rigorously evaluated? We can say therefore that as a general rule this room for interventionism makes it possible to take liberties with the ideal of the cultural abstentionism of states (which can be inaccessible and even harmful), but not with fundamental rights.

Could the foregoing be understood as an acceptance of, if not an incentive to, "majoritarianism" (Pathak, 2008) as well as nationalism in the negative sense that the word usually carries in Europe (that is, the promotion of withdrawal, chauvinism, and confrontation rather than openness and collaboration)?[45] Of course not: what I am saying is just a reminder that it is important, and legitimate, for a nation to preserve its symbolic foundation, and specifically a sense of continuity drawing on founding myths.

In light of the above, it is not surprising that all democratic nation states practise cultural interventionism, even those considered the most liberal or the most "civic." Canada, for example, makes particularly intense (one might sometimes even say excessive) use of it, in spite of its multiculturalism and pluralist allegiance. I am thinking of the reference to the supremacy of God in the preamble to the Constitution, of initiatives to promote "Canadian" values, of the recent reaffirmation of monarchist symbols, of the restrictions (quotas) imposed on the distribution of foreign cultural "products" (e.g., on radio and television), on the sale or disposition of objects considered as heritage symbols, or on the composition of football teams, which are allowed only a certain proportion of American players, among other examples (see R. Edwardson, 2008).

Again with respect to Canada, I am also thinking of the annual ritual of the National Prayer Breakfast, which brings together the speakers of the Senate and the House of Commons, Supreme Court judges, and members of the cabinet in order to call upon "Almighty God," to "ask the Most High for strength and wisdom, to show our faith and renew our devotion and that of our nation to God and to His works," all "in the spirit of Jesus Christ."[46] We are not that far from the time when the French Canadian clergy consecrated the nation to the Sacred Heart.

In the United States, Christian symbols permeate political life, and WASP cultural heritage is still very influential, like the assimilationist model of the melting pot. Great Britain is not to be outdone, in maintaining the official status of the Anglican Church as the national religion and refusing to give a Catholic descendant the right to occupy the throne (close to five hundred years after Henry VIII's schism). Republican France itself, among other measures, refuses Islam (the second biggest religion in the country) the official recognition that it grants to Catholicism, Protestantism, and Judaism (in accordance with the law of 1905), imposes republican values (based on its own history) on the pretext of universalism, and limits the distribution of American songs on its airwaves.

Many of these examples obviously push too far the principle of ad hoc interventionism, to the extent that, without sufficient justification, they violate the fundamental imperatives of pluralism.

In the case of Quebec, the cultural interventionism appears all the more justified, given Quebec's status as a cultural minority on the continent and a national minority within Canada (see R. Poole, 1999, pp. 128–9, and V. Spencer, 2008). This interventionism is actually already in use, as shown by Law 101 on language, the immigrant selection policy (which gives preference to French speakers), the Ethics and Religious Culture course (a course taught in all of the province's elementary and high schools, which pays particular attention to Christian religions – see chapter 5), and the measures to protect heritage associated with the founding majority.

In writing above about what I call the ad hoc cultural interventionism, I have taken special care to specify that this does not amount to decreeing an a priori or formal precedence for the majority (which would result in establishing a hierarchy and creating two classes of citizens). Similarly, the report of the Bouchard-Taylor Commission refers to a "de facto precedence" as opposed to a "precedence of law" (p. 214). Nevertheless, certain observers have not taken this distinction into account and, quite wrongly, have considered only the second meaning; they have thus condemned the idea. In order to avoid any confusion, then, I will now abandon the term "precedence" entirely and restrict

myself to the concept of ad hoc or contextual interventionism, by referring to the well-known theme of the supposed cultural neutrality (or
abstentionism) of governments. It should be clearly understood that this
concept *does not* lead to the institution of a legal hierarchy. On this point,
it should be noted that interculturalism is distinguished once again from
certain republican regimes that, directly or not, on the pretext of universalism give systematic, a priori precedence to what I call the majority or
founding culture. In summary, while interculturalism explicitly recognizes the existence of a majority-minorities relationship, it does so to better
do justice to both the majority and the minorities and to better protect
the rights of all citizens.

Conclusion

Readers may have noted that, in the pages above, I have for the purposes
of the presentation lumped together liberalism and republicanism. This is
because both put special emphasis on rights; but in other respects the two
philosophies differ substantially. One is suspicious of the role of government, the other values it; one is generally resistant to collective rights, the
other accepts them. But above all, liberalism, because it considers itself
very sensitive to individual rights, is largely open to the expression of differences and accommodations, while republicanism considers them contrary to its universalist credo and its concept of equality of citizenship.

All in all, we are thus faced with three options or models for dealing
with diversity among which Quebec will have to choose. One is an assimilationist model, which should be excluded because of the formal hierarchy it establishes among citizens and because of the scant concern it
shows for the fate of minorities, who are required to either sacrifice their
culture or live in exclusion. The second option, based on either classical
liberalism or republican philosophy, advocates a strictly civic and individual approach and establishes a double disjuncture or dichotomy, on
the one hand between the legal and the cultural (or the identity aspect),
on the other hand between the individual and the collective. The majority-minorities relationship is thus marginalized, if not excluded completely, with the result that a basic fact of the ethnocultural reality of
Quebec is ignored.

The third option is interculturalism, which, in a spirit of balance, aims
to overcome these dichotomous elements by promoting the development of bridges and syntheses and by offering a more complete image of
the collective dynamic, which guarantees a better grasp of reality and
opens the door to policies better suited to the Quebec context.

There might be concerns that this concept of interculturalism could neglect the rights of minorities in favour of the majority and thus distance itself from pluralism. I believe that I have shown this is not at all the case. Rather, the search for balance between the majority and minorities has guided my entire reflection, which focuses on a concept of pluralism that is fully adapted to the realities of Quebec.[47] It is in this spirit that I advocate a careful consideration of the majority-minorities relationship and the identity dynamics associated with it.

This is the same general objective that guided the work of the Bouchard-Taylor Commission, and I am certainly not repudiating the positions expressed in that commission's report, which contained many proposals that I have presented here with further explanation: search for balance, majority-minorities relationship, cultural non-neutrality of states, ad hoc cultural interventionism ("de facto precedence," p. 214), founding culture, emphasis on integration with reciprocity, and need for a symbolic foundation in addition to the rule of law, among others. Readers will also note that the report placed great importance on the fate of the cultural majority, on the founding traditions and values that have been forged during its history (pp. 118, 122), on its memory, and on its identity (chap. 6, part C; chap. 10, part C).

I will conclude with a comment on a very rich sociological process that emphasizes not the problem of harmonization of ethnocultural differences, but the social conditions of their production and reproduction. Based on the work of Max Weber, this approach establishes that, to a large extent, differences of origin, religion, language, customs, and "race" are artificially fabricated or amplified by elites (or majorities) who use them as pretexts to exclude a portion of the citizenry and practise various forms of discrimination. This process, and the resulting inequalities, are made possible by the power held by majorities, which establish a relationship of domination over minorities that permits them to impose their world view and their standards.[48]

This concept of the majority-minorities relationship is also based on another Weberian idea according to which identity is formed through relational dynamics: the group that has constructed and promoted its identity always needs to mark its distinctive character by positioning itself in relationship to another group perceived and constructed as different (to become conscious of what we are, it is useful if not necessary to refer to what we are not). Identity and otherness are therefore inseparable. Another characteristic frequently associated with this mechanism is the unequal value assigned to the majority and minority cultures, the former being declared superior to the latter. Finally, it is the minorities that are said to be "ethnic," never or rarely the majorities, which prefer to position themselves as civic, universal, and progressive.

These statements contain a severe criticism of pluralism as it is currently conceived. Since the majority and the minorities are linked by relationships of domination that are sources of tensions and conflicts (which can hardly be disputed), it would be naive to believe that the measures in favour of rapprochement and exchange advocated by interculturalism will produce the expected positive effects. The Weberian process also leads to a criticism of the principle of recognition and accommodations: once established in a dominant position, why would the majority agree to share their advantages?

For interculturalism, these criticisms are an important reminder of the sociological foundations of ethnocultural difference and the attention that must be paid to power relationships, as I have already mentioned on a few occasions. This is the reason why the model places great emphasis on the fight against the various forms of exclusion and discrimination. It is also why it favours the establishment of programs for access to equality and the practice of accommodations as corrective measures. Does this mean that initiatives for rapprochement and exchange, advocated by interculturalism, would be in vain? Of course not; but we can better see how they should be carried out in order to be effective. In short, social and political action should always go hand-in-hand with action on the cultural front.

With respect to majorities and the spontaneous aversion any dominant group feels to disciplining and moderating itself, we clearly have to rely on factors more convincing and more certain than good faith or good intentions to avoid maintaining the status quo. In certain cases, majorities can, via the fear of fragmentation, be persuaded to improve their relationships with minorities and be concerned about their integration. We are observing here, in a way, a self-defence mechanism. Specifically with regard to immigrants, the majority's motivation for conciliation comes in part from anticipated advantages, especially economic ones (see above in this chapter).

Majorities also feel pressure because of the moral authority that pluralism has acquired in democratic societies since the end of the Second World War, and even more since the 1960s. We should not underestimate the influence of international conventions and treaties, and the weight of the prestigious organizations that ensure they are observed. The judiciary, using the charters, is another powerful instrument of regulation and constraint. Finally, the minorities themselves, as they struggle to renegotiate and rebalance their relationship with majorities, play a major role. Their demands, when based on principles of justice defined and professed by the majority itself, will necessarily find allies among the majority population.

In fact, the sociological approach inspired by the Weberian tradition, far from condemning interculturalism, seems instead to be complementary to it. Consequently, authors who subscribe to this tradition maintain that strategies of power and exclusion account for a lot in the development of ethno-cultural minorities but, with certain exceptions,[49] they do not claim that this factor alone accounts for their existence. We almost always find, in the beginning, cultural differences that provide support to strategies of ethnicization (see D. Juteau, 1996). This strictly cultural foundation, often encouraged, perpetuated, and accentuated by the concerned groups themselves, therefore calls for a specific process.

In addition, ethnocultural features, even if they are artificially created or amplified, end up being internalized and experienced as authentic. In other words, with the help of the identity dynamic, these features take on an existence of their own, which confers an additional reality on intercultural differences and contributes to their maintenance.

Finally, groups of citizens who feel excluded for any reason or who do not recognize themselves in common representations of the nation will be naturally induced to form minority communities. In short, independently or on the margins of the power structure, there will always be people who will feel the need to maintain the reference to their culture or group of origin.

5

For an Inclusive Secularism

In this chapter I present a proposal for a secular regime that I consider to be inclusive (following J. Baubérot, 2004, 2006) and that I see as inspired by the philosophy of interculturalism. But I want to point out at the outset that interculturalism can certainly accommodate many other concepts of secularism. The one that I am submitting for discussion is quite simply an extension of my vision of this model.

I also want to express my disagreement with the opinion that reflections on secularism should be carried out independently of reflections on interculturalism, since these are two separate issues. It is true that the current debate on the relationship between the state and religion in Quebec rarely makes reference to interculturalism. And yet, the whole issue of requests for accommodations for religious reasons in government institutions is directly related to interculturalism. In fact, religious diversity appears as one of the main aspects of ethnocultural diversity, which includes a mixture of more or less institutionalized visions of the world, beliefs, values, ideals, allegiances, and traditions. Accordingly, interculturalism and secularism can and even should be dealt with in combination, and on the basis of the same premises.

This chapter also provides an opportunity to show that the regimes of secularism are always hybrids. They are made up of various components, often competing and subject to tensions if not in contradiction. They also always carry the mark of the society in which they operate; they reflect its context, traditions, institutions, sensibilities, history and, inevitably, its divisions. Finally, they are never closed. They constantly require re-evaluations, negotiations, and adjustments. And for all these reasons, they are never immune from controversies and they are difficult to transpose from one society to another.

First of all, a few concepts need to be clarified. I will talk about laicization rather than secularization. In my view, "secularization" refers mainly
(a) to a change over recent centuries in Western culture to a new vision
that gives less and less space to the supranatural dimension, thus opening the way for the rule of positive knowledge, guided by the rigorous
observation of facts; and (b) to a citizen's space in the management of
collective life. "Laicization," by contrast, traditionally refers above all to
institutional arrangements the purpose of which is to regulate relationships between the state and religious life, or between the citizen and
the believer.

Contrary to current usage and in keeping with a definition in the report of the Bouchard-Taylor Commission, I will extend the concept of
religion in using the phrase "convictions of conscience" to designate the
allegiances, beliefs, visions of the world, principles, and ideals (religious
and other) according to which individuals define themselves on a profound level, choose their major goals, and regulate their lives.[1] The
reason for this choice is simple: in a diverse society, all forms of moral
convictions or ideals of primordial nature, religious or not, should be
respected. Failing that, there is a risk of establishing among convictions
of conscience an arbitrary hierarchy in favour of religious beliefs.

Moreover, instead of talking about secularism to characterize the system of a given society, I will talk about a secular regime (once again following the Bouchard-Taylor report[2]). The latter is a more complex and
more comprehensive concept, but also more faithful to reality.

What Is a Secular Regime?

In Quebec and elsewhere, the public debate commonly refers to societies that are considered more or less "secular." This reduces the concept
of secularism to a very restrictive meaning, that of the separation of state
and religion (or convictions of conscience). In reality, secularism covers
a complex set of arrangements; hence the concept of secular regime,
which involves five principles or values:
1. freedom of conscience and religion
2. equality among systems of beliefs (religious and other)
3. the separation or mutual autonomy of state and institutionalized
   systems of beliefs (such as churches)
4. the neutrality of the state with regard to all religions (or systems of
   deeply held beliefs, convictions of conscience based in world views)[3]
5. preservation of customary or heritage values

This last component, which involves the history of a community, is less formalized and does not seem to operate at the same level as the four preceding ones. It is nevertheless sufficiently powerful to sometimes legitimately benefit from a kind of ad hoc precedence over the others – which can occur in particular when it competes with principles as fundamental as the neutrality of the state or the freedom of conscience of individuals (to put it more precisely: the freedom to declare one's beliefs or profound convictions through ritual or other acts).

Here are a few examples from Quebec of this kind of ad hoc precedence: the national funerals for heads of government in a Catholic church, symbols of Christian festivals (Christmas in particular) in public places and in government or paragovernmental buildings, the financial participation of the government in the preservation of old Christian buildings, the biased schedule of legal holidays, the cross on the Quebec flag, the daily ringing of the bells of Catholic churches, and the crosses erected along rural roads. It was in the same spirit that in March 2011 Italy was authorized by the Grand Chamber of the European Court of Human Rights[4] to keep crucifixes on the walls of its schools. It can be seen from these examples that the criterion of customary values can sometimes acquire a significant weight; it adds much more than a marginal component or value. It draws its authority from the usefulness for a community of preserving its symbolic foundation (the sense of its continuity, of its identity).

With respect to the five components, it should be noted that I am talking about values (goals or ideals, sources of motivation) and not only of principles. For the most part, values have taken root in the West through a long history of difficult struggles. This can be seen clearly in the evolution of the separation of state and religion. This principle has acquired the status of a value in many societies because it has made a considerable contribution to the emergence of political freedom, autonomy of citizens, and, ultimately, democracy. It could be said in this sense that France made secularism sacred. In the Quebec framework, we can refer, for example, to the laicization movement (also called declericalization) of the 1960s. It is no surprise that, having been so hard won, these principles have become in many cases fundamental values.[5]

In the daily life of public institutions, the five constitutive values of the secular regime often seem to be in competition. For example, many requests for accommodations result in conflicts between freedom of religion and the separation of state and religion. With respect to government bodies and their extensions, I am referring here to teachers' wearing of the hijab, the reciting of prayers at municipal council meetings, prayer rooms in universities, and so on. In addition, sometimes it is the neutrality of the government and customary values that are in competition – for example, displaying a crucifix on the wall of the National Assembly or putting up a Christmas manger scene in front of a town hall.[6]

In the same spirit, outside the sphere of government freedom of religion is often in conflict with other rights or norms: should Sikh motorcyclists be forced to wear helmets in the name of the standard of protection of the person? Should we allow a pregnant Muslim to be treated only by a female gynecologist or refuse her this prerogative in the name of equality between men and women? Should we forbid the wearing of the hijab in tae kwon do tournaments in the name of safety or an athletic standard?

In a given society, what characterizes a secular regime and gives it its originality is the way in which it defines relationships between these five values or components, and more specifically the way in which each is weighted in comparison to the others, in order to resolve disputes between rights. In this regard, I classify as radical a regime that establishes a formal, a priori hierarchy between the components, which therefore grants to one of them an official, permanent precedence at the expense of the others. And I classify as inclusive a regime that, to the contrary, seeks a balance among these five values in order to better take into account the diversity of situations and arbitrate more equitably between competing rights.

I prefer to say "inclusive secularism" rather than "open secularism" for two reasons. First, the term "inclusive" indicates very well the general orientation of the regime, which pursues an objective of integration of religious diversity in a spirit of respect for individual rights and the fundamental values of society. It also evokes the major goals of regimes of secularism, which are to permit everyone, within prescribed limits, to live according to their convictions of conscience and to display them. In addition, this term is intended to avoid a certain confusion that attaches to "open secularism," which is frequently accused (wrongly in my opinion) of practising indiscriminate openness to requests for religious accommodations ("open to everything"), especially to requests that violate the principle of equality between men and women.[7]

In the spirit of inclusive secularism, conflict situations are arbitrated using what I call derived criteria. These criteria can be socio-legal, functional, or contextual.

1. Some examples of socio-legal criteria: (a) the fundamental values of a society (e.g., fairness, equality between men and women, personal

safety, non-violence); (b) respect for other's rights; (c) respect for the law; (d) preservation of the social order; (e) and the imperatives of collective integration.

2. Examples of functional criteria: (a) the need to preserve the credibility of a fundamental institution (e.g., the legal system, police forces); (b) the need to satisfy the elementary requirements of a job (wearing the burqa, for example, is considered incompatible with the practice of teaching).

3. Contextual criteria are empirical decision-making criteria. They draw from all the unpredictable elements that emerge at random in various situations that could occur in the daily life of institutions. Many possible examples in the area of requests for religious accommodations can be cited:

- A student's refusal to take a class because its content is contrary to the precepts of his or her religion: Is it a mandatory class or an optional course (in which case, the student will simply enrol in another class)?
- A request for a prayer room in public schools: Are we talking about a permanent room or temporary space free at certain hours of the day? A room assigned exclusively to a religious group or a place for reflection open to all?
- In a hospital, a request that the operation of an elevator be programmed to accommodate the members of a religion (in this case, orthodox Jews who are forbidden to operate electronics on the Sabbath): Are the other users inconvenienced? Are there other elevators available?
- Postponement of the date of a school examination when it conflicts with a religious holiday: What type of examination is it? What is the nature of the delay, and the frequency of these requests? Have such postponements already been considered eligible for other reasons under the regulations of the institution?

According to the situations and the arbitration carried out between the competing elements involved, it can happen that one principle or component is given precedence over others, but without establishing a permanent hierarchy. The analysis of specific situations is therefore decisive. This being said, this arbitration exercise is not improvised; it is limited and governed by norms. For example, among the socio-legal criteria, it goes without saying that the so-called fundamental values are supreme. It follows, for example, that except in very exceptional and imperative circumstances any request for religious accommodation should be rejected if it violates the principle of the respective institutional autonomy of state and religion, if it infringes on the principle of equality between men and women, or if it leads to the use of any kind of violence. Fortunately it is often possible to find adjustments that make it possible to overcome the apparent incompatibility between the imperatives involved.

The treatment of these often complex situations can give rise to some inconsistencies. We can also observe that regimes of secularism, precisely because they result from power struggles and varied historical paths, are rarely free from contradictions. Here are a few examples:

- The United States is a secular country that forbids the reciting of prayers in school, but at the same time the Constitution and especially American political discourse are full of references to God, as are the rituals of government (we even find such traces on the banknotes).[8]
- As mentioned already, France does not officially recognize Islam, even though it is the second religion of the country in terms of numbers of followers; Islam therefore does not benefit from the provisions of the law of 1905, unlike Catholicism, Protestantism, and Judaism. Moreover, while France is very fastidious in the area of the separation of state and religion, many of its public holidays coincide with Catholic holidays (Christmas, Easter, Ascension, Pentecost, and so on). It also very generously funds numerous private ("free") schools, many of which are religious. As well, the government owns most religious sites, of which it funds the maintenance and other costs.
- Canada, a pluralist, multicultural nation where de facto separation between government and religion prevails, nevertheless includes in the preamble to its constitution a reference to the supremacy of God (as does Switzerland). In a further contradiction, the same preamble affirms the primacy of law. Among its diverse religions, Canada grants special status to Protestantism and Catholicism. And as we saw in the previous chapter, it perpetuates the institution of the Prayer Breakfast where politicians and judges come together to pray to "Almighty God."
- Ontario funds private Catholic schools but not other religiously affiliated schools.
- Quebec, a secular society that places great emphasis on the institutional separation of church and state and on the neutrality of the

state, decided in 2008 (in a unanimous vote by the members of all parties) to maintain on the wall of the National Assembly a crucifix that was placed there in 1936 by a conservative regime to symbolize the alliance of the church and the government. Quebec also subsidizes private ethno-religious schools and gives tax exemptions to religious institutions. Finally, the Quebec Bar Association marks the beginning of a new year each fall by celebrating a "Red Mass," similar to the Canadian Prayer Breakfast.

We can see from this that each society implements its own secular regime, that is, a particular arrangement among the five components mentioned above, intended to be compatible with the history, institutions, and sensibilities of that society, but which also carries traces of its divisions. That is why, as I have indicated, these regimes are difficult to transpose from one society to another. This also explains why Quebecers often disagree with the judgments of the Supreme Court of Canada in the area of religion (see chapter 2).

Components and Provisions of Inclusive Secularism

On the basis of what I have presented above, I will now review various questions that have been recently fueling controversy in Quebec. I will pay particular attention to the separation of state and religion, and especially to the question of the expression of religious convictions in government institutions.

Fundamental Values

The expression of religious convictions (or any beliefs and rituals associated with them) remains subordinate to respect for the fundamental values of Quebec society. There should be no ambiguity on this point. As mentioned above, the adversaries of what is called open secularism often falsely accuse its defenders of being willing, in the name of pluralism, to sacrifice the fundamental values of Quebec.[9] It should be remembered that in recent years cases of accommodations that have violated the principle of equality between men and women have received a lot of attention and, with good reason, have been strongly protested by the population. However, these cases have been few and far between and, thanks to the vigilance of citizens, the media, and institutions, these blunders have been quickly rectified.

Moreover, there is nothing in the open secularism model that calls for subordination of the fundamental values of Quebec to opposing precepts that might be brought by immigrants or proposed by other members of the host society. As I pointed out with respect to the general practice of accommodations, there have merely been a few errors in judgment by policy-makers, in addition to deficiencies in the application of the general orientations and guidelines used.

The vigilance citizens have shown in this respect is therefore completely founded. In most if not all democratic societies, religions enjoy a kind of privilege that often permits them to maintain or promote practices that are contrary to fundamental values (e.g., a formal hierarchy between men and women, condemnation of homosexuality, opposition to contraception). This is an obvious contradiction, which democracies seem to put up with and which certain liberal thinkers consider acceptable for the reason that the faithful are free to leave their religion if these positions do not suit them; it is assumed that believers can give up their religion the way they would leave any other organization or institution. This state of affairs, which places religions beyond the reach of charters and laws, seems unacceptable to me: I believe it should be corrected.

Rights and Their Application: The Case of Religious Symbols

According to the provisions of Western law, citizens are permitted to display in public their religious beliefs or their convictions of conscience; this is even considered a fundamental right. But all jurists also agree that there are no absolute rights – that all rights, even the most fundamental such as the right to life, to freedom of expression, to property, or to privacy – can be limited in their application when they conflict with other rights or with uncontrollable imperatives.[10] Accordingly, in the spirit of inclusive secularism, we have to permit as much as possible the expression of deeply held beliefs, especially religious beliefs and certain rituals associated with them. This principle extends to all public spaces, including government institutions. However, limitations to this right are acceptable when required by higher motives.

This is the case for some categories of government employees who can be legitimately prohibited from wearing religious symbols because of the specific functions those employees exercise. I am thinking primarily of judges, juries, security officers, prison guards, and members of police and security forces to whom our society grants powers of coercion and even violence (e.g., imprisoning citizens, opening fire on another citizen). In the name of the institutions that they represent, it is imperative that the exercise of these extraordinary powers be restricted not only by neutrality but also by the need for the utmost credibility in everyone's eyes.

It is extremely important that these offices project an image of complete objectivity. We can easily imagine embarrassing situations that could occur in the absence of such a prohibition; for example, a judge wearing a kippah giving a harsh sentence to a Muslim or Palestinian accused. For the same reason, this principle should be extended to officers such as the ombudsman and the chief electoral officer, two other functions of democratic government where there should never be the least appearance of partiality given the nature of the powers granted to these offices.

Readers will note that, in all these cases, I am talking about image or appearance in the eyes of citizens in order to preserve an institutional credibility that must remain spotless. It does not follow from this that the wearing of religious symbols by the officers or the civil servants concerned inevitably leads to an inability to be objective.

The same prohibition should be extended to the speaker and vice-speakers of the National Assembly as well as clerks acting as secretaries at meetings of municipal councils (which can be considered as the counterparts to the National Assembly at another level[11]). These civil servants are the primary representatives of the institution of government, with which they have a structural relationship. They should therefore reflect in the eyes of all citizens two fundamental values of an inclusive secular regime: the neutrality of the government with respect to beliefs or convictions of conscience, and the institutional separation of state and religion. Again for symbolic reasons, this list should perhaps include the administrators of school boards and public educational institutions because of the function of cultural transmission assigned to the education system (values, ethics, civic life).

This standard does not, however, apply to elected officials. The obligations that believers consider themselves held to by virtue of their religion should not prevent them from exercising the most fundamental right there is in democracy, that of seeking an elected position, unless those obligations come into conflict with fundamental values or rules of society. Similarly, I do not believe the wearing of the hijab should be forbidden among teachers, at least as long as it has not been shown that this practice interferes with the requirements of the educational function.

A higher motive, however, requires the prohibition of the full veil (burqa, niqab) in government institutions. In strictly technical terms, wearing this kind of garment is obviously incompatible with various functions such as teaching or providing medical care. More generally, in their interactions with the state (or one of its institutions), citizens can demand that its employees communicate with their faces uncovered. This is a need that has deep roots in the civilization in which we live. The wearing of the full veil should also be forbidden whenever personal identification is required. Moreover, as an employer, the government should set an example by not encouraging the wearing of such clothing, which, furthermore, is not really compatible with the ideal of women's emancipation.

It goes without saying that in the private sector employers can decide otherwise, because they are not directly concerned with the secular regime (while remaining subject to the provisions of laws and the charter). Finally, with respect to public space (streets, parks, etc.), it would be excessive to ban the burqa or the niqab, unless they pose real security problems. In any case, these considerations are somewhat moot since it is estimated that there are currently about thirty Muslim women in Quebec who wear a full veil.[12]

Against Complete Prohibition

Many Quebecers argue in favour of a prohibition of all religious symbols in public and para-public institutions, a measure that I consider excessive.[13] This proposal should be subject to the general criterion mentioned above: What is the higher motive that would legitimize this? What is the argument that would permit it to successfully pass the test of law? I do not see how it is based on higher motives equivalent to those mentioned above.

First of all, no one has yet shown that wearing religious symbols would prevent government employees from doing their jobs with impartiality and satisfying all the requirements of their functions.[14] Similarly, it has not been proven that wearing religious symbols can be identified with proselytism. It would also be wrong to state that all employees in public or para-public institutions are representatives or ambassadors of the secular government and that they should therefore refrain from wearing religious symbols (I am thinking here of not only civil servants in the common sense but also road workers, school janitors, warehouse employees, Hydro-Québec electricians, and so forth).

As for the discomfort citizens say they feel when they have to deal with government employees displaying religious symbols (other than the full veil), this cannot be made a reason for a prohibition that would be admissible in law; the effect would be blatantly disproportionate to the motive. Finally, it is excessive to accuse the government of supporting or endorsing religious symbols just because it permits its employees to wear them.[15]

There is an important distinction to be drawn regarding the type of relationship that an employee or a citizen has with public or para-public institutions. We can talk about a structural relationship, by virtue of the fact that the employee does represent the government, on a permanent basis, because of his or her duties. This is the case with the speaker of the National Assembly. We can also talk about a contextual or circumstantial relationship: this is the case for ordinary employees and citizens who go to government institutions to receive services (hospitals, schools, courts) or people who exercise their duties or rights as citizens (members of the National Assembly, people making submissions to a parliamentary commission, people attending sessions of the National Assembly, etc.). It is commonly said that the state is "secular" but not the citizens who serve it or use its institutions: the principle that religious views should not interfere with the functioning of institutions does not mean that such views cannot be displayed by individuals.

Another distinction needs to be made. The current debate on the relationship between government and religion is very different from what took place in Quebec in the 1960s. There is no question today of redefining the power relationships between the government and the church (which, of the two, should control public institutions?). That question is settled,[16] and no one would today dare to argue in favour of religious bodies regaining powers that they have lost in this area. In fact, the current controversies essentially involve symbols displayed by individuals rather than powers exercised by institutions. That being said, is it reasonable to state that the power relationships between government and religions are today threatened by a small number of employees wearing a headscarf, a kippah, or a cross during their hours of work?

According to another argument, championed by the Mouvement laïque québécois and a few others, religious beliefs are intrinsically alienating and it is therefore a mistake to encourage their expression. This is a very radical position and one that is hard to justify, and it flies in the face of the legal traditions of democracies and the teachings of sociology.[17]

In support of total prohibition, people sometimes invoke the need to counteract the growth of the religious fundamentalisms that are currently emerging in Quebec (mainly among Muslims) and the serious menace they supposedly represent. They also mention the obligation to neutralize the hegemonic and totalitarian ambitions inherent in religion. Assuming that such currents actually exist (and this needs to be demonstrated – see below), how could reducing their visibility by restricting the wearing of religious symbols contribute to weakening them? It could be suggested that such measures would instead produce the opposite effect of creating increased tension in intercultural relationships by hardening differences, by marginalizing groups of citizens and radicalizing them. In other words, not only would it not solve the problem, but it would possibly make it worse.

Some maintain that by permitting the wearing of religious symbols the government favours religions and contributes to their spread. In fact, the government is neither for nor against; it simply respects the legitimate choices of certain citizens. Government should not encourage religion, but neither should it constrain it when it is operating within the limitations of the law.

Granting permission to wear religious symbols has also been referred to as granting privileges. Here again, we have to recall that this permission is valid for any people who want to take advantage of it, whatever their religion or their beliefs. Citizens who, for various reasons, choose not to exercise certain rights should not deprive others of them.

According to various intellectuals,[18] total prohibition of religious symbols is the real route to social integration. But if integration is based on mutual respect, on the acceptance of the fundamental values of Quebec, on respect for diversity, on a desire to participate in civic life, and on a willingness to mobilize around shared ideals and projects, which is the best way to achieve it: by restricting the freedom of certain citizens or by permitting them to express their differences?

Complete prohibition therefore creates a significant problem of law, and it would clearly have had little chance of passing the test of article 9.1 of the Quebec charter, article 1 of the Canadian charter, or international law.[19] In addition, it would lead to harmful social consequences by excluding believers who feel obliged to wear religious symbols from a large number of positions (the public and para-public sectors represent around 20 per cent of jobs in Quebec [Institut de la statistique du Québec, 2008a, table 1]) and by risking marginalizing many citizens (particularly women), which is contrary to the rule of equity and the imperative of integration mentioned above.

The complete prohibition of religious symbols in all government institutions would constitute an unjustified ideological choice directed against the most orthodox or conservative believers. Such a measure would also affect believers who feel obliged to display their religious affiliation by some sort of sign, those for whom faith is indissociable from visible signs or rituals. It would therefore mean penalizing specific concepts of religion that, to be sure, clash with attitudes or opinions in Quebec, but that are nevertheless completely legitimate in the eyes of the law. The acceptance of difference must take precedence here.

Certain proponents of prohibition maintain that this measure would not violate the rights of believers since it permits them to practise their religion in private. This argument is not convincing. Once again, some religions require their adherents to constantly display signs of their faith. And for many other individuals, the display of religious symbols is a matter of choice reflecting convictions of conscience. When all is said and done, the position of these prohibitionists is not unlike that old reasoning, which is still sometimes heard today, according to which homosexuals should not flaunt themselves in public, that their rights would not be infringed on if they were permitted to express their sexuality only in private.

Another argument against total prohibition is the legal battle Quebec would be drawn into, in which it would be embroiled for a long time and out of which, in all likelihood, it would emerge the loser. The price to be paid in terms of tensions and lasting divisions in our society would be heavy, and nothing would be gained.

The Hijab

Specifically with respect to the Muslim headscarf in Quebec, various arguments have been presented in favour of forbidding government employees from wearing it.[20] Once again, I do not believe that these arguments pass the test of the higher motive. Indisputably, for a certain number of women, the headscarf is a symbol of submission and even oppression of women.[21] But for other Muslim women, its meaning is completely different: a freely adopted symbol of their faith, a mark of identity, a customary practice rooted in regional or national traditions,[22] and a sign of the rejection of commercialized Western hedonism, among others.[23] These women, who are simply exercising their rights, would therefore be doubly harmed by a general prohibition in the name of secularism or equality between men and women.

With respect to other women, those who are oppressed in their families or their communities and on whom wearing the headscarf is imposed, again I do not see how their condition would be improved if wearing the headscarf were prohibited. Women subjugated by family oppression could even be in danger of reprisals if they were not allowed to wear the headscarf. In other words, suppressing by force what is seen as a symbol of oppression would not change anything about the reality of the social relationships underlying that oppression. We are faced here with difficult situations that require careful interventions within the families and communities concerned to ensure for these women a greater socioeconomic integration, accelerated learning of French (where the need exists), participation in civic and political life, and protection against their immediate environment.

It is also said by some that the headscarf, independently of the reasons women have for wearing it and the meaning it has for them, is an intrinsically repulsive and reprehensible symbol, like the swastika or the symbols of the Ku Klux Klan. Given the diversity of factors or motivations behind the wearing of the headscarf, it is obvious that this statement is an overgeneralization that does not describe the reality of Quebec. The context is important too: while the hijab can have such associations in certain countries, this is certainly not the case in the Americas.

Others invoke the spectre of an Islamist plot of which wearing the headscarf is the Trojan horse or "standard" (the Point de Bascule group, among others, makes this claim). Through a domino effect, wearing this symbol is said to be opening the door to everything else, that is, to a plan for the political domination of the West accompanied by the destruction of its institutions and the values that support them. This dark vision is astonishing. After all, we are talking here about a rather narrow contingency. According to various estimates (none of which are based on a rigorous survey), between 10 per cent and 20 per cent of Quebec Muslim women wear the hijab, and among these we obviously have to exclude all those who do not define themselves as "soldiers of Allah." But above all, how can we conceive of such a dark scenario coming to pass without an incredibly passive response and even more improbable consent from the whole of Quebec society?

The great vigilance demonstrated by the population instead suggests that, for the time being at least, we are very far from such an outcome. We should refrain from overestimating the Islamist threat in Quebec, as Djemila Benhabib and other participants in the public debate have done. Benhabib sees an "outrageous activism" in the wearing of the hijab (2011, p. 222), which she views as an instrument for the reconquest of power by Islamists (2009). She accuses Quebec women who are not in favour of prohibiting the hijab of being "soldiers in the service of a fascist ideology" (2011, p. 227), and many others call the proponents of pluralism "useful idiots" (to the great Islamist project). We can only be deeply shocked by the horrors that Ms Benhabib experienced in her country of origin. But without in any way denying the fact that a form of Islamist terrorism is active in various countries, we should nevertheless keep things in perspective and ask whether such sombre predictions have much to do with the situation in Quebec – the destruction of democracy? the end of freedoms? stonings? the reign of Muslim fundamentalism? the institution of sharia? assassination of journalists?

Even in the United States, a country traumatized by the attacks of September 2001, a report published in February 2012 by the Triangle Center on Terrorism and Homeland Security concluded that Muslim terrorism is "a minuscule threat" to public security. Out of the some fourteen thousand murders committed in 2011 in that country, none were due to Islamic extremism (*International Herald Tribune*, 8 February 2012, p. 4). On what basis then can anyone claim that Quebec would be an exception?[24]

The idea that only extremist Muslim women wear the headscarf in Quebec is one of the many unproven assertions that abound in this debate. Similarly, it is claimed that the hijab is a political tool, and wearing it is attributed to brainwashing, to a strategy of infiltration ("the tip of the iceberg"), and the like.

In summary, it can be acknowledged that, on the whole, there is some truth to the anti-hijab argument. The problem is the aspects of reality that it ignores. We should certainly pay tribute to the contributions that various people have made to this debate in Quebec by bearing witness to the horrors with which the hijab is associated in some countries. For many women, this symbol is therefore a cruel reminder. But we have to refrain from transposing this uncritically to the Quebec context. The proposed preventative measures, motivated by good intentions, could easily turn into stigmatization and anti-Muslim discrimination by strengthening enduring and very harmful stereotypes. At the same time, vigilance is imperative. It would be unwise to think that Quebec is entirely immune to the radical Islamism that is already rife in many countries in the world. Once again, a balance must be found.

Finally, there is good reason to wonder why this hijab crisis is occurring in Quebec but has not created as much tension in English Canada, where it is also worn. Nor is the hijab viewed with as much suspicion in the United States. How can we explain why these societies show so little concern when some in Quebec see it as a serious threat to be eradicated? Once again, if we are not careful, the current offensive against the hijab and all the evils that are attributed to it could actually produce the effects that are feared, namely the isolation and radicalization of certain communities.

Prayer in Municipal Councils

The controversy that erupted in 2011 around the reciting of a Catholic or Christian prayer at meetings of municipal councils (mainly focused on the city of Saguenay)[25] requires a few comments. This practice goes against the spirit of inclusive secularism and, in legal terms, it seems to have little chance of survival. Municipal councils are of the same deliberative nature as parliaments. From the perspective of secularism, municipalities are therefore subject to the same rules, including the separation of government and religions (or systems of beliefs), and the duty of neutrality.

By virtue of the first obligation, the meeting rooms of councils should therefore not display religious symbols in order to clearly follow the principle of institutional separation. By virtue of the second, reciting a Christian prayer infringes directly on respect for diversity of beliefs (religious and other) in our society. This is a rule that also applies in a society where most members declare themselves to be Catholic. All the citizens of a municipality, regardless of their beliefs, should be able to identify equally with their council. In the area of rights, numbers do not hold sway. If we had reasoned this way in the past, the traditionally marginalized minorities in our societies, such as homosexuals, racial groups, aboriginals, and persons with disabilities, would have perhaps never obtained recognition of their rights.

With respect to Catholic or other prayers, it is easy to imagine alternatives that do not in any way infringe on the rights of believers, for example, the public recitation of a text limited to fundamental values and compatible with all creeds or a period of silence during which each person can engage in reflection or prayer as he or she chooses.

Finally, it should be recalled that the rule of neutrality is intended to prevent any infringement of the rights of people whose beliefs or convictions of conscience differ from those of the majority religion. Here we are in agreement with the general goal of regimes of secularism, which is to allow all citizens to freely express their beliefs or their profound convictions, in a spirit of respect for fundamental values.

Heritage Values

As mentioned previously, it can sometimes happen that the principles or values of neutrality and separation, understood in the strict sense, legitimately yield ground to the argument of heritage or identity. A society does not have to repudiate its history in the name of pluralism, even if that history is strongly identified with the cultural majority.[26] It follows that under certain conditions the religious tradition of the founding majority can manifest its presence in the shared (public) culture, including in government institutions. The scope of application of this argument must, however, be carefully circumscribed.[27]

Some will say that it can be invoked when a religious symbol is very old (and therefore deeply rooted in the collective imaginary) and when it does not violate a basic right in a flagrant or offensive way. It is also necessary that the symbol have taken on a life of its own, separate from its original meaning or references, and that it has entered the broader sphere of civic life or the cultural and identity heritage of a society – as opposed to a current symbol that continues to fully exercise its original function and whose use is essentially limited to a community of believers.

In the Quebec context, we might think of the crosses along rural roads, religious monuments in the public squares of various municipalities, street names in honour of saints, crosses erected in many towns and cities, the cross on the Quebec flag, or Christmas decorations and music (as opposed to other, more specific Catholic symbols such as the nativity scene, the tabernacle, and the sacred vessels). These symbols will for many believers continue to be invested with religious meanings, but on the whole they belong to the public domain and lend themselves to widely varied symbolic appropriations.

To fit the argument of heritage or identity, a symbol of religious origin must therefore, over time, have been deactivated (or reconverted, so to speak) and laicized, being now incorporated within the cultural heritage of a society. But even with deactivated symbols, it does not necessarily follow that they have a place in just any public space, for instance in the inner chambers of the secular government or of its extensions, municipal councils. There is obviously a difference between a Parliament and a hill overlooking a city or a public spot in a village.

The distinction between a living symbol and a deactivated (or recycled) symbol is therefore crucial. Another distinction needs to be drawn between a symbol that can be said to be visual (an icon, a statue, a crucifix, a church) or one that is performative, such as a collective prayer recited out loud accompanied by the sign of the cross; the latter is a much more engaging manifestation, involving more than the simple viewing or contemplation of an object. It is understood that a visual symbol will pass the test of the heritage argument more easily than a performative symbol.

The temptation, for a majority, is to unduly extend the scope of the heritage argument to justify provisions that are clearly in conflict with the foundations of the secular regime. In Quebec, this is obviously the case with the crucifix on the wall of the National Assembly, prayer at meetings of municipal councils, and the crucifix in public schools. The "Red Mass" that accompanies the annual reopening of courts in Quebec poses an analogous problem and should be abolished.[28] Reminders of religion in the name of heritage are legitimate when they express a symbol or ritual that is part of a tradition of identity, but they should not be used to try to revitalize a declining religious tradition.[29]

What emerges from the above is that the principle of neutrality of the government in the area of religion is not and should not be applied in an absolute way. In the name of the preservation of the foundations and symbolic capital of the society, tolerance should be observed, with appropriate caution. This is consistent with the general argument presented in chapters 2 and 4 with respect to the non-neutrality or cultural interventionism of the government.

The guidelines and criteria that have just been outlined provide a useful reference, but inevitably there are still grey areas. How do we decide whether a religious symbol is deactivated? How do we determine if it can legitimately be displayed in public institutions without violating the principle of neutrality of the state? It would be unrealistic to think that we will one day have very precise, definitive indicators in this regard.[30] We will always have to rely on good faith, common sense, and public debate, though the existence of a broad, inter-faith consensus is certainly the clearest sign that a religious symbol is deactivated.

The Problem of Ethno-Religious Private Schools Subsidized by the Government

One of the basic objectives of interculturalism and inclusive secularism is to promote the integration of citizens whatever their cultural differences, especially those related to convictions of conscience and visions of the world. In order for this objective to be attained, it is assumed that citizens share certain fundamental values that the government and civil society have a duty to preserve and promote. It is therefore logical to think that the existence of ethno-religious private schools does not favour the achievement of this objective. More generally, because of the community (if not to say communitarian) divisions such schools are suspected of creating, it is appropriate to ask if they are not obstacles to one of the primary conditions of interculturalism: the rapprochements, interactions, and exchanges necessary for the sharing of the common culture and integration.

Many fear, not without reason, that these schools create cultural semi-enclaves within which can be transmitted and perpetuated values and traditions contrary to those that form the basis for a democratic, liberal society. Finally, one might wonder if these institutions are not outright harmful to the autonomy of students, who may have limited possibilities to make real choices regarding their personal lives. The substantial funding that the government provides to these schools (up to 60 per cent) therefore raises significant questions that deserve attention.

We should, however, avoid giving hasty answers, given the very incomplete empirical data we currently possess on the subject. One of the few studies in the field is by P. Sercia (2009). On the basis of comparative data from 2004, it covers sixty-seven schools (Jewish, Muslim, Greek, and Armenian), but the results are unfortunately not conclusive. First of all, the text contains contradictory statements, suggesting that the students who attend these institutions are either very well integrated (pp. 270, 275) or relatively marginalized compared to students in public schools (they have fewer contacts with other cultural or ethnic groups, they have less of a sense of belonging to the wider society, etc.). Thus the author talks about an "ethnocentric configuration" (pp. 271–3, 275–6). In his conclusion, he contends that on the whole the students in these ethno-religious schools are sufficiently integrated, but this is a statement that the findings of the study do not really support.

Accordingly, there is a need for further studies on the subject, but it is important that they look not only at students' sense of belonging or contacts with other ethnocultural groups, but also at values, perceptions and stereotypes, and attitudes about and knowledge of Quebec society. Only in this way will they provide the information required to make an enlightened judgment on this question. Finally, we need to avoid exaggerating the practical impact of this issue, since these schools account for fewer than one per cent of all Quebec students (preschool, elementary, and secondary levels) (F. Fournier, 2008).

Secularism and Interculturalism

The model of inclusive secularism is based on Quebec interculturalism, which emphasizes respect for ethnocultural (including religious) differences within the limitations of fundamental values, especially equality between men and women. It favours integration and therefore seeks to avoid as much as possible segmentation, divisions, and marginalization, in order to respect the rights of citizens and to avoid profound, lasting divisions. Out of concern for balance and pragmatism, inclusive secularism also avoids establishing a formal, permanent hierarchy among its constitutive five principles or values.[31]

In short, just like interculturalism, the regime of inclusive secularism is intended as a middle-ground model between the republican formula, not concerned enough about the free expression of differences, and individualist neoliberalism, not sensitive enough to collective imperatives. Like interculturalism, inclusive secularism calls for a democratic debate as well as a mixture of firmness and flexibility: firmness on principles and fundamental values and flexibility in how they are applied, all towards a common objective, which is to learn to live together in a spirit of respect for differences and, to this end, to cultivate the necessary virtues of openness, prudence, and reserve.

This is why I support mandatory, nondenominational teaching of religions and other systems of beliefs from a sociological and historical perspective. A measure of this kind – the Ethics and Religious Culture course – was introduced by the Quebec Ministry of Education in autumn 2008. The goal of the course is to familiarize young people with the diversity of systems of beliefs (or convictions of conscience) and help them to understand those belief systems beyond stereotypes, so that this diversity is not spontaneously perceived or experienced as a problem or source of worry, but as one characteristic among others of the cultural landscape of the society. The main message that this kind of teaching should transmit is that systems of beliefs, in spite of their claims to be universal and often exclusive, should coexist with others. As a corollary, students will become aware of the secular, pluralist nature of the government, which serves no particular religion or system of beliefs.[32]

An incident that occurred in January 2011 in Quebec City illustrates the usefulness of this type of teaching. A delegation of four members of the Sikh community wearing their kirpans was refused access to the National Assembly, where they were supposed to present their perspective on a bill concerning their religion. Two reasons motivated this decision. The first was concern for security. This shows a great ignorance of the meaning of wearing the kirpan in the Sikh religion, as one of the delegates explained in an article published in the *Gazette* on 17 February and in a few interviews on radio and television. The kirpan has a strictly spiritual meaning (solicitude towards the disadvantaged, rejection of all forms of oppression) and it is considered sacrilegious to use it for purposes other than its religious symbolism, which is attested by the 115-year non-violent history of Sikh religion in Canada. With regard to the 2011 incident in Quebec City, even supposing that any doubt could remain about security, why not supervise the visitors during their very brief presentation?

This is where the second reason invoked (the "secularism" of the government) comes in. But here again, there is a misunderstanding, this time between what I have called a structural relationship and a circumstantial relationship with government institutions.

Moreover, the members of the National Assembly unanimously approved the decision by the security service even while a crucifix hung over the speaker's chair. Because they were refused entry, the four delegates were prevented from exercising their duty as citizens because their religion obliges them to wear a religious symbol. What is more, the incident made minorities feel ill at ease and misunderstood, something which could have easily been avoided.

In a context of increasing diversity, it would seem sensible, within the limitations mentioned above, to allow the religious plurality to be expressed freely in the public sphere and to be visible in daily life, so that it can become part of the collective imaginary. This is the gamble that seems to be most in keeping with the ideal of a democratic society that wants to respect the rights of all citizens and be sensitive to the various manifestations of cultural difference.

This being said, like any initiative of its kind, the course on ethics and religious culture that was introduced in 2008 is obviously still being fine-tuned, and would benefit if designers acted on some of the criticisms that have been formulated, for example, by ensuring that the course avoids promoting religion, that it shows all of a religion's dimensions (positive and negative), and that gives it appropriate space to non-religious systems of beliefs (or convictions). The course has also received other criticisms that seem unfounded to me: promotion of multiculturalism, indoctrination of young people ("brainwashing"), and encroachment on the rights of parents.[33]

On another issue, many Quebec citizens are currently calling for the adoption of a charter of secularism. I believe that an official document, whether it is a charter, a law, or a declaration, could help to dissipate the current lack of clarity by setting broad parameters and formulating the orientations necessary for the treatment of particular cases. At the same time, one should not expect too much from such a document, since it could not contain answers to all the questions that arise in often unpredictable ways in the daily lives of institutions. It is necessary to preserve some level of flexibility in order to have a balanced, adapted, and complete application of rights.

Moreover, opinions on the subject are currently so divided that we might wonder about the chances of success of such an initiative.[34] However, if the government shows firm political will, it would still be useful to establish the fundamental principles and from them deduce orientations and guidelines, and to formulate precise directives wherever possible and pertinent.[35]

The above is a plea in favour of decision-making mechanisms based on a three-pronged approach: (a) the implementation of a general framework of guidelines; (b) the adoption of ad hoc regulations; and (c) the official definition of a process to deal with cases. Indeed, the overall proposal is intended precisely to be the outline of a model that encompasses the normative (the major orientations, the ethical and legal foundations), the traditional (the customary or heritage values), and regulated empiricism (the processing of cases).

Conclusion

For the various reasons outlined in the preceding chapters, interculturalism appears to be the model that best suits Quebec society, given its history, its situation, and its aspirations. There is, however, still a lot of work
to be done to translate the spirit of the model into policies and original programs, in accordance with the stated objectives. Nonetheless, the
outlook seems promising, not only for Quebec but for all societies where
the ethnocultural realities are viewed through the lens of a majority-
minorities relationship.

Interculturalism: A Model for Quebec

As a form of integrative pluralism, interculturalism places its faith in democracy, that is, in the capacity to achieve consensus on ways to live together peacefully that preserve the fundamental values of the host society
and create a future for all citizens, regardless of their origins and cultural
characteristics. For the majority culture in Quebec, the simplest option
would be to try to protect the old francophone identity to the point of
isolating it, ossifying it and thus impoverishing it, which would endanger
it even more. The most promising course of action, but also the most
difficult, is the one that offers an expanded horizon for that identity and
for the values that sustain it by projecting them into the shared culture.
This option, contrary to what is sometimes claimed, is one not of self-
effacement or self-renunciation, but of a true self-affirmation. This is the
option of expansion and enrichment of heritage. It has also the distinct
advantage of proposing a future mobilization for all the citizens of
Quebec, in particular immigrants and members of minorities, who are
invited to share in nourishing Quebec culture with their heritages.

In short, what is being proposed is a mutual recognition between the majority and the minorities that will provide a basis for a dynamic of exchange, rapprochement, and partial blending as conditions for social cohesion. This mutual recognition must be accompanied by reciprocal accommodations, since (a) minorities need protection to ensure the majority respects their rights; and (b) the founding francophone majority is also a minority that has to be concerned about its survival and development. As the founding majority, it also has the main responsibility for the heritage that forms the basis for Quebec culture and supports social cohesion.

All this brings us back to the shared culture. Its development will be a long process, and it is impossible to know what the future holds for it. Creating this shared culture means nothing less than somehow combining the imaginaries around what I have called master myths, born out of particular historical threads and linked to identities that are sometimes flexible and sometimes deeply rooted. We could say that two major paths are possible. One consists of conceiving new myths that would transcend the existing configurations. The other, much more realistic, is open to a mixing of these configurations. The important thing is to apply a flexible vision of the intercultural dynamic that avoids the hardening ("essentialization") of cultures and identities, but without ignoring their often enduring hold on the society and their legitimacy – that is, a vision that takes into consideration both rootedness and fluidities.

As mentioned, I consider it necessary to open up the field of interculturalism to all aspects of integration and intercultural relations, in particular the social and political dimensions. If culture plays a key role in this, it is as the entry point to a more general set of problems, given that many of the obstacles to economic and social integration and respect for rights arise from cultural factors, factors that sustain prejudices, stereotypes, and intolerance, which in turn lead to discriminatory and racist behaviours.

Interculturalism is also in complete harmony with the new parameters of French-speaking Quebec, which seems to have entered a long-term period of demographic decline, diversification through immigration, and globalization. A minority in its broader environment, this French-speaking population cannot afford to weaken itself by creating long-standing divisions within the nation. On the contrary, it needs all its strength: its future depends on respectful integration of diversity. It is essential to adopt a formula that preserves the achievements of this nation, with all their richness, while at the same time expanding the sphere in which they can be deployed or redeployed. Until there is evidence to the contrary, interculturalism appears to be the model most capable of effectively combining these imperatives and ensuring a decent future for both the majority and the minorities.

Given the situation and specific needs of Quebec, interculturalism, as a middle-ground model, avoids the shortcomings usually associated with the other familiar models: assimilationism is not sensitive enough to minorities and multiculturalism does not do enough for the majority, while republicanism (especially in its French version) does too much. By comparison, the model that I have outlined, in adopting the duality paradigm, is intended first of all to reflect and account for a primary reality of the Quebec ethnocultural landscape, by trying to arbitrate equitably, to mitigate and harmonize the majority-minorities relationship but without aiming for its disappearance, since this relationship is reproduced through the actions of citizens who choose legitimately to cultivate a link with their culture of origin.

I should add that the founding majority's key role as the main vector for integration does nothing, in my view, to jeopardize the rule of equity inherent in pluralism. This arrangement simply reflects the historical demographic and sociological weight of the majority that, in Quebec as in any society, leaves an inevitable imprint on the life of intercultural relations and institutions; it therefore leads to no form of privilege resulting in a hierarchy among citizens.

I have talked a lot about balance with respect to interculturalism. Needless to say, all contemporary democratic nations are faced with the need to reconcile divergent norms and aspirations, and apparently incompatible imperatives: they have to combine the continuation of their culture (or aspects of it), in the sense of their history and their roots, with other cultures and other paths; they have to arbitrate relationships among sometimes very diverse, even incompatible visions of the world; they have a legitimate desire to safeguard their identities and their prerogatives, but must act within the limitations of the laws to which they subscribe; and, as they do this, they have to untangle, among their founding myths and the values that they maintain, which ones should remain unaltered and which ones lend themselves to flexibility or even redefinition.

In this respect, however, the case of Quebec is noteworthy because of the structural factors that make it doubly precarious. First of all, like all democratic nations endorsing pluralism, it has an obligation to build a solid civic foundation with a universal character or vocation to which all ethnocultural minorities and all citizens can rally, whatever their beliefs and allegiances. But in the opposite direction, and unlike sovereign nation states, Quebec has to struggle endlessly to assert its specificity as a nation and ensure itself the greatest possible autonomy, and therefore it feels impelled to affirm its distinctive ethnocultural features.[1] In addition, being in a minority position with a sense of its own fragility, francophone Quebec, as a majority and in a spirit of equity, is nevertheless committed to protecting minority cultures. Finally, many members of the founding majority feel that there are issues from its colonial past that are still unresolved; hence the perpetuation of a memory under pressure, which is central to the national question. But for many members of this majority, it appears difficult and even impossible to instil that living memory in "other" Quebecers, giving rise to their uneasiness with, if not rejection of, pluralism.[2]

Like Scotland, Wales, Catalonia, and other non-sovereign nations characterized by majorities with a double status, Quebec is thus doomed to a constant quest for delicate balances that need to be perpetually renegotiated. It is this complex dynamic that the model I have outlined is intended to reflect. This point also illuminates the difficulty, for a founding culture such as that of Quebec francophones, to always behave as a true majority, sure of itself and its destiny. It is, in fact, sometimes too harshly criticized by those who forget its double condition of minority in Canada and on the continent.

We also see from the above how this Quebec version of interculturalism places certain limitations on the possibilities for transfer to other nations or societies. Many components seem to be easily exportable; this is the case with everything related to pluralism, integration, interactions, the shared culture, and the duality paradigm. However, the majority-minorities relationship can assume various forms, leading to specific configurations for interculturalism. There is a danger that majorities will define themselves as more fragile or more threatened than they actually are and, on that basis, grant themselves excessive advantages. In this regard, like many other models, interculturalism is not immune to certain excesses.

Shortcomings and Priorities for Action

In recent decades, various actors in Quebec society have done a great deal to establish pluralism, in the spirit of interculturalism. In schools, especially in the Montreal region, the achievements have been remarkable.[3] In most municipalities, even small ones, we find structures for receiving and supporting immigrants. The ministry responsible encourages many projects, in spite of very insufficient financial resources. The teaching of languages of origin continues to receive significant support. Special attention has been devoted to francization, as well as to protection of the rights of immigrants and members of minorities. The government carries out campaigns to raise awareness about the problems of discrimination and racism.

Major grey areas remain, however. I am thinking primarily of the lack of a government document officially establishing interculturalism as the model for integration and for the management of diversity in Quebec. Such an initiative might be supported by a broad consensus. Why doesn't the government give interculturalism an official recognition equivalent to that enjoyed by multiculturalism in Canada? Under section 27 of the Canadian charter multiculturalism has the status of an interpretative clause; the same could be done with interculturalism in the Quebec charter (see also L.-P. Lampron, 2010). It is also urgent to give official status to a secular regime, as I have attempted to show in the previous chapter. The very modest efforts that the Liberal government made in these two directions in recent years have consisted of two bills (16 and 94) dealing respectively with cultural diversity (2009) and requests for accommodations in government administration (2010). Both bills failed to pass, while what is needed for Quebec is nothing less than a kind of Law 101 for integration and intercultural relationships.

I am also thinking here of the economic and social integration of immigrants, which is always slower than it should be,[4] of the danger of the ethnicization of inequalities and poverty, of the challenges faced by second-generation immigrants (including the problem of students dropping out of school), of the status of female immigrants, of the underrepresentation of immigrants and members of minorities in public administration,[5] of their low visibility in the media,[6] of the limited resources devoted to concrete programs to fight discrimination and racism (including racial profiling[7]), and of the very modest results of the policies on regionalization of immigration. This list shows clearly that government initiatives to remedy these problems have been insufficient.

Among the causes of underemployment, commonly mentioned (and rightly so) is the non-recognition of degrees (affecting physicians in particular: CDPDJ, 2010) and skills, as well as the mismatch between the needs of the market and the qualifications of immigrants. The auditor general of Quebec criticized these two problems among many others in the report he submitted to the National Assembly in May 2010: the government is not sufficiently concerned about the absorptive capacity of the labour market, which also calls into question the selection criteria for immigrants, many of which remain jobless in spite of their skills.

All of these issues can be seen as priorities for action.[8] As long as significant progress has not been made on all these fronts, the interactions advocated by interculturalism will be of limited effect. In order to fully achieve their objective, they require that the people concerned can first of all consider themselves as full citizens.

According to S. Reichhold (2011), there is an enormous imbalance in the division of funding between ministry services and integration work on the ground. There also seems to be a significant gap between the official discourse on integration and interculturalism and the programs and resources that are actually allocated to them. In this regard, the diagnoses made in the report of the Bouchard-Taylor Commission in 2008 seem to remain completely valid: Quebec has developed a very promising model, but the resources and programs required for its application have not followed as they should have.[9]

However, the development of interculturalism is not only the responsibility of the government. The entirety of Quebec society needs to be mobilized for this purpose: para-public and private institutions, the business community, the union federations, the media, individuals, and pressure groups. The projects conducted at the community or microsocial level at the initiative of citizens have made priceless contributions (as the activists of the Intercultural Institute of Montreal have long maintained). When all is said and done, the fate of interculturalism depends in large part on their dynamism and their inventiveness.

Francization, which would require an increased budgetary effort, remains a permanent challenge (M. Pagé & P. Lamarre, 2010). But beyond the problem of linguistic integration of immigrants, the general situation of French, faced with the hard reality of globalization, needs to be urgently and thoroughly rethought. The current obstacles differ from those against which Quebec has had to defend itself in the past (e.g., the fight against assimilation threats coming from English Canada). We can say that the 1970s, with Law 101, coincided with a reinvention of French-speaking Quebec. From that moment on, the French language, proclaimed the official language of Quebec, was extended beyond French Canadian identity to be transformed into a common denominator for all of public life. Law 101 also contained provisions to make this new status a concrete reality, in particular by making mandatory the francization of the children of immigrants. In the current context, under the pressure of international currents, and marked by bilingualism and multilingualism, these provisions are no longer sufficient.

Quebec now needs to reprogram the future of French to ensure its survival and development in a globalized age. The linguistic integration of immigrants also has to be thought of from this perspective. It has to combine openness to bilingualism and multilingualism with a very firm commitment to French as the only official language of Quebec.

This is also an opportunity for an overall reflection on policies of interaction, so essential to interculturalism. Quebec should distinguish itself in this area through exceptional efforts characterized by creativity and persistence. To all the reasons already mentioned in the preceding chapters, I should add the very particular structure of the ethnocultural map of Quebec, with the strong concentration in Montreal of minorities and immigrants (more than 85 per cent). The metropolis has thus become a hub of immense diversity. More than 60 per cent of students on the island of Montreal have a mother tongue other than French. They come from nearly two hundred nations and speak more than sixty languages.[10]

On this topic, various questions remain unanswered. For example, how are the interactions oriented? Do they really involve the majority and the minorities, or mostly members of minorities and immigrants interacting with each other? Are they limited to contacts within the framework of leisure activities or are they extended to initiatives for change that correspond to concrete needs? There have been criticisms of the communitarian orientation that supposedly informs how the City of Montreal works with immigrants and minorities. What is the actual situation? From the point of view of its ethnocultural composition, Quebec is already divided into two parts because of the homogeneity of the regions. We need to avoid having the metropolis itself become internally polarized in somewhat the same way; the very future of the shared culture is at stake here. Finally, it is important that interactions take place at the individual level and not only at the level of groups or associations.[11] In short, an additional effort is required to better understand the ethnocultural terrain and ensure that policies and programs are better suited to the spirit of interculturalism.

As mentioned above, the practice of accommodations always faces strong opposition in the population. The cultural insecurity that immigration generates among the majority has a lot to do with this.[12] But the alleged reasons are not always well founded; they are based in large part on strong suspicions concerning the administrators of institutions, which feed on insufficient knowledge of the situation. It would be easy to remedy this by creating the Office d'harmonisation ou de médiation interculturelle recommended in the report of the Bouchard-Taylor Commission. One of the functions of this organization would be precisely to organize the relevant data on the practice of accommodations in all public institutions, and in particular to report them to the population, which would then know what is actually occurring. Currently, there is no source of information of this kind, which opens the door to any and all perceptions without any mechanism to criticize or refute them.

Another function of this organization would be to monitor practices of accommodations to ensure that (a) the granting of requests does not infringe on the fundamental values of Quebec; (b) from one institution to another, there is consistency in how administrators proceed; and (c) refusals are, in fact, justified. Such an office would carry out information and consciousness-raising activities with the general public. It would also work with schools, businesses, and other institutions. Finally, it could participate in joint initiatives with other para-public or private civic-oriented organizations.

It would thus accumulate expertise so that it could offer assistance to policy-makers working in both private businesses and public institutions. It could also provide training services and act as a mediator when required. It would therefore operate at a distance from the judiciary and favour the settlement of disputes by citizens themselves, with the courts representing an indispensable body, to be sure, but only as a last resort.[13]

There is a great need for empirical studies: insufficient knowledge of situations and problems is often noted. We do not know enough about the experiences of immigrant families after their arrival on Quebec soil.[14] To this we can add the whole area of discrimination and racism of which immigrants are victims.[15] We need more detailed knowledge of the reality of minorities: What is their composition? What is their degree of institutionalization and organization? How are feelings of belonging and solidarity expressed in them, and with what intensity? How do these feelings combine with a sense of belonging to Quebec? To what extent are cultures of origin perpetuated and how are they related to the shared culture? What is the status of women in these communities? What forms does discrimination take? What is the role of religion?[16]

With respect to integration, various studies conducted in the United States and English Canada have shown that members of well-structured cultural minorities or immigrant groups have better chances of integrating into the wider society. This result goes against commonly held beliefs. What is the actual situation in Quebec? It would also be useful to have indicators to measure the impact of interactive programs and monitor the progress of the shared culture. For the time being, except for the measurement of francization, we have to rely on very imprecise data.

Immigrants are often criticized for introducing and perpetuating in Quebec values and customs that are contrary to modernity and incompatible with the values and customs prevailing in Quebec. They are also accused of not wanting to integrate. But what do we know about this exactly? We are also lacking longitudinal studies that would show the process of integration over two or three generations. Similarly, what are the daily lives of immigrants like in the regions? What are the conditions of their integration, and how do the reception mechanisms operate? What is the source of those difficulties of rootedness that are so commonly talked about? Is it impossible to turn around the current trend that concentrates immigrants in the Montreal region?

But in spite of the controversies that divide the population and the discontent that is sometimes felt, the perspectives that are opening up for integration and pluralism remain good because Quebecers maintain a positive attitude towards immigration and an openness with regard to diversity. From this point of view, the Quebec case compares favourably with that of Canada. With the exception of the sometimes acrimonious babble of blogs and a few Internet sites, anti-immigration discourse is rarely heard in Quebec (one could say that the book by Dubreuil and Marois, commented on in chapter 4, is the first real expression of this view in the public debate).[17]

As stated in the report of the Bouchard-Taylor Commission (pp. 36, 66, 186, 231), we do not have sufficient data to affirm that Quebec, in comparison to anglophone Canada, is lacking tolerance, reception mechanisms, or pluralism. Various polls producing comparative data even suggest the opposite.[18]

Similarly, with respect to the number of immigrants accepted as a proportion of the total population, we can recall that for the entire period since the end of the Second World War, Quebec ranked tenth among industrialized nations of more than one million inhabitants (M. Paillé, 1993, pp. 15–16). We also need to take into consideration that over that same period close to 90 per cent of immigrants settled in the metropolitan region of Montreal, thus increasing the pressure on the host society without ever causing any major conflicts. On this point, the Quebec case therefore appears enviable, especially when we consider the unfavourable structural factors mentioned earlier in this chapter. All these data show that the members of the majority culture have largely succeeded in overcoming their concerns, as shown by E. Gidengil et al. (2003).

This being said, Quebecers (francophones, in the main) stand out generally on one point: their attitude towards religion, which reflects the particular history of the Catholic clergy in Quebec and its controversial heritage. To no one's surprise, another characteristic that emerges from the compared data of polls is that the members of the cultural majority have recently shown themselves to be more aware than in the past of the fragility arising from their status as a minority on the continent.

Finally, I have already underlined on a few occasions the essential role of national history in the activation and promotion of shared values, in dialogue and intercultural rapprochement, and in the strengthening of the symbolic foundation of Quebec society. I join my voice to all those who, in the last decade, have called for an increased role for this kind of teaching in educational curriculum and, beyond school, for an enhancing of collective memory for all citizens of Quebec.

Perspectives for Interculturalism and for Quebec

The disfavour that multiculturalism has fallen into in many European countries and the rejection of assimilationist formulas in most of these countries opens up a broad horizon for interculturalism, as attested by the results of a large-scale consultation the Council of Europe carried out in 2006–2007 among its forty-seven member states (following the Summit of Warsaw in 2005).[19] Questioned on the best model to promote in the area of interethnic relations, all those countries arrived at a consensus on three points: (a) the rejection of multiculturalism, associated with the risk of fragmentation and seen as harmful for social cohesion; (b) the rejection of assimilation, because of the violation of individual rights to which it leads; (c) the choice of interculturalism as a middle path, as the model of balance and equity. The consultation also showed that this model retained the best of multiculturalism (sensitivity to diversity) and of republicanism (sensitivity to the universality of rights) (see G. Battaini-Dragoni, 2009, as well as M. Emerson, 2011).

Interculturalism was already established in many member countries, but mainly theoretically and as a practice of interculturality in the field of education and at the microsocial level.[20] However, mostly because of the Muslim presence, we have observed over the last few years a growing feeling that this process is showing its limitations, that it is colliding with an otherness structured in terms of identity, belonging, traditions, and values. To this is added the perception of a threat not only to the culture and cohesiveness of host societies, but also to the physical safety of citizens.

Finally, intercultural dialogue (made a priority by the Council of Europe) can be compromised by the inequalities and relationships of domination that structure any ethnocultural reality. Intercultural reflection is then concerned with the general problematic of integration. At the same time, this reflection seems to gradually embrace the duality paradigm, which tends to feed on the dichotomies of white–non-white, native-foreign, secular-religious, homogeneity-diversity, and majority-minority.[21] In this context, European interculturalism is bound to be deployed equally at the macrosocial and political level, as is the case in Quebec.[22]

I will conclude with a few thoughts on the future of Quebec. Beyond simple misunderstandings about pluralism's true meaning, the reservations and oppositions that have been expressed with regard to it are based on various motivations. Some of them, the most powerful perhaps, are rooted in the master myths of the founding majority, that is: (a) the feeling of being, within Canada and on this continent, a fragile minority whose weight is gradually diminishing; and (b) the memory of various dominations suffered in the past, which call for collective correction that has still not been achieved. To this is added, to varying degrees according to generations and social groups, a third legacy of the past in the form of suspicion of churches and religions. At various moments in the contemporary history of Quebec, these three undercurrents brought about salutary movements of resistance and reform and, inevitably, they are now contributing to shaping Quebec interculturalism. The danger is that they will come to jeopardize it by inspiring an overestimation of the risks and dangers associated with ethnocultural diversity.

I have tried to show in this book that under certain conditions, pluralism is entirely compatible with the aspirations of the founding majority and can even contribute to their fulfilment. My intention was also to show that communitarianism as well as assimilationism (with their corollaries of creating marginalization and hierarchies) have no future. The destiny of the founding majority, and French-speaking Quebec as a whole, will come through careful management of diversity, in the sense proposed by interculturalism. The coming years, of course, will bring their share of misunderstandings and controversies; what matters is to be clear about the principles and values that will make it possible to discuss them effectively and solve them for the sake of the higher interests of Quebec.

Afterword

This book had already been written when the governing Parti Québécois released its proposal for a charter of Quebec values. This initiative requires a few comments since, being related to intercultural issues, it is expected to bear heavily on the relationship between the francophone majority and the ethnocultural minorities in Quebec.

The proposed charter announced on 10 September 2013 had three components: first, an official definition of the principles of a secular regime for Quebec (e.g., separation of state and religion); second, changes in the practice of religious and cultural accommodations; and third, a requirement that government employees (including those in government-run agencies) no longer wear religious symbols at work.

The first component enjoys a wide consensus and attracted little attention in the public debate. In its report, the Commission on Accommodation Practices that I co-chaired with Charles Taylor in 2007–2008 asked the government to produce a White Paper on secularism in Quebec. However, this recommendation, like many others, has not been acted upon, and such a study is long overdue.

The second component is more controversial; it is also an area of profound misunderstanding among the population. Indeed, there is a widespread belief that the practice of accommodations in public institutions (education, health care, and elsewhere) violates the Quebec Charter of Human Rights and Freedoms, particularly regarding women's rights. Although no research whatsoever has documented this view (and none was commissioned by the government before it released its proposal), the minister responsible, Bernard Drainville, constantly repeated that the practice of accommodations urgently needs to be corrected. This kind of discourse has inspired a deeply negative view of accommodations.

The last component aroused a heated debate in the province of Quebec, and put Quebec society in danger of losing its ability to function as a cohesive, progressive state with respect to the management of ethnocultural diversity. Over recent decades, Quebec has developed interculturalism as an effective model to manage intercultural relationships in a reasonable way. Unfortunately, the considerable progress that has been made was put under threat.

The Quebec government argued that for the state to be secular, its employees should not wear religious symbols at work. Employees are said to be representatives (or ambassadors) of the secular state, and therefore the wearing of religious symbols is seen as a form of proselytism that is not compatible with the rule of professional impartiality. It is also said to contradict the separation of state and religion as well as the rule of neutrality of the state with respect to religions.

According to opponents of the proposed charter, this requirement would have violated a fundamental right without a legitimate or superior motive. They argued that the institutional separation of state and religion does not imply that employees should be prohibited from wearing religious symbols, contending that it is the state as an institution that is "secular," not the individuals. What really matters is that there be no interference by any religion in the state's responsibilities, and vice versa. In fact, it has never been demonstrated that this rule would be broken by the wearing of religious symbols. Opponents also said that the proposed charter would discriminate against certain groups of citizens, especially Muslim women, possibly forcing some of them to give up their jobs. Ironically, one major goal of the charter trumpeted by the government was better protection for gender equality.

The debate was complicated by a number of factors. For instance, supporters of the charter include an assortment of strange bedfellows. According to various polls conducted over the months before the election, it was estimated that about half of them belong to a core of francophones nostalgic for the old "French Canadian" Quebec. The remaining supporters included a number of feminists concerned about the patriarchal bias of major religions; aging baby-boomers who fought for the Quiet Revolution and the end of the Catholic clergy's abusive power in Quebec society, and thus have an enduring distrust of religion per se; individuals who take their cues from Republican France; some members of minorities who, having immigrated from North Africa where they witnessed (sometimes in their own families) the horrors committed by Islamist extremists, warn the population against an ongoing, hidden

Islamist plot and an imminent upsurge of violence in Quebec; and not very well informed (or deeply concerned) citizens who, in good faith, embrace the government discourse. This mixture made it all the more difficult to isolate the central issues of the proposal and build an effective, well-targeted counterdiscourse.

Political dimensions also obscured the issues. For instance, as a minority government, it was unlikely that the Parti Québécois would be able to rally a majority in the National Assembly, since all the other parties rejected the plan. So we have to ask what motivated the government. The recent leadership of the Parti Québécois seems out of step with a party that was known for combining a vigorous form of nationalism with a true liberal, progressive philosophy (a not-so-frequent occurrence in the history of democracy). One is therefore justified in wondering if this shift was motivated by ideology or just callous (and rather cynical) electoralism. This question is all the more relevant given that, judging from their track records, there is good reason to believe many representatives of the party disagreed on the third component of the proposal. But not one dissident voice was heard from the government benches – although four former sovereignist party leaders have denounced the proposed charter.

Opposing it were people who hold less radical views on secularism and give a higher priority to the protection of human rights. I, for one, was strongly critical of this component of the charter. Here are a few of my objections:

- There is an obvious imbalance between the moral and societal benefits pursued through the proposal versus the damage that would be inflicted on some citizens.
- The then-government evoked the rule of neutrality of the state to justify the ban, but this reasoning is deficient. The rule of neutrality means that the state must refrain from privileging one religion at the expense of others – including deep moral non-religious convictions. From this, one could infer that no sign or symbol should be tolerated. However, one could infer the opposite as well: that all signs should be allowed everywhere. In both cases, neutrality is achieved. On the face of it, a better way of thinking would rely on the rule of institutional separation. But then one would have to demonstrate that wearing religious symbols jeopardizes this rule.
- The argument claiming that all public employees are representative of the state rings hollow. Consider, for instance, service employees such as a Hydro-Québec maintenance crew or workers in hospital

cafeterias. Even if they do represent the state, it is a feeble ratio-
nale for restricting or suppressing a fundamental right. There is no
basis for comparison here with Law 101, the Charter of the French
Language, introduced in 1977, whose purpose was no less than to
secure the future of francophone Quebec (an objective that has been
recognized as legitimate by the Supreme Court of Canada).

- There is no empirical evidence that the wearing of religious symbols
  violates the rule of impartiality and prevents a worker from carrying
  out his or her duties satisfactorily.
- The ban would create two classes of citizens and deprive some of
  them from access to quality jobs (we are talking about some six hundred thousand public service jobs).
- The proposed charter was said to be aimed at countering fundamentalism and thereby reducing the Islamist terrorist threat in Quebec.
  One suspects that such a ban will only stoke resentment and favour
  radicalization.
- The government also claimed that the ban would help Muslim wom-
  en who, under pressure from their families, are compelled to wear
  the hijab. Again, one wonders how this would reduce the oppression
  that they endure.
- As hard as it is to believe, it has now been confirmed that the government conducted no research whatsoever prior to engaging in this
  major initiative. In other words, it intended to legislate on matters of
  which it had very little knowledge.[1]

Finally, despite the outcome of the provincial election, it will not be
easy to repair the major damage that has been caused. One negative effect has been the demonization of religious symbols, particularly the hijab. Another is the anti-immigrant sentiment that has been aroused. A
third is the rift that has been created in Quebec society between the francophone majority and many members of minorities. A de facto coalition
was created to unite the latter in their fight against the charter – this is
a rare sociological occurrence, since in most societies minorities tend to
promote their interests separately, if not in competition with each other.

A fourth damaging effect is the break with decades of pluralism in
Quebec and, potentially, the end of a very successful combination of nationalism and liberalism. A fifth is the harm to Quebec's image internationally as a society respectful of diversity and rights, with a capacity to
maintain good relationships with its minorities. Finally, this debate opened
a can of worms because of the way it was conducted by Mr Drainville, who,
perhaps unwillingly, publicly expressed xenophobic views.[2]

In a reply to a very critical op-ed about the proposed charter published in the *New York Times* ("Quebec's Tea Party Moment," 13 November 2013), two government ministers (Bernard Drainville and Jean-François Lisée) argued that, with the proposed charter, Quebec was only replicating what Jefferson himself had done in the United States in his time, that is, clearly separating state and religion ("Jefferson in Quebec," *NYT*, 23 November 2013). Their argument is deeply flawed. Certainly, Jefferson and other American founding fathers were eager to ensure institutional separation between the state and religions. However, their guiding rule was tolerance, acceptance of diversity. In their minds, this arrangement did not preclude a particularly close association between the state and religion construed as a general body of beliefs, ideals, and principles that should serve as the symbolic foundation of the political life, what R.N. Bellah (1967) called the "civil religion" of America. Actually, it is well known that this conflation has always been a characteristic of American public culture right up to the present. The idea of banning religious symbols among public servants in the name of secularism would have seemed preposterous to Jefferson and his fellow founding fathers.

Not only did the proposed charter do damage to Quebec society that will not be easy to repair – mostly because of the bitter debate it ignited – but it is not needed to preserve Quebec culture or values. Surveys carried out by several public and private institutions since the beginning of the debate showed that these institutions have experienced no serious difficulties and the practice of accommodations is under control. This was clearly the case of a solution – and a wrongheaded one at that – in search of a problem.

This being said, prospects were not all that bleak. Every opposition party in the National Assembly came out against the proposed charter and close to half of Quebecers rejected the charter.

Charles Taylor and I, just six years ago, co-chaired a commission on cultural and religious accommodations in Quebec. In our report, we concluded that interculturalism has been developing as a unique strength of Quebec society. We pointed to a way forward in which ethnocultural diversity would exist comfortably alongside and within a French-speaking core. We also pointed out that, preferably, integration and ethnocultural differences must be negotiated between citizens, at the microsocial level, rather than through government diktats or court intervention.

We also wrote that, rather than focusing on their differences, the people of Quebec needed to move forward to build a common identity, with common values and one inclusive collective memory. Quebec, we said, could not afford to be permeated with fear and mistrust, but required instead an identity and a citizen culture in which all Quebecers would be able to invest and thrive.

I still fully endorse these views today. The overall goal of interculturalism, as outlined in this book, is to manage the relationship between the majority and minorities in a way that is in accordance with human rights and pluralism, with a view to promoting dialogue, mutual understanding, and rapprochement. Sadly, the recent proposal clearly ran counter to this goal. According to the premier at the time, the charter was supposed to bring all Quebecers together and to create harmony. What we saw instead was a situation of conflict, deep divisions, and growing resentment, along with promises of civil disobedience from some institutional bodies. To sum up, this proposed charter was in many respects obviously an ill-advised initiative that would have involved Quebec society in very long court battles with no clear benefits in sight.

While conducting hearings on accommodations, our commission heard numerous appeals for tolerance, moderation, and respect from Quebecers of all cultures and persuasions, including immigrants. One of them was Karina Chami, who said: "Let us avoid bequeathing to our children a Quebec that is too narrow for them." Fortunately, the defeat of the Parti Québécois in the last April general election put an end to this project, which was rejected by the new government of the Liberal party. However, the debate on this issue is undoubtedly far from over.[3]

Notes

Introduction

1 The same is true for aboriginal populations. See, for example, L. Elenius (2010).

2 In spite of the various criticisms that have been made of Law 101, it needs to be pointed out that this law, by establishing French as the official public language, made it an indispensable shared resource for all civic life. French thus became a common denominator open to all cultures and not only an identity attribute for the old-stock francophone majority. It has also favoured participation in political life and access for everyone to public institutions and services. See F. Giroux (1997), G. Rocher (2006), and C. Taylor (2003).

3 I explain these concepts of majority and minorities in chapters 1 and 2.

4 An excellent summary can be found in F. Rocher, M. Labelle, A.-M. Field, and J.-C. Icart (2007).

5 Powerful sites for promotion and reflection can be found, for instance, in the European Union and the Council of Europe. A review of all this background would, however, require a whole other study.

6 The Consultation Commission on Accommodation Practices Related to Cultural Difference (created in February 2007 by the Quebec government). I co-chaired this commission with philosopher Charles Taylor. The report of the commission was released in May 2008 (see G. Bouchard & C. Taylor, 2008).

7 According to this model, immigrants should completely give up their own cultures and their original identities.

8 Recent history shows that societies can achieve democracy and pluralism by various routes. For example, Great Britain allows public schools to organize classes in religious education. In the United States, this arrangement would

be seen as contrary to the separation of church and state. But are we to conclude from this that freedom of religion is better protected in Great Britain
than in the United States? (See J. Gray, 2000, 2002.)

9 We could mention in this regard a widespread rejection of pure and simple
  assimilation, the frequent maintenance among immigrants of close links
  with the society of origin through new communication technologies, the
  diversification of places of origin and ethnocultural baggage, and very high
  levels of education (among immigrants settling in Quebec and elsewhere
  in Canada).

10 This model, for reasons that will be outlined below, has very bad press
   in Quebec.

11 For a detailed definition of this concept, along with a set of empirical indicators, see Council of Europe (2005). For the purposes of this book, I will
   adopt a general definition that refers to (a) the minimal social bond that
   permits a society to function and develop towards the goals it has set for
   itself, and (b) the conditions and mechanisms required by the creation and
   maintenance of this bond.

12 This means that I share the opinion of I. Angus (1998), according to which
   pluralism can only be achieved within the diversity paradigm. Interculturalism is an authentic pluralism, despite the fact that it is most often based on
   a duality paradigm (see chapter 1).

13 This is according to two resolutions adopted by the National Assembly of
   Quebec, one dated 20 March 1985 (on the recognition of aboriginal rights)
   and the other 30 May 1989 (on the recognition of the Malecite nation).
   These provisions were strongly reaffirmed in 2002 with the "Peace of the
   Braves" agreement as well as in May 2011 when Quebec signed a "nation-
   to-nation" cooperation agreement with the Cree.

14 In particular, A.-G. Gagnon (2000b), A.-G. Gagnon and R. Iacovino (2003;
   2007, chap. 4), F. Rocher et al. (2007), M. Labelle (2000, 2008a), F. Rocher
   and M. Labelle (2010), M. McAndrew (1995, 2007), D. Juteau (1994), G.
   Baril (2008), and Intercultural Institute of Montreal (2007a). See also G.
   Bouchard and C. Taylor (2008, pp. 116–18) and G. Bouchard, G. Battaini-
   Dragoni, C. Saint-Pierre, G. Nootens, and F. Fournier (2011b).

15 Criticisms that have been formulated on the basis of preliminary presentations that I made on the subject in recent years (in particular, G. Bouchard,
   2011; G. Bouchard et al., 2011b).

1. Conditions and Foundations of Quebec Interculturalism

1 *House of Commons Debates*, 39th Parliament, 1st session, vol. 141, no. 87
  (27 November 2006).

2 With respect to language, the story has been told in various studies. See, for example, the collection edited by M. Plourde (2000).

3 Rightly or wrongly, this is a criticism that has often been made of the report of the commission that I co-chaired with Charles Taylor in 2007–2008. It has been accused of not being sensitive enough to the problems of the majority, which is itself a minority.

4 Sociologist M. Lamont (2002) has shown that unlike their French counterparts, for example, American workers are characterized by a mentality (a "repertoire") based mainly on individualist references. On the subject of collective rights versus individual rights, see M. Seymour (2008) and P. Leuprecht (2009).

5 It is clear that my position on this point is – and always will be – in opposition to the so-called civic model of the nation, inspired in particular by the constitutional patriotism of Jürgen Habermas. A criticism of this model can be found in G. Bouchard (1999, pp. 20–30; 2001c). It is surprising that J.-Y. Thériault (2010, pp. 147–8) and a few others refer to that same text to show that I am instead a proponent of the civic nation. See also G. Bouchard (1995).

6 There are abundant studies dealing with the controversies surrounding the models of the civic nation and the ethnic nation. See, for example, W. Kymlicka (1995, in particular p. 188), G. Nootens (1999), and G. Bouchard (1999, pp. 20–30; 2001c).

7 These reflections owe a great deal to discussions I had with Charles Taylor. They also echo a few passages from the report of the commission that we co-chaired (for example, pp. 126–7).

8 The expression "Franco-Québécois" is sometimes used in this sense, but I reject it because it is not precise enough; strictly speaking, it includes all francophones living in Quebec (French, Belgian, Haitian, etc.). What we have to say here, obviously, is "Quebecers of French Canadian origin," in order to clearly distinguish them from francophone Quebecers of other origins. It is well known (and acknowledged by everyone) that before the 1960s the vast majority of the members of the francophone population in Quebec referred to themselves as "French Canadians." But reference (even for the past) to this ethnonym nowadays can antagonize some Quebecers (of French Canadian origin), even though it is still emphatically claimed today by a certain number of francophones and is sometimes used by various authors who cannot be suspected of ethnic prejudice (for example, M. McAndrew, 2001, p. 219; L. Meney, 2010, p. 292, passim; J. Létourneau, 2008; M. Labelle et al., 2007, p. 102; L. Rousseau, 2012, pp. 5, 11).

9 Diversity was enshrined as a fundamental characteristic by a motion in the House of Commons in 1971 and by the 1988 law on multiculturalism.

10 In Australia, the official conversion to diversity coincided with the adoption of multiculturalism in 1973 (for an overview of how well this vision has now taken root in the population, see J. Brett and A. Moran, 2011).

11 Ethnocultural diversity is so great in this country that, in order to transcend this diversity, the unity of the nation is based largely on the state and its ramifications (N. Subramanian, 2013). As well, the constitution of the country (article 51-A) establishes for each citizen the duty "to promote harmony and the spirit of common brotherhood amongst all the people of India transcending religious, linguistic and regional or sectional diversities."

12 A document issued by the Swedish government in 2006 officially defined that country with reference to ethnocultural diversity (K. Hamdé, 2008, p. 89).

13 Some have called such a country a "fractured nation" (A. Chollet, 2011) or even a "multi-nation" (W. Kymlicka, 1995).

14 In Quebec, we find a trace of this paradigm in the special status recognized for English Quebecers (elements of bilingualism in public life, separate education system, etc.).

15 These have been extensively studied, for example, by A.-G. Gagnon (2007).

16 In the sense that the members of the founding majority have no legal status that would elevate them officially above other citizens (see chapter 4).

17 On the concept of founding majority, see also chapter 2.

18 These criticisms are summarized in G. Bouchard and C. Taylor (2008, pp. 215–16). According to some government documents, Quebec society includes no fewer than 130 "communities." We do not know, however, where this surprising number comes from. Elsewhere, some authors talk of around 100 "communities" (M. Labelle, 2008a, p. 35).

19 On the ethnocultural categorizations and the attendant risks of creating exclusion or hierarchies within the Quebec framework, see Y. Shiose and L. Fontaine (1995).

20 A study done in 1978 showed that Montreal Jews recruited close to 90 per cent of their friends within their community (M. Weinfeld & W.W. Eaton, 1979). These results are reported in P. Anctil (1984, p. 444).

21 The same thing happens in France, where, to designate immigrants, the media sometimes talk about "Français issus de la diversité" [French from diversified communities]; diversity becomes a trait falsely identified with foreigners, the excluded, and minorities. Moreover, this concept, at least in the minds of the majority, can have negative connotations.

22 See D. Moïsi (2007) and P. Pathak (2008). Yet according to other observers (for example, R. Brubaker, 2001), what we are seeing is instead a return to the homogeneity-assimilation paradigm.

23 For a detailed discussion on the subject, see T. Todorov (2008). I will leave aside the question of whether or not duality already existed in a latent form

in the culture of these countries; in that case, it should then be understood as having been masked by ideologies and policies of openness that do not resonate with the populations.

24 Consociationalism is a model that advocates the proportional sharing of power among two or more intranational groups (sometimes combined with a veto right) and the exercise of authority through delegated elites (A. Lijphart, 1968).

25 I have not mentioned federalism, since this concept seems to refer primarily to a model of the distribution of political powers among various national or other entities, rather than a management model per se for dealing with ethnocultural reality and relations. It is true, however, that any federal regime is based on certain values that are not without consequence for the management of diversity (for example, the idea of pluralism or respect for communities or constituent identities) (F. Rocher, 2008).

26 Canada had first considered the hypothesis of duality or bipolarity (a binational state based on the equality between two founding peoples). The Royal Commission on Bilingualism and Biculturalism (also known as the Laurendeau-Dunton Commission) had this as one of its main recommendations in its preliminary report (see A. Laurendeau & A.D. Dunton, 1965, p. 3). This idea of Canadian duality then found many expressions, in particular in the well-known notion of the two solitudes. In 1971 the Leader of the Official Opposition in the House of Commons, Robert L. Stanfield, spoke about "the basic duality of our country" (*House of Commons Debates*, 8 October 1971, pp. 8545–8).

27 An important current of thinking at present tends to give credence to a dualist vision of the nation. I am thinking, for instance, of David Goodhart (2006) and *Prospect* magazine, of which he is the founder and editor.

28 This number does not include temporary migrants from the south on their way to northern countries (mainly the United States).

29 In 1991, the Salinas government had article 4 of the Constitution amended to officially establish the multicultural character of the country (G. de la Peña, 2006).

30 A key reference on this uneasy relationship is the incisive and very controversial book by S. Huntington (1996).

31 See B. Gregg (2003), who contrasts nations with a "dual" structure and nations with a "mosaic" structure.

2. Quebec Interculturalism: A Definition

1 I refer readers in particular to F. Rocher et al. (2007), F. Rocher and M. Labelle (2010), Denise Helly (1996), Pierre Anctil (1996), Danielle Juteau

(2002), Gladys Symons (2002), M. McAndrew (2002), F. Harvey (1986), D. Salée (2007), and R. Iacovino and C.-A. Sévigny (2010). I will also base my analysis on various government documents, which I will mention in the course of these pages.

2 French, which had been one of the main foundations of French Canadian identity, thus gave way to a broader vocation by becoming a foundation for civic life in Quebec. This change would accelerate at the same time as the shift from the French Canadian nation to the more inclusive concept of the Quebec nation.

3 Under this accord, which extended three previous agreements, Quebec obtained the right to select so-called independent immigrants (excluding refugees) and responsibility for their integration.

4 The main points in this proposal are presented in a preparatory document for the Forum national sur la citoyenneté et l'intégration [National Forum on Citizenship and Integration], held in September 2000 (Quebec, MRCI, 2000).

5 See the document *Shared Values, Common Interests* (Quebec, MRCI, 2004), accessible at http://www.micc.gouv.qc.ca/publications/en/planification/PlanAction20042007-summary.pdf.

6 Pioneering actions had, however, already taken place beginning in the 1950s, in particular the submission in 1954 of a remarkable brief by the Société d'assistance aux immigrants [Society for Aid to Immigrants] (Montreal) to the Tremblay Commission on constitutional problems (F. Harvey, 1986, p. 224). The Royal Commission of Inquiry on Education, created in 1961 and chaired by Alphonse-Marie Parent, had also stimulated discussions on the subject (M. Milot, 2009, pp. 40–3).

7 As stated, for example, in this excerpt from a government text (the Quebec government's 1978 white paper on cultural policy, *La Politique du québécoise développement culturel*): "Entre l'assimilation lente ou brutale et la conservation d'originalités incluses dans les murailles des ségrégations, il est une autre voie praticable: celle des échanges au sein d'une culture québécoise" [Between slow or brutal assimilation and the conservation of originality inside the walls of segregation, there is another possible way, that of exchanges within a Quebec culture] (vol. 1, p. 79). We find a similar statement in a paragovernmental document from 1994 according to which Quebec is searching for a model "à égale distance d'une politique assimilationniste ou d'une politique multiculturaliste" [equidistant from an assimilationist policy and a multiculturalism policy] (Conseil des communautés culturelles et de l'immigration du Québec [Council of Cultural Communities and of Immigration], 1994, p. 3).

8 In a similar vein, I should mention pioneering proposals of *indépendantiste* leader Pierre Bourgault dating back to the 1960s to 1970s: rejection of withdrawal into ethnic identity, pluralism (ahead of his time), political and sociological definition of Quebec identity, emphasis on common values, and openness to immigrants (see J.-F. Nadeau, 2007, passim). The same can be said for Hubert Aquin (1962), one of the first of his time to adopt a pluralist vision of the nation. Similarly, still outside government circles, the Intercultural Institute of Montreal began in the 1960s to promote the principles of pluralism and interculturalism (R. Vachon, 1986).

9 Little is known about its origin in Quebec. It was, however, in use among senior civil servants in the early 1980s (L. Bernier, 2008). The first comment on the concept was published during that period (A. Laperrière, 1985, p. 190). Researchers connected to the Council of Europe and the Belgian government also used the word beginning in 1981 (L. Porcher, 1981; R. Detry, 1981). As for the concept of the intercultural (at the microsocial level), it has an older origin, in particular in Quebec.

10 These projects have been the subject of a few presentations at the International Symposium on Interculturalism, held in Montreal in May 2011 on the initiative of Interculturalism 2011 (see G. Bouchard, G. Battaini-Dragoni, C. Saint-Pierre, G. Nootens, and F. Fournier, 2011a, 2011b). It should be noted, however, that interculturality does not exclude duality. In fact, the majority-minorities relationship can also manifest itself at the microsocial level. During a workshop held in January 2011 in Montreal, again under the auspices of Interculturalism 2011, experts in intercultural mediation showed that this relationship was very active in business, school, and neighbourhood life. Some have explained, for example, that resistance to pluralism often came from members of the majority culture.

11 This seven-point definition matches in various ways, but with differences in emphasis, a few previous proposals, in particular those of A.-G. Gagnon and R. Iacovino (2002; 2007, chap. 4) and F. Rocher et al. (2007, pp. 48–52). Note also the absence of references to the aboriginal populations, for the reason stated in the previous chapter.

12 For a presentation and critical discussion of this topic, see C. Taylor (1992), Axel Honneth (1995), and R. Bhargava (2010).

13 Those who are first and foremost concerned here are immigrants and members of minorities, but also members of the cultural majority.

14 For an overview of this program, which reaches sixty-five hundred students annually, see Quebec, MELS (2009).

15 The same can be said for accommodations, which will be discussed in chapter 4.

16 Among many other references, see M. Mendelsohn (1999), D. Helly and
    N. Van Schendel (2001), M. Waters (2000), I. Bloemraad (2006), and R.
    Ruiz (2010). The huge international Intercultural Cities project, conducted
    under the auspices of the Council of Europe and the European Union,
    produced many similar conclusions.
17 For the Montreal context, a demonstration of this can be found in A.M. Fiore
    (2010). On the same subject, still in the Quebec context, see J. Erfurt (2010).
18 Or, to use A.-G. Gagnon's expression (2000b, p. 20), "a focal point of the
    collective identity" that includes majority and minorities. On this subject,
    see also F. Rocher, G. Rocher, and M. Labelle (1995) and F. Giroux (1997).
19 Polls conducted over many years show that in recent decades the propor-
    tion of citizens who identify as Quebecers has been constantly increasing
    (for a summary of this topic, see M. Labelle et al., 2007, p. 56ff.); see also
    the results of a poll conducted in October 2011 (*La Presse,* 7 April 2012, sec-
    tion "Enjeux," p. 5). This statement also seems to apply to Anglo-Quebecers
    (J.-F. Lisée, 2012, p. 26).
20 On this subject, see M. Pagé (2006) and the comments of J. Maclure (2006).
21 The right of all citizens (especially the members of minorities) to maintain
    links with their cultures of origin is recognized, for example, by the Inter-
    national Covenant on Civil and Political Rights (1966), by the UNESCO
    Convention on Cultural Diversity (article 2), by the Fribourg Declaration
    on Cultural Rights (2007), and by the Quebec Charter of Human Rights
    and Freedoms (article 43). On the origin and meaning of the concept of
    cultural rights, see G. Rocher (2000).
22 On this subject, see G. Nootens (2010a) as well as the theoretical reflection
    developed by E. Winter (2010).
23 There is abundant literature on the subject. For an introduction, it is useful
    to read D. Gratton (2009), G. Legault (2000), M. Cohen-Emerique and
    S. Fayman (2005), C. Delcroix (1996), Y. Leanza (2006), and C. Eberhard
    (2001). See also a special issue of the review *INTERCulture* devoted to this
    topic (Intercultural Institute of Montreal, 2007).
24 Once again, I need to mention here the groundbreaking work carried out
    since the 1960s by the organizers at the Intercultural Institute of Montreal.
    See, for example, Intercultural Institute of Montreal (2007b).
25 For example, J. Brett and A. Moran (2011), T. Caponio and M. Borkert
    (2010), A.-C. Fourot (2010), and F. J. Lechner (2011).
26 As Dominique Schnapper (2007) shows so well.
27 In Quebec, there is a consensus on this, including among immigrants and
    members of minorities (see, for example, M. Labelle, F. Rocher, & R. Anto-
    nius, 2009a, pp. 119–120, 126, 129ff.).

28 A similar distinction can be found in F.J. Lechner (2011).

29 The book that first spread the use of this term is not recent (G.W. Allport, 1954; republished 1979).

30 See, for example, P. Thomas (2011), M. Hewstone, E. Cairns, A. Voci, J. Hamberger, and U. Niens (2006), R. Brown and M. Hewstone (2005), M. Hewstone (2009), and F. Stoeckel (2012).

31 See M. Girard (2008, pp. 48, 90–4). The process was also the subject of an experiment in the Quebec school system; see a review in M. McAndrew (2013, chap. 2).

32 Rocher is moreover very critical of the concept of a shared public culture, which he says should be "consigned to history" (p. 161).

33 In light of this comment, one can understand the discomfort that can be created among members of the francophone majority by these words from Marco Micone's well-known poem "Speak What," in which he says he is expressing the feelings of immigrants: "We are strangers to the anger of Félix/ Speak to us of your Charter/of the vermilion beauty of your autumn." In fact, if we carefully examine the sources of "the anger of Félix," we discover that it arises directly from the old struggles for rights of which the Quebec charter is one of the culminations and from which all Quebec citizens now benefit. Quebec citizenship and the culture that nourishes it should be seen as the products of a living, developing heritage of which all Quebecers are stakeholders. For a very enlightening statement on this subject, see Quebec, MRCI (2000, p. 8). The claim that all Quebecers are immigrants gives rise to a similar discomfort since it seems to deny the history of the founding majority and its old roots in the soil of Quebec.

34 This concept of the negotiable versus non-negotiable deviates from the definition proposed by J. Rawls (1971, 1993), which tries to limit public culture to its most universal and most consensual (or potentially consensual) content, in this case, basic liberal values (see also D. Weinstock, 1995).

35 The above statements cover the four constitutive elements of shared culture (or "civic identity") as defined by M. Seymour (2001, pp. 17ff.).

36 To borrow the words of Rachida Azdouz (speaking at a Quebec Liberal Party conference held 28 May2011 in Montreal).

37 This position is in keeping with the teachings of sociology and liberal philosophy (see, for example, J. Maclure, 2006, p. 155).

38 For a summary of this idea, see G. Bouchard (2003). Y. Lamonde's *The Social History of Ideas in Quebec* (2013) provides a useful point of reference here. In that work he studies the Patriote movement and the Rebellions of 1837–38 in detail, but also from the broad perspective of national revolutions in the nineteenth century. A similar process was the impetus for my book on the

emergence of nations and national identities in the societies of the New World (G. Bouchard, 2000). While giving full justice to the substance of the Quebec past, the book attempts to bring out both what distinguishes that past and how it is part of transcontinental developments.

39 See the analysis by Y. Lamonde (2010).

40 On the above, see G. Bouchard (1999, part 2).

41 A similar argument can be found in the report of the Bouchard-Taylor Commission (G. Bouchard & C. Taylor, 2008, pp. 125–7).

42 Taken too far, pluralism can turn into compartmentalization and ethnicization of difference. I am thinking here of the critique of Canadian multiculturalism formulated by Neil Bissoondath (1994). Similarly, it has been shown that liberal discourse on ethnicity in the United States has contributed to the hardening of stereotypes associated with the African American minority (J. Pierre, 2004). Every person should therefore benefit from what some call a "right to leave," which is moreover recognized by the Fribourg Declaration on Cultural Rights (2007, art. 4).

43 It is useful therefore to avoid what T. Cantle (2011) calls the "paradox of diversity," namely the fact that, among the individuals who are most exposed to diversity, some will have the reflex of adopting an inward-looking identity.

44 For a particularly representative example of this line of thought, see D.A. Hollinger (1996). On the same subject, see G. Bouchard (2000, p. 348–66).

45 See on this topic the critical reflection by M. Abdallah-Pretceille (2006), who even proposes doing away with using the concept altogether – which seems excessive.

46 Among the many titles, see M. Labelle (2001), R.G. Rumbaut (1997), M.C. Waters (1990), M. Labelle and J.J. Lévy (1995), J. Brett and A. Moran (2011), P. Kasinitz, J.H. Mollenkopf, and M.C. Waters (2004), and P. Kasinitz, J.H. Mollenkopf, and M.C. Waters (2008).

47 This dimension should not be underestimated in a society such as Quebec, which belongs to the minority nations struggling with an anguished memory and the pursuit of ancient unfulfilled dreams.

48 Pessimists will compare this challenge to squaring the circle. See, for this point of view, the critical reflection by D. Weinstock (2009) on P.-E. Trudeau's great Canada-wide project, a project that (from the Canadian perspective) came to naught in that it failed to deal with or reduce the francophone-anglophone duality. But in this case, the process was governed by a strongly centralizing (if not to say assimilationist) tendency.

49 I reiterate here a statement from the report of the Bouchard-Taylor Commission (G. Bouchard & C. Taylor, 2008, chap. 7).

50 P. Drouilly (2007), table 9, p. 14.

51 The idea of including in the charter an article to protect and promote Quebec identity – an idea put forward by the Parti Québécois in 2007 – is in principle legitimate (Bill 195, "Québec Identity Act," First Session, Thirty-Eighth Legislature). The problem lies with the definition of "Quebec identity" and how to translate this idea into law.

52 For a more recent statement of this argument, see S. Lecce (2008).

53 On this subject and for a general criticism of the neutrality argument, see W. Kymlicka (2000, esp. pp. 185–7).

54 See also J. Maclure (2006, p. 155). A similar idea is expressed in R. Poole (1999, pp. 128–9).

55 See the observations of L. Cardinal (2010, 2011).

56 On this subject, see M. Labelle and J.J. Lévy (1995), M. Labelle, F. Rocher, and G. Rocher (1995), M. Labelle and D. Salée (2001), M. McAndrew (2001, pp. 178ff.), F. Rocher et al. (2007), E. Brouillet (2005), M. Labelle and F. Rocher (2004, 2006, 2009b), and L. Cardinal (2010, 2011). For a very empirical overview based on testimony from immigrants, see D. Helly and N. Van Schendel (2001). This general problem of duplication was very clearly formulated in 1990 in a document from the Quebec Ministry of Cultural Communities and Immigration (Quebec, MCCI, 1990b, pp. 49–50).

57 Section 27 of the Canadian Charter of Rights and Freedoms stipulates that any interpretation that is made "shall be interpreted in a manner consistent with the preservation and enhancement of the multicultural heritage of Canadians." The text does not, however, provide a definition of the term "multicultural."

58 Referring to how the Supreme Court of Canada defines federalism, A.-G. Gagnon (2010, p. 261) speaks also of "a space of democratic affirmation … that should be fostered."

59 On this subject and the discussion above, in addition to the references listed in chapter 1 (point 3, pp. XX–XX), see M. Labelle et al. (1995); F. Rocher et al. (1995); M. Seymour (1999); A.-G. Gagnon (2000a, 2000b, 2010); Quebec, MRCI (2000, pp. 17–18); M. Labelle and F. Rocher (2004); D. Turp (2005); F. Rocher et al. (2007); A. Brochu (2008); R. Iacovino and C.-A. Sévigny (2010); and M. Seymour and G. Laforest (2011).

60 F. Rocher and M. Labelle (2010, p. 193) also give an expanded definition of citizenship, similar to the one proposed here.

61 This is an old idea in Quebec and is frequently found in the writing of those contributing to the current debate. See, for example, Conseil des communautés culturelles et de l'immigration du Québec (CCCI) (1994, p. 3), M. McAndrew (2001, pp. 118–19), A.-G. Gagnon and M. Jézéquel (2004), G. Rousseau (2006), and J. Maclure (2006). It is also a key aspect of the

approach of the Council of Europe in the area of diversity; see G. Battaini-
Dragoni (2009) and Council of Europe (2008).

62 A.-G. Gagnon (2000b, p. 23) makes this search for balance "the main virtue
of the Quebec model." See also A.-G. Gagnon and R. Iacovino (2002,
pp. 329, 333–4; 2003, pp. 418, 433) and A.-G. Gagnon (2011, pp. 178–80).

63 See in particular P. Anctil (1996), A.-G. Gagnon (2000b, 2010), M. Labelle
(2000), A.-G. Gagnon and R. Iacovino (2003; 2007, chap. 4), A.-G. Gagnon
and M. Jézéquel (2004), F. Rocher et al. (2007, pp. 49ff.), G. Baril (2008),
and G. Bouchard and C. Taylor (2008). In various other texts, we find definitions that support the points just made, for example, R. Vachon (1997),
B. Pelletier (2010, pp. 264ff.), and Conseil du statut de la femme (2011a).

64 See in particular the texts published in S. Gervais, D. Lamoureux, and
D. Karmis (2008).

3. Interculturalism and Multiculturalism

1 The initial decision was made by the (federalist) Robert Bourassa government. It was conveyed to the prime minister of Canada, Pierre Elliott
Trudeau, in a letter dated 11 November 1971.

2 It is useful here to draw a comparison with the situation in New Zealand, a
country that is officially defined as binational (Maoris and Pakehas). However, the Maoris have the same suspicion of multiculturalism that Quebec
francophones have; it is fueled by the same reasons and is expressed in
practically the same terms (S. May, 2002; G. Bouchard, 2000).

3 I refer here to the latest annual reports on the application of the law on
multiculturalism, the Canadian Heritage website in recent years, the text of
the Canadian Multiculturalism Act (1985, 1988), statements by Jason Kenney,
minister of Citizenship, Immigration and Multiculturalism (as reported by
the journalist Hélène Buzzetti in *Le Devoir* of 10 February 2009 as well as by
Joe Friesen and Bill Curry in the *Globe and Mail* of 13 November 2009), a
double issue of the journal *Canadian Ethnic Studies* (vol. 40, nos. 1–2, 2008),
the study by F. Rocher et al. (2007), the new version of the citizenship guide
(*Discover Canada*, 2009, rev. 2011), a government status report on multiculturalism (*Building a Stronger Canada*) published in 2010 by Citizenship and
Immigration Canada, and a text by N. Girard (2011) written for Citizenship
and Immigration Canada.

4 On the other hand, on the Quebec side, few commentators pay attention
to various rather communitarian government documents, including the
Charter of Human Rights and Freedoms of 1975 – section 43 ("Persons belonging to ethnic minorities have a right to maintain and develop their own

cultural interests with the other members of their group"). This formulation was repeated in a section of a draft constitution developed by the Parti Québécois at the time of the 1995 referendum (as reported by *La Presse* of 14 April 2012, p. A18). Support for the development of the "cultural communities" and their specificity has a similar aim.

5 The idea of interactions and intercultural initiatives is now making inroads in English Canada, as evidenced, for example, by the rapid expansion of the Intercultural Dialogue Institute, now established in nine cities.

6 On this subject, see M. Labelle and F. Rocher (2006), who attribute all these shifts to various factors such as the growth of conservatism, a desire to counteract the secessionist threat coming from Quebec, the reaction to the attacks of September 11, and fear of terrorism.

7 Thus Quebec interculturalism is said to be "a superficial exercise in rebranding" (J. Jedwab, 2011).

8 The motion passed by the House of Commons in 2006 recognizing that the Québécois form a nation seems to contradict this proposition. In reality, that declaration has no value in law and therefore entails no statutory recognition. It is essentially a political gesture that resulted in no concrete measures.

9 According to I. Angus (1997, 1998), Canadian multicultural identity is based on an "us/we" association rather than on an "us/them" dichotomy. See also M. Adams (2007, p. 126).

10 To the above, we could add that Canadian literature on diversity, citizenship, and multiculturalism commonly uses concepts of majority and cultural minorities or ethnic groups.

11 This has already been pointed out by A.-G. Gagnon and R. Iacovino (2007, pp. 99, 110–11). Should this be seen as a French and/or republican influence in Quebec interculturalism? I see it more as the result of a continuity strongly rooted in the past of a dominated, fragile minority that has learned to band together in order to survive and develop. On this subject, see P. Donati (2009).

12 I intentionally use the term "tension" rather than "roadblock" or "stalemate." It would be a mistake to think that this question, as difficult as it is, rules out any solution, as is currently suggested by some very pessimistic discourse in Quebec. See, for example, a proposition that could overcome this difficulty in G. Bouchard (1999, pp. 81–137; 2003).

13 Once again, this distinction is important, but it is not always taken into account. Many authors identify pluralism with multiculturalism, which creates confusion (e.g., P. Savidan, 2009; M. Wieviorka, 2005; various texts published in newspapers and magazines). Others (such as A. Nugent, 2006, and

L. Pietrantonio et al., 1996) conclude that there are similarities between interculturalism and multiculturalism, but they do this by reducing the content of the two models to pluralist orientations (which they actually do share).

4. Criticism and Defence of Interculturalism

1 Especially in the kirpan and sukkah cases (for a detailed presentation, see G. Bouchard and C. Taylor, 2008, chap, 2).
2 Which, to no one's surprise, opens the door to the concept of treason (and even of "collaboration"), of which the dissidents are considered guilty (see, for example, M. Laroche, 2011).
3 An effort of this kind can be found in C. Belkhodja (2008), who analysed the contents of two magazines, *L'Action nationale* and *Argument*. See also M. Labelle (2008b).
4 For the purposes of general orientation, I will list various writings by Mathieu Bock-Côté, Jacques Beauchemin, Joseph-Yvon Thériault, Charles-Philippe Courtois, Éric Bédard, Joseph Facal, Serge Cantin, and Joëlle Quérin; chapters of the anthology edited by Bernard Gagnon (2010); many articles published in *L'Action nationale* over the last ten years; literature from the Institut de recherche du Québec and the Réseau Liberté-Québec; texts from the journal *Égards*; and a few Internet sites such as Vigile.net and Point de Bascule.
5 This is a position regularly found in the writings of Mario Roy, an editorialist with *La Presse*. Quebec, like other Western societies, is said to have given in, losing sight of its fundamental values. Energetic correction is therefore required.
6 The survey was conducted by Environics Research Group, and the results were made public at a conference of the Trudeau Foundation (17–19 November 2011).
7 He also observed the same phenomenon among the immigrants in Australia (A. Bilodeau, I. McAllister, & M. Kanji, 2010).
8 On this, see the relevant comment by R. Azdouz (2009).
9 Léger Marketing poll for the Fondation Emergence (results reported in *La Presse* of 16 May 2009, p. A25). Somewhat in the same vein, although in a different context, K.L. Gibson, S.J. McKelvie, and A.F. de Man (2008) were able to show, on the basis of samples, that Quebec francophones and anglophones shared a very similar profile in terms of values, orientations, and the like.
10 I mention collective affirmation as being among the civic or shared values because, for a nation such as Quebec, a cultural minority on the continent,

this value can have meaning for all citizens. It can, in fact, inspire the most various kinds of commitments, individual or collective, in a wide range of spheres. In politics, it can also be expressed in various ways inside or outside the Canadian constitutional framework.

11 We find, for example, in the Scottish identity a heritage of values remarkably similar to that of francophone Quebec (collective sensibility, social justice, egalitarianism, etc.). See references in A. Henderson and N. McEwen (2005, p. 184).

12 For example: the latitude that was shown, years ago, by the Quebec Automobile Insurance Corporation towards certain strict Jews and Muslims with respect to the choice of male or female examiners for driving tests. A strict procedure has never been instituted.

13 The idea of a hierarchy of values encounters even greater difficulties because of the insoluble problem of the assessment required (multiplicity of categories and levels, lack of precision of concepts, etc.). See on this the brief comment by T. Bennett, L. Grossberg, and M. Morris (2005, pp. 365–7). Moreover, with respect to the principle of the interdependence of rights, see the critical reflection by L.-P. Lampron (2012). Through an analysis of Canadian jurisprudence, the author shows that this principle is not always followed.

14 For a more detailed critique of this argument, see G. Nootens, 2010b, chap. 5).

15 Here again, the literature is voluminous. Here are a few starting points to the debate: K. Banting and W. Kymlicka (2006), D. Goodhart (2004), I. Bloemraad (2007), and C. Kesler and I. Bloemraad (2010). I also mention a study on the state of Kerala, in India, showing that ethnocultural diversity is compatible with cohesiveness and social development as long as efforts are made to ensure integration into a shared identity (P. Singh, 2011).

16 In most countries, traditional law was conceived for societies that were either homogeneous or assimilationist.

17 We then talk about a contextualization or a differentialist philosophy of law. With respect to Quebec, see, for example, D. Howes (2005) and J.-F. Gaudreault-Desbiens and D. Labrèche (2009). In the European context see C. Eberhard (2011).

18 This is the kind of argument that has led some people to identify Quebec interculturalism with a form of ethnic nationalism (C. Blad & P. Couton, 2009, pp. 651ff.).

19 Among these, we can mention N. Gagnon (2000, pp. 547, 563, passim), C.-P. Courtois (2008), D. Latouche (1990, pp. 101–2), J. Larose (1997, p. 79), J. Facal (2009), and D. Benhabib (2011a, pp. 262–3).

20 Among the current defenders of the argument, there is J. Beauchemin
    (2002, 2010b), M. Bock-Côté (2008), C.-P. Courtois and G. Rousseau
    (2010), and B. Landry (2010). For Dumont, the model of cultural conver-
    gence was combined with a project to create a broad political community
    that had the effect of mitigating the assimilationist orientation. On this sub-
    ject, see G. Mathieu (2001, pp. 29–32) and G. Bouchard (2001b). Finally,
    some advocates of the convergence model also identify themselves with
    republican views.
21 This concept should not be confused with that of A.-G. Gagnon (2000b,
    p. 20), who also talks about a "nexus of convergence" ("foyer de conver-
    gence"), but by referring to the shared public culture rather than to only
    the culture of the founding majority.
22 For further analyses critical of the convergence model, see D. Helly (1996),
    G. Bouchard (2001b), E. Brouillet (2005), and M. Pagé (2006).
23 It should be added that in the next twenty years, in a context of demograph-
    ic decline (due to natural movement in the population), Quebec will have
    to replace a quarter of the people currently on the labour market. Sources:
    news release from the Institut de recherche en économie contemporaine
    (institute for research in contemporary economics) (Montreal, May 12,
    2010); A. Grenier (2011, pp. 6, 10).
24 This is the case at the level of Quebec as well as of Canada: Quebec fran-
    cophones represented 29 per cent of the population in 1951 and 18.8 per
    cent in 2006 (Statistics Canada, "Population by Mother Tongue and Age
    Groups, 2006 Counts, for Canada, Provinces and Territories – 20% Sample
    Data." These are the only data currently available.
25 A particularly convincing demonstration was made with respect to the
    Catholics of Northern Ireland (J. Nagle and M.-A.C. Clancy, 2010).
26 Readers will recognize here Max Weber's theory of ethnic relations; this
    very rich perspective inspired studies by D. Juteau (1999), E. Winter (2011),
    and others, on which I will comment at the end of this chapter.
27 See on this topic F. Rocher et al. (2007). Even the "moral contract" of 1990,
    Let's Build Quebec Together (Quebec, MCCI, 1990a), which tried to distance
    itself from duality, maintained that affirmation of the francophone collectiv-
    ity and its institutions as the site for the integration of new arrivals repre-
    sented a vital necessity (p. 17). See also the study by L. Pietrantonio (2002)
    that offers a content analysis of seven official documents produced from
    1965 to 2000 by the ministry responsible for culture and communications.
    Once again, the analysis focuses on the concept of majority group.
28 This statement can be verified even among intellectuals and researchers
    who are reluctant to accept this relationship, as we can see, for example, in

the last book by M. McAndrew (2013) on "fragile majorities" or in various texts by Micheline Labelle. The majority-minorities relationship also enters into reflections on contemporary nationalisms (A.-G. Gagnon, A. Lecours, & G. Nootens, 2007).

29 I am referring in particular to papers presented by Robert Vyncke (Groupe Conseil Continuum), Alain Robichaud (Robichaud Conseil Inc.), and Marie-Claire Rufagari (TCRI) at the workshop on interculturalism held in January 2011 in Montreal (under the auspices of Interculturalism 2011).

30 On the general theme of the majority-minorities relationship in the recent past of Quebec thought and in a more general sociological context, see also G. Rocher (2000), L. Pietrantonio (2000), F. Rocher et al. (2007), and P.-L. Déry (2009).

31 The accommodations crisis, for example, showed clearly that requests did not all come from minorities or immigrants. See on this topic P. Eid (2009).

32 This issue has been analysed by various feminist authors, for example S. Okin (2005), C. Kukathas (2001), and A. Shachar (2001).

33 I use the word in an entirely neutral, sociological sense to designate a particular type of collective representation that is a vehicle for values and beliefs, that can be true or false, beneficial or harmful, but that has the power to impose itself on individuals as well as communities by virtue of the sacred character associated with it (see G. Bouchard, 2007).

34 A similar argument was formulated by M. Castells (1997).

35 I am referring here to an intellectual tradition based on Jürgen Habermas and (early) John Rawls. It is usually associated with the model of the so-called civic nation. In Quebec, C. Bariteau (1996, 1998) and J.-P. Derriennic (1995) are among its most influential representatives.

36 W.H. Sewell (1985) has shown how, even before the end of the eighteenth century, French revolutionaries had to go beyond the disembodied concept of "contract" to wrap it in the "hot" symbolism of homeland and the nation, defined in deeply ethnic terms. On this subject, see, among others, J. Krulic (1988), G. Noiriel (1988, 2001), M. Segalen (1989), A.-G. Dieckhoff (2000), D. Schnapper (2003, pp. 80–1), P. Tevanian (2007), and C. Laborde (2010).

37 A similar tension exists between multiculturalism and liberalism (A.-G. Gagnon and R. Iacovino, 2003).

38 For a brilliant example, see E. Winter (2011).

39 Many liberal authors could be cited to support this claim: J. Raz (1988), C. Taylor (1988, 1989, 1992), I.M. Young (1990), A. Margalit and J. Raz (1990), W.A. Galston (1991), S. Macedo (1991), Y. Tamir (1993), D. Miller (1995), W. Kymlicka (1995, 2000, 2007b), J. Couture (1995; 1999, pp. 293ff.), M. Canovan (1996), A.-G. Dieckhoff (2000, chap. 3), U. Özkirimli (2003),

V. Bader (2007), A. Lecours and G. Nootens (2007), M. Seymour (2008), and M.J. Sandel (2010). See also the reflections of D. Weinstock (2003), who argues for a state "as culturally neutral as possible" (p. 380). For a review of this debate, see D. Helly (2002) and F. Fournier and É.-D. Bellemarre (2012).

40 Other authors (such as Will Kymlicka and Michel Seymour), addressing this topic, talk of "societal culture." The concepts of culture and national identity are also very much related to the concept of symbolic foundation, and they have been the subject of arguments similar to those that I am presenting here (D. Miller, 1995; Y. Tamir, 1993; C. Calhoun, 2007; M. Guibernau, 2007).

41 See M. Guibernau (2007) and D. Brown (2008). The argument in favour of cultural continuity can also be verified at the microsocial level: intergenerational cultural breakdowns, which often result from immigration, create among children or grandchildren a context of uncertainty and anxiety. The identity crises characteristic of aboriginal communities offer an even more striking example of the same phenomenon.

42 Universal Declaration on Cultural Diversity, as the "the common heritage of humanity." The Convention on the Protection and Promotion of the Diversity of Cultural Expressions was adopted on 20 October 2005 by the General Conference of UNESCO.

43 Examples of abuses are a single system of public holidays modelled only on the majority religion, textbooks that ignore minority experiences, and uniform menus in the cafeterias of public institutions.

44 On this topic, other authors talk about "ethnocracy" (O. Yiftachel, 1999) or "majoritarianism" (P. Pathak, 2008). This latter concept, which comes from political philosophy, is an old one; it refers traditionally to a system that grants majorities excessive privileges.

45 This (rightly) assumes that there are positive forms of nationalism. A society that has relentlessly contributed to improving the condition of human beings and pursued the advancement of peace and social justice can legitimately take pride in its accomplishments and use them to feed a national consciousness. We also know that the decolonization process in the Third World was made possible thanks to a collective mobilization largely driven by nationalism. In several European cases as well, nationalism was instrumental in the establishment of democracy in the nineteenth century.

46 According to the text of an invitation card. See also .

47 As I noted in the introduction to this book, pluralism, like liberalism, is a general orientation, and each society or nation must specify how it will be applied according to its context.

48 Among others, see on this topic L. Wirth (1945), C. Guillaumin (1972), E.W. Said (1994), D. Juteau (1999), L. Pietrantonio (2000), M. James (2008), E. Winter (2010, 2011), A. Wimmer (2002), and D. Salée (2001, 2010).

49 For example, C. Guillaumin (1972), L. Pietrantonio (2000, pp. 161–2), and C. Delphy (2002). According to Delphy, ethnocultural differences are "created from scratch in order to establish groups" (p. 9).

5. For an Inclusive Secularism

1 These are what the Supreme Court of Canada calls "profoundly personal beliefs" (A. Decroix, 2011, p. 262). See also J. Maclure and C. Taylor (2011, pp. 79–80, 89ff.).

2 On many points, my presentation repeats proposals formulated in chapter 7 of this report. It departs on other points, reflecting the evolution of my thinking in recent years.

3 It has been suggested that the concept of neutrality be replaced by that of equity (G. Lévesque, 2010). This seems inappropriate given that all regimes of secularism should be guided by the rule of equal treatment.

4 Overturning a previous judgment by the European Court.

5 I consider the difference to be that a principle is based mainly on rational thought while a value is an internalized category or form belonging more to myth and imaginary (in the sociological sense).

6 In these two cases, as we will see, we are talking about customary values because the object of the request concerns a symbol that is supposed to have lost its original religious resonance (at the very least, for a very large part of the population).

7 The concept of open secularism was put forward in 1999 by a task force created by the minister of education (see J.-P. Proulx, 1999). It was then taken up by many Quebec authors. For a recent presentation see J. Maclure and C. Taylor (2011). These two authors also use the expression "liberal-pluralist secularism." Similarly, J. Baubérot and M. Milot (2011) talk about a "secularism of recognition." See also G. Leroux (2007) as well as "Manifeste pour un Québec pluraliste" (http://www.ledevoir.com/societe/actualites-en-societe/282309/manifeste-pour-un-quebec-pluraliste); this is a text signed by a group of Quebec intellectuals, also published in *Le Devoir* of 3 February 2010. For a brief defense of the principle of open secularism, see D. Weinstock (2011).

8 In November 2011, the House of Representatives adopted a motion confirming that the phrase "In God We Trust" is indeed the national motto of the United States.

9 According to the Conseil du statut de la femme (CSF; Quebec Council on the Status of Women), open secularism "means Quebec giving way to others, supposedly to welcome them" (CSF, 2011, p. 66).

10 With respect to the basic right to life, soldiers are nevertheless sent to the front, and we tolerate the deaths caused by mountain climbing, car racing, and snowmobile accidents (there were more than five hundred fatal snowmobile accidents from 2002 to 2011 in Quebec, according to the Institut de la statistique). On the other hand, according to the courts, the right to life prevails when Jehovah's Witnesses, in the name of their religion, oppose blood transfusions for their children.

11 Municipalities are in a way extensions of the National Assembly by virtue of the powers delegated to them.

12 Personal communication with Frédéric Castel, researcher at the Université du Québec à Montréal and expert on Islam, September 2012.

13 This position is defended by various organizations such as the Parti Québécois, the Mouvement laïque québécois (Quebec Secular Movement), the Conseil du statut de la femme, the Coalition Laïcité Québec (Quebec Secularism Coalition), and the Collectif citoyen pour l'égalité et la laïcité (CCIEL, Citizens' Collective for Equality and Secularism). See also P. Joncas (2009) and L. Mailloux (2010a). Among the texts published in newspapers, of particular interest is the "Déclaration des intellectuels pour la laïcité" (Le Devoir, 16 March 2010, p. A7) as well as another piece signed by a group of academics including a few jurists (Le Devoir, 27 September 2010, p. A7). In addition to demanding the end of all accommodations for religious reasons, these authors argue for "secular social relationships in public space" (and not only in public institutions; wearing religious symbols would be forbidden on the streets and in parks, businesses, and other such public spaces).

14 The same could be said for judges, members of police forces, and other officials targeted by selective prohibition. But, as I have pointed out, in these particular cases, there is in addition to the rule of objectivity an obligation to give the *appearance* of objectivity, given the exceptional nature of the functions involved.

15 This is an argument made, for example, by the Conseil du statut de la femme (CSF, 2011, p. 102).

16 The long process of secularization of the Quebec government can be considered as having essentially been completed in 2000 when teaching of the Catholic and Protestant religions in public schools came to an end.

17 On this, see also L. Mailloux (2011). Others, in a similar vein, propose nothing less than the suppression of religions. But how can we suppress religion, which is one of the oldest and most widespread ways in which humans express their need for transcendence?

18 Including the signatories of the "Déclaration des intellectuels pour la laïcité" (*Le Devoir*, 16 March 2010).

19 I could also mention the Universal Declaration of Human Rights, the two United Nations Human Rights Covenants, and the Inter-American Convention on Human Rights. The case of the European Convention on Human Rights is more complicated because of the national margin of appreciation granted to the member countries, which permits them to contravene certain provisions of the convention (this provision has created embarrassing contradictions, as shown by F. Ast, 2011).

20 The debate on this subject dates to the 1990s in Quebec (C. Ciceri, 1999).

21 Some critics call it the "extension of the harem" (L. Mailloux, 2010b, p. 13).

22 It has been shown, in the European context, that this feature is associated with families that have abandoned Islam but want to perpetuate certain rituals as part of their heritage (J. Laurence, 2012).

23 I am relying here mainly on the many submissions made to the Bouchard-Taylor Commission (during the public and private hearings). Empirical data on the subject are insufficient in Quebec. See, however J.-R. Milot and R. Venditti (2012, pp. 259–62).

24 For more balanced comments on this subject, see the editorial by Mario Roy ("Choisir ses peurs" [Choosing Your Fears]) in *La Presse*, 2 December 2011, p. A22, and another by Bernard Descôteaux ("À prendre au sérieux, mais ..." [To Be Taken Seriously, but ...]) in *Le Devoir*, 28, 29 August 2010, p. C4.

25 In 2011, the mayor of that municipality appealed a judgment of the Quebec Human Rights Tribunal, which had ordered him to stop the ritual. On 27 May 2013 Quebec's Court of Appeal ruled that reciting a prayer did not violate the religious neutrality of a city.

26 The merits of this statement have been recognized by the Supreme Court of Canada (A. Decroix, 2011, p. 167).

27 Some liberal-minded authors have shown themselves to be very open to this affirmation of the majority religion, arguing that it would not contravene the principle of the equality of religions. I, however, believe that extreme caution is required here. For a theoretical discussion on this subject, see R. Ahdar and I. Leigh (2004).

28 On this I agree with the opinion of the Conseil du statut de la femme on secularism (CSF, 2011, p. 66).

29 In this regard, we have to be wary of certain commentators who, when they come to the defence of the foundations of Quebec identity, arbitrarily condemn certain religious symbols in the name of secularism while justifying others in the name of heritage.

30 A recent collection of essays (S. Lefebvre, 2009) illustrates this problem effectively. From author to author, the concepts of heritage and religious

differ; see, for example, the chapters by P. Lucier, M. Pelchat, C. Cheyrou, F.-M. Gagnon, R. Brodeur, L. Turgeon, and L. Saint-Pierre.

31 This proposal may be seen as a response to the call formulated by J. Baubérot (2008, pp. 205–54) for what he calls an intercultural secularism, the expression also used by the Québec solidaire party in its brief to the Bouchard-Taylor Commission (p. 9).

32 On this subject, see N. Bouchard and J. Pierre (2006), G. Leroux (2007a, 2007b), and P. Donovan, S. Fournier, A. Gignac, and S. Lavallée (2011). For a broader perspective, see R. F. Magsino (2003).

33 See, for example, J. Quérin (2009), M. Bock-Côté (2009b), M.-M. Poisson (2011), and A. Malenfant-Veilleux (2011). For a succinct defense see L. Rousseau (2011); see also the account by teacher Martin Dubreuil in *Le Devoir,* 7 March 2012, p. A9.

34 With respect to, for example, the wearing of religious symbols by employees of the government and its institutions, all polls show that at least half the population is opposed. However, the proportion of respondents in favour is still substantial (M. Girard, 2008).

35 This chapter was been written before the crisis triggered by the project of the Charter of Quebec Values initiated in September 2013 by the Parti Québécois government.

Conclusion

1 E. Winter (2011, p. 79) expressed a similar idea.

2 This whole problematic operates at the national level, but also within regional frameworks. For example, it is perfectly reproduced, on a reduced scale, in a conflict that occurred in the Saguenay region at the beginning of the twentieth century with respect to a plan for the immigration of Finns who wanted to found a "colony" in that region (G. Bouchard, 1989).

3 There are abundant references on this. Some of the primary sources are M. McAndrew (2001; 2013, chap. 2; 2011a; 2011b), F. Ouellet (1995, chap. 1), and P. Toussaint (2010).

4 As can be seen in the unemployment rate (almost twice as high among immigrants than among other Quebecers) and in the situation of racialized minorities. An equal level of education does not guarantee equality in employment (B. Boudarbat & M. Boulet, 2010); identical jobs can have different pay levels (S. Reichhold, 2011), and immigrants from North Africa are especially affected even when they have superior education (A. Lenoir-Achdjian, S. Arcand, D. Helly, I. Drainville, & M. Vatz Laaroussi, 2009).

5 This problem is also observed at the Canadian level. At the beginning of the decade 2001–2010, racialized minorities made up 6.8 per cent of employees

in the federal public service but represented 13 per cent of the population (P.S. Li, 2003). These data have not changed significantly since.

6 Where they also constitute a small proportion of the labour force. See the excellent study produced in 2009 by the Conseil des relations interculturel-les [Intercultural Relations Council] (CRI, 2009).

7 The existence of this practice was clearly attested by a study by the Commission des droits de la personne et des droits de la jeunesse [Quebec Human Rights and Youth Rights Commission] (CDPDJ, 2011).

8 These observations are based mainly on summary documents from the proceedings of Interculturalism 2011 (G. Nootens & C. Saint-Pierre, 2011; G. Bouchard et al., 2011a). They have been supplemented by many interviews with professionals working in the reception and integration of immigrants in Montreal.

9 On this topic, the Table de concertation des organismes au service des personnes réfugiées et immigrantes (TCRI; Coalition of Organizations Working with Refugees and Immigrants) has drawn up a very critical report on government policies (see the "Bulletin de performance à l'endroit du gouvernement du Québec" published 12 April 2010). The exercise was repeated in spring 2011 with appreciably the same conclusions. This coalition includes 139 organizations working across Quebec (see its website: www.tcri.qc.ca).

10 For a more concrete description of this reality at the level of daily life, see J.-C. Laurence and L.-J. Perreault (2010).

11 A criticism of this kind has been made of British policies. By giving priority to representatives or spokespeople of diversity, they are said to have generated institutional compartmentalization as well as creating a multiethnic mosaic. This is thought to have blocked the integration of young people while favouring the development of fundamentalist movements (K. Malik, 2011).

12 According to a survey conducted in April–June 2011 by Léger Marketing for Hebdos Québec, 42 per cent of respondents believe that immigration is a threat to Quebec culture.

13 We see from this outline that the proposed organization would go far beyond the mandate of the advisory service created by the government in 2008 and attached to the Commission des droits de la personne et des droits de la jeunesse.

14 I should, however, mention here a few recent positive initiatives, for example, F. Kanouté and G. Lafortune (2011) and M. Vatz-Laaroussi (2009).

15 This deficiency has been criticized for a long time; see, for example, M. Potvin (2004, 2005), J. Renaud, A. Germain, and X. Leloup (2004), and M. McAndrew (2007, p. 147). For a recent contribution see M. Labelle (2010).

16 It will be necessary to increase the number of focused studies, such as those presented in L. Rousseau (2012), that look at various ethnocultural minorities in Quebec (Tamil, Cambodian, Congolese, Algerian, etc.).

17 This statement should be qualified in light of the debate around the project of a charter of values that took place between the summer of 2013 and the winter of 2014.

18 We can refer, for example, to the following: an Environics poll of August 2002 on openness to immigration, whose results are summarized in M. Labelle (2006, p. 105); indexes of self-declared discrimination (data from 2002) reported in J.G. Reitz et al. (2009, p. 131); a poll on the perception of various ethnocultural minorities sponsored by the Association for Canadian Studies, reported in *La Presse*, 23 April 2003, p. A5; a June 2007 Ipsos poll on the perception of immigration, reported by *The Gazette*, 20 August 2007, p. A8; an Angus Reid poll on the perception of immigration, September 2010, reported in *Le Devoir*, 10 September 2010, pp. A1, A10; and a study of the Institut de recherche en politiques publiques on support for immigration, commented on in *Le Devoir*, 18 October 2011. Polls conducted during the 1990s had similar results. It should be remembered, however, that other polls carried out on the same subject during the same years gave different results that shed light on and sometimes contradict the polls I have just mentioned. For example, a study carried out recently by A. Bilodeau, L. Turgeon, and E. Karakoç (2012) shows that Quebecers are very open to immigration but rather hesitant with regard to what are called visible minorities. This suggests that we should always take a critical view of the results of this kind of exercise, which are useful, certainly, but sometimes misleading. It is therefore advisable to also refer to in-depth studies, for example, J.H. Carens (1995), E. Grabb and J. Curtis (2004), V. Spencer (2008), and M. Adams (2003, 2007). (Note, however, that these last two books also make extensive use of polls.) Other results have a high level of reliability; this is the case, for example, for data coming from Statistics Canada, and reproduced in *Le Devoir*, 13 April 2012, showing that the rate of hate crimes for the year 2010 was much lower in Quebec than in Ontario (2.7 as opposed to 5.7 per 100,000 inhabitants).

19 Council of Europe, 118th Ministerial Session, White Paper on Intercultural Dialogue: "Living Together as Equals in Dignity" (2008).

20 This is perhaps what explains that, in the review he offers of the major integration models, T. Modood (2012, pp. 10–11, 26–9) gives little space to interculturalism. For a different point of view, see T. Cantle (2011).

21 The approach developed by C. Karnoouh (1998) at the transnational level is an exception. According to this view, interculturalism concerns relations

between nations and civilizations while multiculturalism concerns intercultural relations within nations.

22 This overview of the European situation obviously calls for much more development and many qualifications. I will have to limit myself here to this very brief outline.

Afterword

1 One indication of this lack of knowledge is a statement by the then premier of Quebec, Pauline Marois, touting France as the model to replicate in the area of the integration of immigrants, especially immigrants from North Africa.

2 I am referring in particular to an interview he gave to talk show host Denis Lévesque on the TVA network on 15 May 2013.

3 This afterword is an extended and modified version of Bouchard 2013b.

References

Abdallah-Pretceille, M. (2006). Interculturalism as a Paradigm for Thinking about Diversity. *Intercultural Education, 17*(5), 475–83. http://dx.doi.org/10.1080/14675980601065764.

Abu-Laban, Y., & Gabriel, C. (2002). *Selling Diversity: Immigration, Multiculturalism, Employment Equity and Globalization.* Peterborough: Broadview Press.

Ackerman, B.A. (1980). *Social Justice in the Liberal State.* New Haven: Yale University Press.

Adams, M. (2003). *Fire and Ice: The United States, Canada and the Myth of Converging Values.* Toronto: Penguin.

Adams, M. (2007). *Unlikely Utopia: The Surprising Triumph of Canadian Pluralism.* Toronto: Viking.

Ahdar, R., & Leigh, I. (2004). Is Establishment Consistent with Religious Freedom? *McGill Law Journal/Revue de droit de McGill, 49*(3), 635–81.

Allport, G.W. (1954). *The Nature of Prejudice.* Cambridge, MA: Addison-Wesley.

Anctil, P. (1984). Double majorité et multiplicité ethnoculturelle à Montréal. *Recherches Sociographiques, 25*(3), 441–56. http://dx.doi.org/10.7202/056117ar.

Anctil, P. (1996). La trajectoire interculturelle du Quebec City: La société distincte vue à travers le prisme de l'immigration. In A. Lapierre, P. Smart, & P. Savard (Eds.), *Langues, cultures et valeurs au Canada à l'aube du xxie siècle* (pp. 133–54). Ottawa: Conseil international d'études canadiennes/Carleton University Press.

Angus, I. (1997). *A Border Within: National Identity, Cultural Plurality, and Wilderness.* Montreal/Kingston: McGill-Queen's University Press.

Angus, I. (1998). The Originality of the Multicultural Context. In D. Haselbach (Ed.), *Multiculturalism in a World of Leaking Boundaries* (pp. 65–99). Münster: Literatur Verlag.

Apparicio, P., & Séguin, A.-M. (2008). *Retour sur les notions de ségrégation et de ghetto ethniques et examen des cas de Montréal, Toronto et Vancouver.* Montreal: Institut national de la recherche scientifique, Urbanisation, Culture et Société.

Aquin, H. (1962). La fatigue culturelle du Canada français. *Liberté, 4*(23), 299–325.

Armony, V. (2010). Les rapports majorité/minorités au Quebec City: Question culturelle ou enjeu de pouvoir? In B. Gagnon (Ed.), *La Diversité québécoise en débat: Bouchard, Taylor et les autres* (pp. 77–92). Montreal: Québec Amérique.

Ast, F. (2011). La capacité de l'Europe à accommoder les autres cultures: La diabolisation de l'interculturalisme? In G. Bouchard, G. Battaini-Dragoni, C. Saint-Pierre, G. Nootens, & F. Fournier (Ed.), *L'Interculturalisme: Dialogue Québec-Europe.* Actes du Symposium international sur l'interculturalisme, Montreal, 25–27 May 2011. http://www.symposium-interculturalisme.com.

Azdouz, R. (2009). Libre opinion – L'État de droit et le manichéisme. *Le Devoir,* 10 December, p. A6.

Bader, V. (2007). Defending Differentiated Policies of Multiculturalism. *National Identities, 9*(3), 197–215. http://dx.doi.org/10.1080/14608940701406187.

Banting, K., & Kymlicka, W. (Eds.). (2006). *Multiculturalism and the Welfare State: Recognition and Redistribution in Contemporary Democracies.* New York: Oxford University Press. http://dx.doi.org/10.1093/acprof:oso/9780199289172.001.0001.

Baril, G. (2008). L'Interculturalisme: Le modèle québécois de gestion de la diversité culturelle. Master's thesis, Université de Montréal.

Bariteau, C. (1996). Pour une conception civique du Québec. *L'Action Nationale (Toulouse), 86*(7), 105–68.

Bariteau, C. (1998). *Québec 18 septembre 2001: Le monde pour horizon.* Montreal: Québec Amérique.

Barnes, L., & Hall, P.A. (2013). Neoliberalism and Social Resilience in the Developed Democracies. In M. Lamont & P.A. Hall (Eds.), *Social Resilience in the Neo-Liberal Era* (pp. 209–38). Cambridge: Cambridge University Press. http://dx.doi.org/10.1017/CBO9781139542425.013.

Barth, F. (Ed.). (1969). *Ethnic Groups and Boundaries: The Social Organization of Culture Difference.* Bergen, Norway: Universitetsforlaget.

Battaini-Dragoni, G. (2009). *Address to the Conference "Human Rights in Culturally Diverse Societies."* Strasbourg: Council of Europe, Directorate General of Human Rights and Legal Affairs.

Baubérot, J. (2004). Voile, école, femmes, laïcité. In A. Houziaux (Ed.), *Le voile, que cache-t-il?* (p. 49–78). Ivry-sur-Seine, France: Les Éditions de l'Atelier.

Baubérot, J. (2006). *L'Intégrisme républicain contre la laïcité*. La Tour-d'Aigues: Éditions de l'Aube.

Baubérot, J. (2008). *Une laïcité interculturelle: Le Québec, avenir de la France?*. La Tour-d'Aigue: Éditions de l'Aube.

Baubérot, J., & Milot, M. (2011). *Laïcité sans frontières*. Paris: Seuil.

Beauchemin, J. (2002). Le poids de la mémoire franco-québécoise dans un Québec pluraliste. *GLOBE: Revue Internationale d'Etudes Quebecoises, 5*(2), 21–55. http://dx.doi.org/10.7202/1000678ar.

Beauchemin, J. (2003). Qu'est-ce qu'être Québécois? In A.-G. Gagnon, Ed., *Québec: État et Société* (vol. 2, pp. 27–43). Montreal: Québec Amérique.

Beauchemin, J. (2004). Entre la loi du marché et l'individualisme. *Le Devoir,* 12 July, p. A7.

Beauchemin, J. (2005). *La Société des identités: Éthique et politique in le monde contemporain*. Outremont, QC: Éditions Athéna.

Beauchemin, J. (2010a). Accueillir sans reconcer à soi-même. *Le Devoir,* 22 January, p. A9.

Beauchemin, J. (2010b). Le pluralisme identitaire et le conflit des mémoires au Québec. In J.-F. Plamondon & A. de Vaucher (Eds.), *Les Enjeux du pluralisme: L'actualité du modèle québécois* (pp. 77–90). Bologna: Edizioni Pendragon.

Belkhodja, C. (2008). Le discours de la 'nouvelle sensibilité conservatrice' au Québec. *Études ethniques canadiennes, 40*(1), 79–100.

Bellah, R.N. (1967). Civil Religion in America. *Daedalus, 96*(1), 1–21.

Benhabib, D. (2011). *Les Soldats d'Allah à l'assaut de l'Occident*. Montreal: VLB.

Bennett, T., Grossberg, L., & Morris, M. (Eds.). (2005). *New Keywords: A Revised Vocabulary of Culture and Society*. Malden, MA: Blackwell.

Bernier, L. (2008). *Recherche sur l'origine du vocable "interculturalisme" au Québec*. Montreal: Consultation Commission on Accommodation Practices Related to Cultural Differences, 22 March. Document no. 23.

Bhargava, R. (2010). Hegel, Taylor and the Phenomenology of Broken Spirits. In M. Seymour (Ed.), *The Plural States of Recognition: Citizenship and Identity* (pp. 37–60). Basingstoke: Palgrave Macmillan.

Bilodeau, A. (2011). Is Democracy the Only Game in Town? Tension Between Immigrants' Democratic Desires and Authoritarian Imprints. Paper presented at the conference "The Political Incorporation of Immigrants: Progress, Prospects and Pitfalls in Europe and North America." University of California Berkeley, 4–5 March.

Bilodeau, A., McAllister, I., & Kanji, M. (2010). Adaptation to Democracy among Immigrants in Australia. *International Political Science Review, 31*(2), 141–65. http://dx.doi.org/10.1177/0192512110364737.

Bilodeau, A., Turgeon, L., & Karakoç, E. (2012). Small Worlds of Diversity: Views toward Immigration and Racial Minorities in Canadian Provinces. *Revue canadienne de science politique, 45*(3), 579–605. http://dx.doi.org/10.1017/S0008423912000728.

Bissoondath, N. (1994). *Selling Illusions: The Cult of Multiculturalism in Canada 1994.* Toronto: Penguin.

Blad, C., & Couton, P. (2009). The Rise of an Intercultural Nation: Immigration, Diversity and Nationhood in Quebec. *Journal of Ethnic and Migration Studies, 35*(4), 645–67. http://dx.doi.org/10.1080/13691830902765277.

Bloemraad, I. (2006). *Becoming a Citizen: Incorporating Immigrants and Refugees in the United States and Canada.* Berkeley: University of California Press.

Bloemraad, I. (2007). Unity in Diversity? Bridging Models of Multiculturalism and Immigrant Integration. *Du Bois Review: Social Science Research on Race, 4*(2), 317–36.

Bock-Côté, M. (2006). Penser à l'abri du pluralisme: Genèse du multiculturalisme in la politique contemporaine. *Controverses, 1,* 122–46.

Bock-Côté, M. (2007). *La Dénationalisation tranquille: Mémoire, identité et multiculturalisme in le Québec postréférendaire.* Montreal: Boréal.

Bock-Côté, M. (2008). À défaut de convaincre le peuple, en fabriquer un nouveau. *L'Action Nationale (Toulouse), 98*(7), 107–32.

Bock-Côté, M. (2009a). L'identité occidentale du Québec ou l'émergence d'une "cultural war" à la québécoise. *Recherches Sociographiques, 50*(3), 537–70.

Bock-Côté, M. (2009b). La fabrique du multiculturalisme: Le cours éthique et culture religieuse en contexte. *L'Action Nationale (Toulouse), 99*(7), 18–31.

Bock-Côté, M. (2010). Dérapage à la française? Le débat sur l'identité nationale française. *L'Action Nationale (Toulouse), 100*(2), 67–76.

Bosset, P. (2009). Accommodement raisonnable et égalité des sexes: Tensions, contradictions et interdépendance. In P. Eid, P. Bosset, M. Milot, & S. Lebel-Grenier (Eds.), *Appartenances religieuses, appartenance citoyenne: Un équilibre en tension* (pp. 181–206). Quebec City: Presses de l'Université Laval.

Bouchard, G. (1989). Les Saguenayens et les immigrants au début du xxe siècle: Légitime défense ou xénophobie. *Canadian Ethnic Studies/Études ethniques au Canada, 21*(3), 20–36.

Bouchard, G. (1990). Représentations de la population et de la société québécoises: L'apprentissage de la diversité. *Cahiers Quebecois de Demographie, 19*(1), 7–28. http://dx.doi.org/10.7202/010031ar.

Bouchard, G. (1995). La nation au singulier et au pluriel: L'avenir de la culture nationale comme "paradigme" de la société québécoise. *Cahiers de Recherche Sociologique, 25*(25), 79–99. http://dx.doi.org/10.7202/1002292ar.

Bouchard, G. (1999). *La Nation québécoise au futur et au passé.* Montreal: VLB.

Bouchard, G. (2000). *Genèse des nations et cultures du Nouveau Monde: Essai d'histoire comparée.* Montreal: Boréal.

Bouchard, G. (2001a). Nation et co-intégration: Contre la pensée dichotomique. In J. Maclure & A.-G. Gagnon (Eds.), *Repères en mutation. Identité et citoyenneté in le Québec contemporain* (pp. 21–36). Montreal: Québec Amérique.

Bouchard, G. (2001b). Sur le modèle de la nation québécoise et la conception de la nation chez Fernand Dumont. *Bulletin d'Histoire Politique, 9*(2), 144–59.

Bouchard, G. (2003). Promouvoir ce qu'il y a de plus universel in notre passé. *Le Devoir,* 30 January, p. A9.

Bouchard, G. (2007). "Le mythe: Essai de définition." In G. Bouchard & B. Andrès, *Mythes et sociétés des Amériques* (pp. 409–26). Montreal: Québec Amérique.

Bouchard, G. (2011). What Is Interculturalism? *McGill Law Journal/Revue de Droit de McGill, 56*(2), 435–68.

Bouchard, G. (2013a). Neoliberalism in Québec: The Response of a Small Nation under Pressure. In P.A. Hall & M. Lamont (Eds.), *Social Resilience in a Liberal Era* (pp. 247–92). Cambridge: Cambridge University Press.

Bouchard, G. (2013b). The Struggle about Secularism in Quebec. *News and Ideas,* no. 8 (November).

Bouchard, G., Battaini-Dragoni, G., Saint-Pierre, C., Nootens, G., & Fournier, F. (2011a). *Symposium international sur l'interculturalisme: Rapport d'activités.* Université du Québec à Chicoutimi, Document I-E-45 de la Chaire de recherche du Canada sur l'étude comparée des imaginaires collectifs, 26 May.

Bouchard, G., Battaini-Dragoni, G., Saint-Pierre, C., Nootens, G., & Fournier, F. (Eds.) (2011b). *L'Interculturalisme: Dialogue Québec-Europe.* Actes du Symposium international sur l'interculturalisme, Montreal, 25–27 May 2011. http://www.symposium-interculturalisme.com.

Bouchard, G., & Taylor, C. (2008). *Building the Future: A Time for Reconciliation.* Report of the Consultation Commission on Accommodation Practices Related to Cultural Differences. Quebec City: Gouvernement du Québec.

Boudarbat, B., & Boulet, M. (2010). *Immigration au Québec: Politiques et intégration au marché du travail.* Montréal: CIRANO.

Brett, J., & Moran, A. (2011). Cosmopolitan Nationalism: Ordinary People Making Sense of Diversity. *Nations and Nationalism, 17*(1), 188–206. http://dx.doi.org/10.1111/j.1469-8129.2010.00451.x.

Bribosia, E., & Rorive, I. (2010). *In Search of a Balance between the Right to Equality and Other Fundamental Rights.* Brussels: Publications Office of the European Union.

Brochu, A. (2008). L'assimilation soft: Libre réflexion sur un sujet tabou. *L'Inconvénient, 35,* 23–32.

Brouillet, E. (2005). *La Négation de la nation: L'identité culturelle québécoise et le fédéralisme canadien.* Sillery, QC: Septentrion.

Brown, D. (2008). The Ethnic Majority: Benign or Malign? *Nations and Nationalism, 14*(4), 768–88. http://dx.doi.org/10.1111/j.1469-8129 .2008.00330.x.

Brown, R., & Hewstone, M. (2005). An Integrative Theory of Intergroup Contact. *Advances in Experimental Social Psychology, 37,* 255–343. http://dx.doi .org/10.1016/S0065-2601(05)37005-5.

Brubaker, R. (1998). Myths and Misconceptions in the Study of Nationalism (pp. 272–306). In J.A. Hall (Ed.), *The State of the Nation: Ernest Gellner and the Theory of Nationalism.* Cambridge: Cambridge University Press. http://dx.doi .org/10.1017/CBO9780511897559.013.

Brubaker, R. (2001). The Return of Assimilation? Changing Perspectives on Immigration and Its Sequels in France, Germany and the United States. *Ethnic and Racial Studies, 24*(4), 531–48. http://dx.doi.org/10.1080/ 01419870120049770.

Brubaker, R. (2004). *Ethnicity without Groups.* Cambridge, MA: Harvard University Press.

Brudny, Y. (2013). Mythology, National Identity, and Democracy in Post-Communist Russia. In G. Bouchard (Ed.), *National Myths: Conflicted Pasts, Contested Presents* (pp. 133–56). New York: Routledge.

Calhoun, C. (2007). *Nations Matter: Culture, History, and the Cosmopolitan Dream.* London: Routledge.

Canada. (2011). *Inter-Action: Canada's New Multiculturalism Grants & Contributions Program.* Ottawa: Citizenship and Immigration Canada. http://www.cic .gc.ca/english/multiculturalism/funding/Inter-Action_Events_Guidelines .pdf.

Canada. Statistics Canada. Minister of Industry. (2010). *Projections of the Diversity of the Canadian Population, 2006 to 2031.* No. 91–551-x. Ottawa: Statistics Canada.

Canovan, M. (1996). *Nationhood and Political Theory.* Cheltenham, UK: Edward Elgar.

Cantin, S. (2002). Quel avenir pour notre mémoire? *Possibles, 26*(1–2), 40–54.

Cantle, T. (2011). Cohesion and Integration: From "Multi" to "Inter" Culturalism. In G. Bouchard, G. Battaini-Dragoni, C. Saint-Pierre, G. Nootens, & F. Fournier (Eds.), *L'Interculturalisme: Dialogue Québec-Europe.* Actes du Symposium international sur l'interculturalisme, Montreal, 25–27 May 2011. http://www.symposium-interculturalisme.com.

Caponio, T., & Borkert, M. (Eds.). (2010). *The Local Dimension of Migration Policymaking.* Amsterdam: Amsterdam University Press. http://dx.doi.org/ 10.5117/9789089642325.

Cardinal, L. (2010). Language Policy-Making and Planning in Quebec and in Canada. In R. Jarrett, S. Gervais, & C. Kirkey (Eds.), *Quebec Questions: Quebec Studies for the Twenty-First Century* (pp. 186–203). Oxford: Oxford University Press.

Cardinal, L. (2011). L'avenir du français in un Québec interculturel. In G. Bouchard, G. Battaini-Dragoni, C. Saint-Pierre, G. Nootens, & F. Fournier (Eds.), *L'Interculturalisme: Dialogue Québec-Europe*. Actes du Symposium international sur l'interculturalisme, Montreal, 25–27 May 2011. http://www.symposium-interculturalisme.com.

Carens, J.H. (1995). *Is Quebec Nationalism Just? Perspectives from Anglophone Canada*. Montreal/Kingston: McGill-Queen's University Press.

Castells, M. (1997). *The Power of Identity*. Malden, MA: Blackwell.

Chollet, A. (2011). Switzerland as a "Fractured Nation." *Nations and Nationalism*, *17*(4), 738–55. http://dx.doi.org/10.1111/j.1469-8129.2011.00520.x.

Ciceri, C., in collaboration with the Centre de recherche interuniversitaire de Montréal sur l'immigration l'intégration et la dynamique urbaine. (1999). *Le Foulard islamique à l'école publique: Analyse comparée du débat in la presse française et québécoise francophone (1994–1995)*. Montreal: Immigration et métropoles.

Cohen-Emerique, M., & Fayman, S. (2005). Médiateurs interculturels, passerelles d'identités. *Connexions*, *83*(1), 169–90. http://dx.doi.org/10.3917/cnx.083.0169.

Coleman, J.S. (1990). *Foundations of Social Theory*. Cambridge, MA: Belknap.

Commission des Droits de la personne et des droits de la Jeunesse. (CDPDJ). (2010). *Enquête systémique dans le dossier des médecins diplômés hors du Canada et des États-Unis (DHCEU)*. Montreal: CDPDJ.

Commission des Droits de la personne et des droits de la Jeunesse. (CDPDJ). (2011). *Profilage racial et discrimination systémique des jeunes racisés: Rapport de la consultation sur le profilage racial et ses conséquences*. Montreal: CDPDJ.

Conseil des communautés culturelles et de l'immigration du Québec (CCCI). (1988). *Avis à la ministre des Communautés culturelles et de l'Immigration du Québec relatif au projet de Loi C-93 sur le maintien et la valorisation du multiculturalisme au Canada*. Montreal: CCCI.

Conseil des communautés culturelles et de l'immigration du Québec (CCCI). (1993). *Gérer la diversité dans un Québec francophone, démocratique et pluraliste: Principes de fond et procédure pour guider la recherche d'accommodements raisonnables*. Supplementary study submitted to the Ministre des Communautés culturelles et de l'Immigration. Montreal: CCCI.

Conseil des Relations Interculturelles (CRI). (2009). *Une représentation et un traitement équitables de la diversité ethnoculturelle in les médias et la publicité au Québec*. Brief submitted to the Minister of Immigration and Cultural Communities, Montreal, June.

Conseil du Statut de la Femme (CSF). (2011). *Avis: Affirmer la laïcité, un pas de plus vers l'égalité réelle entre les femmes et les hommes.* Quebec City: CSF.

Corbeil, J.-C. (2009). La langue française au Québec face à ses défis. In R. Laliberté (Ed.), *À la rencontre d'un Québec qui bouge: Introduction générale au Québec* (pp. 107–20). Paris: Éditions du CTHS.

Council of Europe (2005). *Methodological Guide to the Concerted Development of Social Cohesion Indicators.* Strasbourg: Council of Europe Publishing.

Council of Europe (2008). *White Paper on Intercultural Dialogue: "Living Together As Equals in Dignity."* Strasbourg: Council of Europe Publishing.

Courtois, C.-P. (2008). Bouchard-Taylor: Lectures malcommodes – Un rapport trudeauiste. *L'Action Nationale (Toulouse), 98*(9–10), 60–80.

Courtois, C.-P. & Rousseau, G. (2010). Intégration et laïcité: D'autres voies sont possibles. *Le Devoir,* 25 January, p. A7.

Couture, J. (1995). Pourquoi devrait-il y avoir un conflit entre le nationalisme et le libéralisme politique? In F. Blais, G. Laforest, & D. Lamoureux (Eds.), *Libéralismes et Nationalismes* (pp. 51–75). Quebec City: Presses de l'Université Laval.

Couture, J. (1999). Pour une démocratie globale: Solidarité cosmopolitique ou solidarité nationale? In M. Seymour (Ed.), *Nationalité, citoyenneté et solidarité* (pp. 289–321). Montreal: Liber.

Decroix, A. (2011). Pluralisme et idéologie: L'exemple canadien. In O. Benoist & H. Isar (Eds.), *Pluralisme, pluralismes* (pp. 151–68). Aix-en-Provence: Presses universitaires d'Aix-Marseille.

de la Peña, G. (2006). A New Mexican Nationalism? Indigenous Rights, Constitutional Reform and the Conflicting Meanings of Multiculturalism. *Nations and Nationalism, 12*(2), 279–302. http://dx.doi.org/10.1111/j.1469-8129.2006.00241.x.

Delcroix, C. (1996). Rôles joués par les médiatrices socioculturelles au sein du développement local et urbain. *Espaces et Sociétés (Paris, France), 84–85,* 153–176.

Delphy, C. (2002). *L'Ennemi principal: Penser le genre.* Vol. 2. Paris: Syllepse.

Derriennic, J.-P. (1995). *Nationalisme et Démocratie: Réflexion sur les illusions des indépendantistes québécois.* Montreal: Boréal.

Déry, P.-L. (2009). Le rapport entre la majorité et les minorités in la formation de l'identité nationale québécoise. Master's thesis, Université du Québec à Montréal.

Detry, Robert (1981). Les adolescents migrants en crise d'intégration scolaire et sociale: Témoignages et expériences à propos de l'interculturalisme. *Les Cahiers JEB.* Belgium: Ministère de l'Éducation nationale et de la Culture française, Direction générale de la jeunesse et des loisirs, no. 1.

Dieckhoff, A. (2000). *La Nation dans tous ses États: Les identités nationales en mouvement.* Paris: Flammarion.

Doane, A.W., Jr., (1993). Bringing the Majority Back In: Towards a Sociology of Dominant Group Ethnicity. Paper presented at the annual meeting of the Society for the Study of Social Problems, Miami Beach, FL, 10–13 August.

Donati, P. (2009). Beyond the Dilemmas of Multiculturalism: Recognition through "Relational Reason." *International Review of Sociology, 19*(1), 55–82. http://dx.doi.org/10.1080/03906700802613947.

Donovan, P., Fournier, S., Gignac, A., & Lavallée, S. (2011). *La Religion sans confession: Regards sur le cours d'éthique et culture religieuse.* Montreal: Médiaspaul.

Drouilly, P. (2007). *L'élection fédérale du 23 janvier 2006: Au Québec, une élection toute en ambiguïtés.* Montreal: Institut du Nouveau Monde. http://archives .inm.qc.ca/pdf/publications/annuaire/2007/ann0013.pdf.

Dubreuil, B. & Marois, G. (2011). *Le Remède imaginaire.* Montreal: Boréal.

Dumont, F. (1995). *Raisons communes.* Montreal: Boréal.

Dworkin, R. (1978). *Taking Rights Seriously.* Cambridge, MA: Harvard University Press.

Dworkin, R. (1985). Liberalism. In Dworkin, *A Matter of Principle* (pp. 181–204). Cambridge, MA: Harvard University Press.

Eberhard, C. (2001). Towards an Intercultural Legal Theory: The Dialogical Challenge. *Social & Legal Studies, 10*(2), 171–201.

Eberhard, C. (2011). *Droits de l'homme et dialogue interculturel.* Paris: Éditions Connaissances et Savoirs.

Edwardson, R. (2008). *Canadian Content: Culture and the Quest for Nationhood.* Toronto: University of Toronto Press.

Eid, P. (Ed.). (2009). *Pour une véritable intégration: Droit au travail sans discrimination.* Montreal: Fides.

Elenius, L. (2010). Symbolic Charisma and the Creation of Nations: The Case of the Sami. *Studies in Ethnicity and Nationalism, 10*(3), 467–82. http://dx.doi .org/10.1111/j.1754-9469.2011.01088.x.

Emerson, M. (2011). Summary and Conclusions. In Emerson (Ed.), *Interculturalism: Europe and Its Muslims in Search of Sound Societal Models* (pp. 1–16). Brussels: Centre for European Policy Studies.

Erfurt, J. (2010). Interculturalisme: Les défis glottopolitiques pour l'État québécois et pour la nouvelle francophonie. In Y. Lamonde & J. Livernois (Eds.), *Culture québécoise et valeurs universelles* (pp. 417–35). Quebec City: Presses de l'Université Laval.

Eriksen, T.H. (2007). Ernest Gellner and the Multicultural Mess. In S. Malesevic & M. Haugaard (Eds.), *Ernest Gellner and Contemporary Social Thought* (pp. 168–86). Cambridge: Cambridge University Press.

Facal, J. (2009). L'idéologie multiculturaliste contre la nation québécoise. In L.-A. Richard (Ed.), *La Nation sans la religion? Le défi des ancrages au Québec* (pp. 155–85). Quebec City: Presses de l'Université Laval.

Facal, J. (2010). *Quelque chose comme un grand peuple: Essai sur la condition québécoise.* Montreal: Boréal.

Fiore, A.M. (2010). La communauté sud-asiatique de Montréal: Urbanité et multiplicité des formes de capital social immigrant. Doctoral dissertation, Institut national de la recherche scientifique (INRS).

Fontaine, Louise (1993). *Un labyrinthe carré comme un cercle: Enquête sur le ministère des Communautés culturelles et de l'Immigration et sur ses acteurs réels et imaginés.* Montreal: Étincelle Éditeur.

Forbes, D. (2007). Immigration and Multiculturalism vs. Quebec Separatism: An Interpretation of Canadian Constitutional Politics since 1968. Paper presented at the annual meeting of the American Political Science Association, Chicago, 1 September.

Fournier, F. (2008). *Les Écoles privées ethniques de confession juive, musulmane et orthodoxe.* Memo no. 14, Consultation Commission on Accommodation Practices Related to Cultural Differences. Québec: Gouvernement du Québec.

Fournier, F., & Bellemare, É.D. (2012). *Neutralité et neutralité culturelle de l'État: Revue de la littérature.* Document I-E-51 de la Chaire de recherche du Canada sur l'étude comparée des imaginaires collectifs, Université du Québec à Chicoutimi, May.

Fourot, A.-C. (2010). Managing Religious Pluralism in Canadian Cities: Mosques in Montreal and Laval. In T. Caponio & M. Borkert (Eds.), *The Local Dimension of Migration Policymaking* (pp. 135–59). Amsterdam: Amsterdam University Press.

Gagnon, A.-G. (2000a). Unity and Diversity in Canada – Under Trudeau and Chrétien. In D. Austin & M. O'Neill (Eds.), *Democracy and Cultural Diversity* (pp. 12–26). Oxford: Oxford University Press.

Gagnon, A.-G. (2000b). Plaidoyer pour l'interculturalisme. *Possibles*, 24(4), 11–25.

Gagnon, A.-G. (2007). *Au-delà de la nation unificatrice: Plaidoyer pour le fédéralisme multinational.* Barcelona: Institut d'Estudis Autonòmics (Generalitat de Catalunya).

Gagnon, A.-G. (2010). La diversité et la place du Québec au sein de la fédération canadienne. In B. Gagnon (Ed.), *La Diversité québécoise en débat: Bouchard, Taylor et les autres* (pp. 247–61). Montreal: Québec Amérique.

Gagnon, A.-G. (2011). *L'Âge des incertitudes: Essais sur le fédéralisme et la diversité nationale.* Quebec City: Presses de l'Université Laval.

Gagnon, A.-G., & Iacovino, R. (2002). Framing Citizenship Status in an Age of Polyethnicity: Quebec's Model of Interculturalism. In H. Telford & H. Lazar

(Eds.), *Canadian Political Culture(s) in Transition* (pp. 313–42). Montreal/
Kingston: McGill-Queen's University Press.

Gagnon, A.-G., & Iacovino, R. (2003). Le projet interculturel québécois et
l'élargissement des frontières de la citoyenneté. In A.-G. Gagnon (Ed.),
Québec: État et société, vol. 2 (pp. 413–38). Montreal: Québec Amérique.

Gagnon, A.-G., & Iacovino, R. (2007). *De la nation à la multination: Les rapports
Québec-Canada*. Montreal: Boréal.

Gagnon, A.-G., & Jézéquel, M. (2004). Pour une reconnaissance mutuelle et un
accommodement raisonnable: Le modèle québécois d'intégration culturelle
est à préserver. *Le Devoir*, 17 May, p. A7.

Gagnon, A.-G., Lecours, A., & Nootens, G. (Eds.) (2007). *Les Nationalismes majoritaires contemporains: Identité, mémoire, pouvoir*. Montreal: Québec Amérique.

Gagnon, B. (Ed.). (2010). *La Diversité québécoise en débat: Bouchard, Taylor et les
autres*. Montreal: Québec Amérique.

Gagnon, G. (1988). Plaidoyer pour la convergence culturelle. *Possibles*, *12*(3),
37–44.

Gagnon, N. (2000). Comment peut-on être Québécois? *Recherches Sociographiques*,
41(3), 545–66. http://dx.doi.org/10.7202/057396ar.

Galston, W.A. (1991). *Liberal Purposes: Goods, Virtues, and Diversity in the Liberal
State*. Cambridge: Cambridge University Press. http://dx.doi.org/10.1017/
CBO9781139172462.

Gaudreault-Desbiens, J.-F., & Labrèche, D. (2009). *Le Contexte social du droit in le
Québec contemporain: L'intelligence culturelle in la pratique des juristes*. Cowansville,
QC: Éditions Yvon Blais.

Geadah, Y. (2007). *Accommodements raisonnables: Droit à la différence et non différence
des droits*. Montreal: VLB.

Gervais, S., Lamoureux, D., & Karmis, D. (2008). *Du tricoté serré au métissé serré?
La culture publique commune au Québec en débats*. Quebec City: Presses de
l'Université Laval.

Gibson, K.L., McKelvie, S.J., & de Man, A.F. (2008). Personality and Culture: A
Comparison of Francophones and Anglophones in Québec. *Journal of Social
Psychology*, *148*(2), 133–65. http://dx.doi.org/10.3200/SOCP.148.2.133-166.

Gidengil, E., Blais, A., Nadeau, R., & Nevitte, N. (2003). La langue française
et l'insécurité culturelle. In A.-G. Gagnon (Ed.), *Québec: État et société* (vol. 2,
pp. 389–412). Montreal: Québec Amérique.

Girard, M. (2008). *Résumé de résultats de sondages portant sur la perception des
Québécois relativement aux accommodements raisonnables, à l'immigration, aux com-
munautés culturelles et à l'identité canadienne-française*. Report no. 19. Quebec
City: Consultation Commission on Accommodation Practices Related to
Cultural Differences.

Girard, N. (2011). Le pari moderne et civique du multiculturalisme canadien. In G. Bouchard, G. Battaini-Dragoni, C. Saint-Pierre, G. Nootens,
& F. Fournier (Eds.), *L'Interculturalisme: Dialogue Québec-Europe*. Actes du
Symposium international sur l'interculturalisme, Montreal, 25–27 May 2011.
http://www.symposium-interculturalisme.com.

Giroux, F. (1997). Le nouveau contrat national est-il possible in une démocratie
pluraliste? Examen comparatif des situations française, canadienne et québécoise. *Politique et Sociétés, 16*(3), 129–47. http://dx.doi.org/10.7202/040086ar.

Goodhart, D. (2004). Too Diverse? *Prospect, 95*, 30–7.

Goodhart, D. (2006). *Progressive Nationalism: Citizenship and the Left*. London:
Demos.

Grabb, E., & Curtis, J. (2004). *Regions Apart: The Four Societies of Canada and the
United States*. Toronto: Oxford University Press.

Grammond, S. (2009). Conceptions canadienne et québécoise des droits fondamentaux et de la religion: Convergence ou conflit? *Revue juridique Thémis,
43*(83), 83–108.

Gratton, D. (2009). *L'Interculturel pour tous: Une initiation à la communication pour
le troisième millénaire*. Anjou, QC: Éditions Saint-Martin.

Gray, J. (2000). *Two Faces of Liberalism*. New York: New Press.

Gray, J. (2002). The Myth of Secularism. *New Statesman, 15* (16–30 December),
69–71.

Gregg, B. (2003). *Thick Moralities, Thin Politics: Social Integration Across
Communities of Belief*. Durham, NC: Duke University Press. http://dx.doi.org/
10.1215/9780822384526.

Grenier, A. (2011). Les pénuries de main-d'oeuvre guettent-elles le marché du
travail québécois? *Regards sur le travail, 7*(2), 1–12.

Guibernau, M. (2007). *The Identity of Nations*. Malden, MA: Polity.

Guillaumin, C. (1972). *L'Idéologie raciste: Genèse et langage actuel*. Paris: Mouton.

Hamde, K. (2008). The Current Debate on Cultural Diversity in Sweden.
Journal of Cultural Diversity, 15(2), 86–92.

Harvey, F. (1986). L'ouverture du Québec au multiculturalisme (1900–1981).
Etudes Canadiennes/Canadian Studies, 21(2), 219–28.

Helly, D. (1996). *Le Québec face à la pluralité culturelle 1977–1994: Un bilan docu-
mentaire des politiques*. Sainte-Foy, QC: Institut québécois de recherches sur la
culture/Presses de l'Université Laval.

Helly, D. (2000). Le multiculturalisme canadien: De la promotion des cultures
immigrées à la cohésion sociale, 1971–1999. *Cahiers de l'URMIS, 6*, 7–20.

Helly, D. (2002). Cultural Pluralism: An Overview of the Debate since the 60s.
Global Review of Ethnopolitics, 2(1), 75–96. http://dx.doi.org/10.1080/
14718800208405126.

Helly, D., & Van Schendel, N. (2001). *Appartenir au Québec. Citoyenneté, nation et société civile. Enquête à Montréal, 1995.* Sainte-Foy, QC: Presses de l'Université Laval.

Henderson, A., & McEwen, N. (2005). Do Shared Values Underpin National Identity? Examining the Role of Values in National Identity in Canada and the United Kingdom. *National Identities, 7*(2), 173–91. http://dx.doi.org/10.1080/14608940500144286.

Hewstone, M. (2009). Living Apart, Living Together? The Role of Intergroup Contact in Social Integration. *Proceedings of the British Academy, 162,* 243–300.

Hewstone, M., Cairns, E., Voci, A., Hamberger, J., & Niens, U. (2006). Intergroup Contact, Forgiveness and Experience of "The Troubles" in Northern Ireland. *Journal of Social Issues, 62*(1), 99–120. http://dx.doi.org/10.1111/j.1540-4560.2006.00441.x.

Hewstone, M., Tausch, N., Hughes, J., & Cairns, E. (2007). Prejudice, Intergroup Contact and Identity: Do Neighbourhoods Matter? In M. Wetherell, M. Laflèche, & R. Berkeley (Eds.), *Identity, Ethnic Diversity and Community Cohesion* (pp. 102–112). London: Sage. http://dx.doi.org/10.4135/9781446216071.n9.

Hollinger, D.A. (1996). *Postethnic America: Beyond Multiculturalism.* New York: Basic.

Honneth, A. (1995). *The Struggle for Recognition: The Moral Grammar of Social Conflicts.* Trans. J. Anderson. Cambridge, UK: Polity. Originally published as *Kampf um Anerkennung, 1992.*

Howes, D. (2005). Introduction: La culture dans le domaine du droit. *Revue Canadienne Droit et Société, 20*(1), 31–42.

Huntington, S.P. (1996). *The Clash of Civilizations and the Remaking of World Order.* New York: Simon & Schuster.

Iacovino, R. (2009). En matière de reconnaissance du pluralisme ethnoculturel, le Québec a-t-il les moyens de ses ambitions? In B. Gagnon (Ed.), *La Diversité québécoise en débat: Bouchard, Taylor et les autres* (pp. 204–22). Montreal: Québec Amérique.

Iacovino, R., & Sévigny, C.-A. (2010). Between Unity and Diversity: Examining the Quebec Model" of Integration. In S. Gervais, C. Kirkey, & J. Rudy (Eds.), *Quebec Questions: Quebec Studies for the Twenty-First Century* (pp. 249–66). Don Mills, ON: Oxford University Press.

Intercultural Institute of Montreal. (2007a). *Le Québec pluraliste à la lumière d'une pratique interculturelle.* Brief presented to the Consultation Commission on Accommodation Practices Related to Cultural Differences.

Intercultural Institute of Montreal. (2007b). Médiation interculturelle. *INTERculture,* no. 153.

James, M. (2008). *Interculturalism: Theory and Policy.* London: Baring Foundation.

Jedwab, Jack (2011). Multicultural vs. Intercultural: A Superficial Exercise in Branding. *The Gazette*, 8 March, p. A25.

Joncas, P. (2009). *Les Accommodements raisonnables. Entre Hérouxville et Outremont. La liberté de religion in un État de droit.* Quebec City: Presses de l'Université Laval.

Juteau, D. (1994). Multiculturalisme, interculturalisme et production de la nation. In M. Fourier & G. Vermès (Eds.), *Ethnicisation des rapports sociaux: Racismes, nationalismes, ethnicismes et culturalismes* (pp. 55–72). Paris: L'Harmattan.

Juteau, D. (1996). Theorising Ethnicity and Ethnic Communalisations at the Margins: From Quebec to the World System. *Nations and Nationalism, 2*(1), 45–66. http://dx.doi.org/10.1111/j.1354-5078.1996.00045.x.

Juteau, D. (1999). *L'Ethnicité et ses frontières.* Montreal: Presses de l'Université de Montréal.

Juteau, D. (2002). The Citizen Makes an Entrée: Redefining the National Community in Quebec. *Citizenship Studies, 6*(4), 441–58. http://dx.doi.org/10.1080/1362102022000041268a.

Juteau, D., McAndrew, M., & Pietrantonio, L. (1998). Multiculturalism à la Canadian and Integration à la Québécoise. In R. Bauböck & J. Rundell (Eds.), *Blurred Boundaries: Migration, Ethnicity, Citizenship* (pp. 95–110). Aldershot, UK: Ashgate.

Kalbach, M., & Kalbach, W. (Eds.). (2000). *Perspectives on Ethnicity in Canada.* Toronto: Harcourt.

Kanouté, F., & Lafortune, G. (Eds.). (2011). *Familles québécoises d'origine immigrante.* Montreal: Presses de l'Université de Montréal.

Karnoouh, C. (1998). Logos without Ethos: On Interculturalism and Multiculturalism. *Telos,* 1998(110), 119–33. http://dx.doi.org/10.3817/1298110119.

Kasinitz, P., Mollenkopf, J.H., & Waters, M.C. (Eds.). (2004). *Becoming New Yorkers: Ethnographies of the New Second Generation.* New York: Russell Sage.

Kasinitz, P., Mollenkopf, J.H., & Waters, M.C. (2008). *Inheriting the City: The Children of Immigrants Come of Age.* Cambridge, MA: Harvard University Press.

Kaufmann, E. (2008). Themed Section on Dominant Groups. *Nations and Nationalism, 14*(4), 739–42. http://dx.doi.org/10.1111/j.1469-8129.2008.00370.x.

Kesler, C., & Bloemraad, I. (2010). Does Immigration Erode Social Capital? The Conditional Effects of Immigration-Generated Diversity on Trust, Membership, and Participation across 19 Countries, 1981–2000. *Canadian Journal of Political Science, 43*(2), 319–47. http://dx.doi.org/10.1017/S0008423910000077.

Krulic, J. (1988). L'immigration et l'identité de la France: Mythes et réalités. *Pouvoirs, 47,* 31–43.

Kukathas, C. (2001). Is Feminism Bad for Multiculturalism? *Public Affairs Quarterly*, *15*(2), 83–98.

Kymlicka, W. (1995). *Multicultural Citizenship: A Liberal Theory of Minority Rights*. Oxford: Clarendon.

Kymlicka, W. (1998). *Finding Our Way: Rethinking Ethnocultural Relations in Canada*. New York: Oxford University Press.

Kymlicka, W. (2000). Nation-Building and Minority Rights: Comparing West and East. *Journal of Ethnic and Migration Studies*, *26*(2), 183–212. http://dx.doi.org/10.1080/13691830050022767.

Kymlicka, W. (2003). Multicultural States and Intercultural Citizens. *Theory and Research in Education*, *1*(2), 147–69. http://dx.doi.org/10.1177/1477878503001002001.

Kymlicka, W. (2007a). Ethnocultural Diversity in a Liberal State: Making Sense of the Canadian Model(s). In K. Banting, T.J. Courchene, & F. Leslie Seidle (Eds.), *Belonging? Diversity, Recognition and Shared Citizenship in Canada* (pp. 39–86). Montreal: Institute for Research on Public Policy.

Kymlicka, W. (2007b). *Multicultural Odysseys: Navigating the New International Politics of Diversity*. Oxford: Oxford University Press.

Kymlicka, W. (2010). *The Current State of Multiculturalism in Canada and Research Themes on Canadian Multiculturalism 2008–2010*. Ottawa: Citizenship and Immigration Canada.

Kymlicka, W. (2011). The Evolving Canadian Experiment with Multiculturalism. In G. Bouchard, G. Battaini-Dragoni, C. Saint-Pierre, G. Nootens, & F. Fournier (Eds.), *L'Interculturalisme: Dialogue Québec-Europe*. Actes du Symposium international sur l'interculturalisme, Montreal, 25–27 May. http://www.symposium-interculturalisme.com.

Kymlicka, W. (2012). *Multiculturalism: Success, Failure, and the Future*. Washington, DC: Migration Policy Institute.

Labelle, M. (2000). La politique de la citoyenneté et de l'interculturalisme au Quebec City: défis et enjeux. In H. Greven-Borde & J. Tournon (Eds.), *Les Identités en débat: Intégration ou multiculturalisme* (pp. 269–94). Paris: L'Harmattan.

Labelle, M. (2001). Options et bricolages identitaires in le contexte québécois. In J. Maclure & A.-G. Gagnon (Eds.), *Repères en mutation. Identité et citoyenneté in le Québec contemporain* (pp. 295–320). Montreal: Québec Amérique.

Labelle, M. (2006). Racisme et multiculturalisme/interculturalisme au Canada et au Québec. In M.-H. Parizeau & S. Kash (Eds.), *Néoracisme et dérives génétiques* (pp. 85–119). Quebec City: Presses de l'Université Laval.

Labelle, M. (2008a). De la culture publique commune à la citoyenneté: Ancrages historiques et enjeux actuels. In S. Gervais, D. Karmis, & D. Lamoureux (Eds.),

Du tricoté serré au métissé serré? La culture publique commune au Québec en débats (pp. 19–43). Quebec City: Presses de l'Université Laval.

Labelle, M. (2008b). Les intellectuels québécois face au multiculturalisme: Hétérogénéité des approches et des projets politiques. *Canadian Ethnic Studies, 40*(1–2), 33–56.

Labelle, M. (2010). *Racisme et antiracisme au Québec: Discours et déclinaisons.* Quebec City: Presses de l'Université du Québec.

Labelle, M., & Dionne, X. (2011). *Les Fondements théoriques de l'interculturalisme.* Report presented to the Direction de la gestion de la diversité et de l'intégration sociale, ministère de l'Immigration et des Communautés culturelles, Québec, Montréal, Chaire de recherche en immigration, ethnicité et citoyenneté (CRIEC), UQAM, September.

Labelle, M., Field, A.-M., & Icart, J.-C. (2007). *Les Dimensions d'intégration des immigrants, des minorités ethnoculturelles et des groupes racisés au Québec.* Working document presented at the Consultation Commission on Accommodation Practices Related to Cultural Differences, Montreal, August.

Labelle, M., & Lévy, J.J..(1995). *Ethnicité et enjeux sociaux: Le Québec vu par les leaders de groupes ethnoculturels.* Montreal: Liber.

Labelle, M., & Rocher, F. (2004). Debating Citizenship in Canada: The Collide of Two Nation-Building Projects. In P. Boyer, L. Cardinal, & D. Headon (Eds.), *From Subjects to Citizens: A Hundred Years of Citizenship in Australia and Canada* (pp. 263–86). Ottawa: University of Ottawa Press.

Labelle, M., & Rocher, F. (2006). Pluralisme national et souveraineté au Canada: Luttes symboliques autour des identités collectives. In J. Palard, A.-G. Gagnon, & B. Gagnon (Eds.), *Diversité et identités au Québec et in les régions d'Europe* (pp. 145–68). Brussels/Sainte-Foy, QC: P.I.E.-Peter Lang/ Presses de l'Université Laval.

Labelle, M., Rocher, F., & Antonius, R. (2009a). *Immigration, diversité et sécurité: Les associations arabo-musulmanes face à l'État au Canada et au Québec.* Quebec City: Presses de l'Université du Québec.

Labelle, M., & Rocher, F. (2009b). Immigration, Integration and Citizenship Policies in Canada and Quebec. Tug of War between Competing Societal Projects. In R. Zapata-Barrero (Ed.), *Immigration and Self-Government of Minority Nations* (pp. 57–83). Brussels: P.I.E.-Peter Lang, coll. "Diversitas."

Labelle, M., Rocher, F., & Rocher, G. (1995). Pluriethnicité, citoyenneté et intégration de la souveraineté pour lever les obstacles et les ambiguïtés. *Cahiers de Recherche Sociologique, 25*(25), 213–45. http://dx.doi.org/10.7202/1002297ar.

Labelle, M., & Salée, D. (2001). Immigrant and Minority Representations of Citizenship in Quebec. In T.A. Aleinikoff & D. Klusmeyer (Eds.), *Citizenship Today: Global Perspectives and Practices* (pp. 278–315). Washington, DC: Carnegie Endowment for International Peace.

Laborde, C. (2010). *Français, encore un effort pour être républicains!* Paris: Seuil.

Lamonde, Y. (2010). Rapailler l'homme québécois: Miron et la catharsis du temps (1945–1970). *Les Cahiers des Dix, 64*(64), 47–82. http://dx.doi.org/10.7202/045788ar.

Lamonde, Y. (2013). *The Social History of Ideas in Quebec, 1760–1896.* Vol. 1, trans. P. Aronoff & H. Scott. Montreal/Kingston: McGill-Queen's University Press. Originally published as *Histoire sociale des idées au Québec (1760–1896),* 2000.

Lamont, M. (2002). *La Dignité des travailleurs: Exclusion, race, classe et immigration en France et aux États-Unis.* Paris: Presses de Sciences Po.

Lampron, L.-P. (2009). Convictions religieuses individuelles *versus* égalité entre les sexes: Ambiguïtés du droit québécois et canadien. In P. Eid, P. Bosset, M. Milot, & S. Lebel-Grenier (Eds.), *Appartenances religieuses, appartenance citoyenne: Un équilibre en tension* (pp. 207–59). Quebec City: Presses de l'Université Laval.

Lampron, L.-P. (2010). La gestion du pluralisme religieux au Quebec City: Comment déroger à la Charte canadienne sans déroger à la liberté de religion. *Le Devoir,* 8 March, p. A7.

Lampron, L.-P. (2012). *La Hiérarchie des droits: Convictions religieuses et droits fondamentaux au Canada.* Brussels: P.I.E.-Peter Lang. coll. "Diversitas."

Landry, B. (2010). Multi et interculturalisme. *La Semaine,* 11 March. http://www.vigile.net/Multi-et-interculturalisme.

Laperrière, A. (1985). Les paradoxes de l'intervention culturelle: Une analyse critique des idéologies d'intervention britanniques face aux immigrant-es. *Revue internationale d'action communautaire, 14*(54), 187–98.

Laroche, M. (2011). L'Hydre multiculturaliste. *L'Action Nationale (Toulouse), 101*(8), 45–69.

Larose, J. (1997). Entretien avec Jean Larose. In M. Ancelovici & F. Dupuis-Déri (Eds.), *L'Archipel identitaire: Recueil d'entretiens sur l'identité culturelle* (pp. 69–81). Montreal: Boréal.

Latouche, D. (1990). *Le Bazar: Des anciens Canadiens aux nouveaux Québécois.* Montreal: Boréal.

Laurence, J. (2012). Integrating Europe's Muslims. *International Herald Tribune,* 25 January, p. 8.

Laurence, J.-C., & Perreault, L.-J. (2010). *Guide du Montréal multiple.* Montreal: Boréal.

Laurendeau, A., & Dunton, A.D. (1965). *Preliminary Report of the Royal Commission on Bilingualism and Biculturalism.* Ottawa: Queen's Printer.

Leanza, Y. (2006). L'interprète médiateur communautaire: Entre ambiguïté et polyvalence. *L'Autre: Cliniques, cultures et sociétés, 7*(1), 109–124.

Lecce, S. (2008). *Against Perfectionism: Defending Liberal Neutrality.* Toronto: University of Toronto Press.

Lechner, F.J. (2011). The Travails of Integration in the Netherlands. In G. Bouchard, G. Battaini-Dragoni, C. Saint-Pierre, G. Nootens, & F. Fournier (Eds.), *L'Interculturalisme: Dialogue Québec-Europe*. Actes du Symposium international sur l'interculturalisme. Montreal, 25–27 May. http://www.symposium-interculturalisme.com.

Lecours, A., & Nootens, G. (2007). Comprendre le nationalisme majoritaire. In A.-G. Gagnon, A. Lecours, & G. Nootens (Eds.), *Les Nationalismes majoritaires contemporains: Identité, mémoire, pouvoir* (pp. 19–45). Montreal: Québec Amérique.

Lefebvre, S. (Ed.). (2009). *Le Patrimoine religieux du Québec: Éducation et transmission du sens*. Quebec City: Presses de l'Université Laval.

Legault, G. (Ed.). (2000). *L'Intervention interculturelle*. Montreal/Paris: Gaëtan Morin Éditeur.

Leloup, X. (2011). Détournement d'inquiétude à Montréal. *Le Devoir*, 23 April, p. B5.

Leloup, X., & Apparicio, P. (2010). Montréal, ville plurielle! – Bilan des travaux et perspectives de recherche sur la concentration ethnique. *Nos diverses cités*, 7, 185–94.

Lenoir-Achdjian, A., Arcand, S., Helly, D., Drainville, I., & Vatz Laaroussi, M. (2009). Les difficultés d'insertion en emploi des immigrants du Maghreb au Québec: Une question de perspective. Étude IRPP. Montreal: Institut de recherche en politiques publiques, 15(3).

Leroux, G. (2007a). *Éthique, culture religieuse, dialogue: Arguments pour un programme*. Montreal: Fides.

Leroux, G. (2007b). Un nouveau programme pour l'école québécoise: Éthique et culture religieuse. In M. Venne & M. Fahmy (Eds.), *L'Annuaire du Québec 2008* (pp. 154–60). Montreal: Fides.

Létourneau, J. (2008). La raison de Bouchard et Taylor. *Le Devoir*, 19 June, p. A7.

Leuprecht, P. (2009). Droits humains: Individuels et/ou collectifs? In M. Seymour (Ed.), *La Reconnaissance in tous ses états: Repenser les politiques de pluralisme culturel* (pp. 185–98). Montreal: Québec Amérique.

Leuprecht, P. (2011). Présentation au Symposium sur l'interculturalisme. In G. Bouchard, G. Battaini-Dragoni, C. Saint-Pierre, G. Nootens, & F. Fournier (Eds.), *L'Interculturalisme: Dialogue Québec-Europe*. Actes du Symposium international sur l'interculturalisme, Montreal, 25–27 May. http://www.symposium-interculturalisme.com.

Lévesque, G. (2010). Équité de l'État: Un devoir supérieur du Québec laïque. *L'Action Nationale (Toulouse)*, *100*(8), 38–58.

Li, P.S. (2003). The Place of Immigrants: The Politics of Difference in Territorial and Social Space. *Canadian Ethnic Studies*, *35*(2), 1–13.

Lijphart, A. (1968). *The Politics of Accommodation: Pluralism and Democracy in the Netherlands*. Berkeley: University of California Press.

Lisée, J.-F. (2012). Anglos-Québécois: Quel paradoxe! *L'Actualité*, 15 April, p. 26.

Macedo, S. (1991). *Liberal Virtues: Citizenship, Virtue, and Community in Liberal Constitutionalism*. New York: Oxford University Press.

Maclure, J. (2006). Politique linguistique ou politique d'intégration? La promotion de la langue in une communauté politique libérale, démocratique et pluraliste. In M. Pagé & P. Georgeault (Eds.), *Le Français, langue de la diversité québécoise: Une réflexion pluridisciplinaire* (pp. 153–70). Montreal: Québec Amérique.

Maclure, J., & Taylor, C. (2011). *Secularism and Freedom of Conscience*. Trans. Jane Marie Todd. Cambridge, MA: Harvard University Press. Originally published as *Laïcité et liberté de conscience*, 2010.

Magsino, R.F. (2003). Study of Religions for Citizenship: Why Not? *Canadian Diversity*, *2*(1), 24–7.

Mailloux, L. (2010a). La religion in l'espace public. *Bulletin d'Histoire Politique*, *19*(1), 197–203.

Mailloux, L. (2010b). Un manifeste raciste et antiféministe. *L'Action Nationale (Toulouse)*, *100*(4), 11–15.

Mailloux, L. (2011). Une laïcité menacée. In N. Baillargeon & J.-M. Piotte (Eds.), *Le Québec en quête de laïcité* (pp. 129–43). Montreal: Éditions Écosociété.

Malenfant-Veilleux, A. (2011). L'école québécoise à l'aune du pluralisme normatif: Une analyse philosophique du cours *Éthique et culture religieuse*. Master's thesis, Université du Québec à Trois-Rivières.

Malik, K. (2011). How Multiculturalism Failed. *International Herald Tribune*, 7 July, p. 6.

Margalit, A., & Raz, J. (1990). National self-determination. *Journal of Philosophy*, *87*(9), 439–61. http://dx.doi.org/10.2307/2026968.

Marhraoui, A. (2004). Nationalisme et diversité ethnoculturelle au Québec (1990–2000). Divergences et convergences à propos du projet de citoyenneté québécoise. Doctoral dissertation, Université du Québec à Montréal.

Mathieu, G. (2001). *Qui est Québécois? Synthèse de débat sur la redéfinition de la nation*. Montreal: VLB.

May, S. (2002). Accommodating Multiculturalism and Biculturalism in Aotearoa New Zealand: Implications for Language Education. *Waikato Journal of Education*, *8*, 5–26.

McAndrew, M. (1995). Multiculturalisme canadien et interculturalisme québécois: mythes et réalités. In M. McAndrew, R. Toussaint, & O. Galatanu (Eds.), *Pluralisme et éducation: Politiques et pratiques au Canada, en Europe et in les pays du Sud: L'apport de l'éducation comparée* (pp. 22–51). Montreal/Paris: Publications de la Faculté des sciences de l'éducation/Association francophone d'éducation comparée.

McAndrew, M. (2001). *Immigration et diversité à l'école: Le débat québécois in une perspective comparative.* Montreal: Presses de l'Université de Montréal.

McAndrew, M. (2002). De l'interculturel au civique: 20 ans d'approche québécoise. La redéfinition des politiques publiques de gestion du pluralisme au Canada et au Quebec City: Vers quelle citoyenneté? In L.K. Sosoe (Ed.), *Diversité humaine: Démocratie, multiculturalisme et citoyenneté* (pp. 537–40). Sainte-Foy, QC: Presses de l'Université Laval.

McAndrew, M. (2005). Québec Immigration, Integration and Intercultural Policy: A Critical Assessment. Paper presented at the International Conference on Multiculturalism, Public Policy and Problem Areas in Canada and India, New Delhi, 5–7 December.

McAndrew, M. (2007). Quebec's Interculturalism Policy: An Alternative Vision. In K. Banting, T.J. Courchene, & F.L. Seidle (Eds.), *Belonging? Diversity, Recognition and Shared Citizenship in Canada* (pp. 143–54). Montreal: Institut de recherche en politiques publiques.

McAndrew, M. (2011a). Immigration and Diversity in Quebec's Schools: An Assessment. In S. Gervais, C. Kirkey, & J. Rudy (Eds.), *Quebec Questions: Quebec Studies for the Twenty-First Century* (pp. 287–304). Don Mills, Ontario: Oxford University Press.

McAndrew, M. (2011b). L'éducation au Québec contribue-t-elle au développement d'une société pluraliste et inclusive? Les acquis et les limites. In G. Bouchard, G. Battaini-Dragoni, C. Saint-Pierre, G. Nootens, & F. Fournier (Eds.), *L'Interculturalisme: Dialogue Québec-Europe.* Actes du Symposium international sur l'interculturalisme, Montreal, 25–27 May. http://www.symposium-interculturalisme.com.

McAndrew, M. (2013). *Fragile Majorities and Education: Belgium, Catalonia, Northern Ireland, and Quebec.* Trans. M. O'Hearn. Montreal/Kingston: McGill-Queen's University Press. Original published as *Les Majorités fragiles et l'éducation: Belgique, Catalogne, Irlande du Nord, Québec,* 2010.

McRoberts, K. (1997). *Misconceiving Canada: The Struggle for National Unity.* Toronto: Oxford University Press.

Meer, N., & Modood, T. (2011). How Does Interculturalism Contrast with Multiculturalism? *Journal of Intercultural Studies.* http://www.tandfonline.com/doi/abs/10.1080/07256868.2011.618266.

Mendelsohn, M. (1999). Measuring National Identity and Patterns of Attachment: The Case of Quebec. Paper presented at the conference Ethnicity and Culture: The Reciprocal Influences, Savannah, GA, 18 February.

Meney, L. (2010). *Main basse sur la langue.* Montreal: Liber.

Miller, D. (1995). *On Nationality.* Oxford: Oxford University Press.

Milot, J.-R., & Venditti, R. (2012). Impact de la migration sur l'identité ethnoreligieuse de musulmans d'origine maghrébine. In L. Rousseau (Ed.),

Le Québec après Bouchard-Taylor: Les identités religieuses de l'immigration
(pp. 241–93). Quebec City: Presses de l'Université du Québec.

Milot, M. (2009). L'émergence de la notion de laïcité au Québec: Résistances,
polysémie et instrumentalisation. In P. Eid, P. Bosset, M. Milot, & S. Lebel-
Grenier (Eds.), *Appartenances religieuses, appartenance citoyenne: Un équilibre
en tension* (pp. 29–73). Quebec City: Presses de l'Université Laval.

Modood, T. (2012). *Post-Immigration "Difference" and Integration: The Case of
Muslims in Western Europe*. London: British Academy.

Moïsi, D. (2007). The Clash of Emotions: Fear, Humiliation, Hope, and the
New World Order. *Foreign Affairs, 86*(1), 8–12.

Nadeau, J.-F. (2007). *Bourgault*. Montreal: Lux Éditeur.

Nagle, J., & Clancy, M.-A.C. (2010). *Shared Society or Benign Apartheid?
Understanding Peace-Building in Divided Societies*. Basingstoke, UK: Palgrave
Macmillan. http://dx.doi.org/10.1057/9780230290631.

Noiriel, G. (1988). *Le Creuset français: Histoire de l'immigration, XIXe–XXe siècle.*
Paris: Seuil.

Noiriel, G. (2001). *État, nation et immigration: Vers une histoire du pouvoir.* Paris:
Belin.

Nootens, G. (1999). Vers une théorie libérale de l'identité. In M. Seymour
(Ed.), *Nationalité, citoyenneté et solidarité* (pp. 389–417). Montreal: Liber.

Nootens, G. (2010a). Penser la diversité: Entre monisme et dualisme. In
B. Gagnon (Ed.), *La Diversité québécoise en débat: Bouchard, Taylor et les autres*
(pp. 56–73). Montreal: Québec Amérique.

Nootens, G. (2010b). *Souveraineté démocratique, justice et mondialisation: Essai sur
la démocratie libérale et le cosmopolitisme*. Montreal: Liber.

Nootens, G., & Saint-Pierre, C. (2011). *Atelier sur l'interculturalisme (synthèse).*
Document I-E-4 of the Canada Research Chair in Comparative Dynamics of
Collective Imaginary, Université du Québec à Chicoutimi, January.

Nugent, A. (2006). Demography, National Myths, and Political Origins:
Perceiving Official Multiculturalism in Quebec. *Canadian Ethnic Studies,
38*(3), 21–36.

Okin, S.M. (2005). Multiculturalism and Feminism: No Simple Question, No
Simple Answer. In A. Eisenberg & J. Spinner-Halev (Eds.), *Minorities within
Minorities, Equality, Rights and Diversity* (pp. 67–89). Cambridge: Cambridge
University Press. http://dx.doi.org/10.1017/CBO9780511490224.004

Ouellet, F. (Ed.). (1995). *Les Institutions face aux défis du pluralisme ethnoculturel.*
Quebec City: Institut québécois de recherche sur la culture.

Özkirimli, U. (Ed.). (2003). *Nationalism and Its Futures*. London: Palgrave.
http://dx.doi.org/10.1057/9780230524187

Pagé, M. (2006). Propositions pour une approche dynamique de la situation
du français dans l'espace linguistique québécois. In M. Pagé & P. Georgeault

(Eds.), *Le Français, langue de la diversité québécoise: Une réflexion pluridisciplinaire* (pp. 27–76). Montreal: Québec Amérique.

Pagé, M. (2011). *Le français, langue de cohésion sociale.* Québec: Conseil supérieur de la langue française.

Pagé, M., & Lamarre, P. (2010). *L'intégration linguistique des immigrants au Québec. Étude IRPP,* no. 3. Montréal: Institut de recherche en politiques publiques.

Paillé, M. (1993). *Aménagement linguistique, immigration et population.* Quebec City: Conseil de la langue française.

Paquin, S. (1999). *L'Invention d'un mythe: Le pacte entre deux peuples fondateurs.* Montreal: VLB.

Pathak, P. (2008). The Rise of the Majority. *The Journal,* 2 October. http://www.journal-online.co.uk/article/3222-the_rise_the_majority.

Pelletier, B. (2010). *Une certaine idée du Québec. Parcours d'un fédéraliste. De la réflexion à l'action.* Quebec City: Presses de l'Université Laval.

Pierre, J. (2004). Black Immigrants in the United States and the "Cultural Narratives" of Ethnicity. *Identities: Global Studies in Culture and Power, 11*(2), 141–70. http://dx.doi.org/10.1080/10702890490451929.

Pietrantonio, L. (2000). Une dissymétrie sociale: Rapports sociaux majoritaires/minoritaires. *Bastidiana. Racisme et relations raciales, 29–30,* 151–176.

Pietrantonio, L. (2002). Who Is We? An Exploratory Study of the Notion of "the Majority" and Cultural Policy. *Canadian Ethnic Studies, 34*(3), 142–56.

Pietrantonio, L., Juteau, D., & McAndrew, M. (1996). Multiculturalisme ou intégration: Un faux débat. In K. Fall, R. Hadj-Moussa, & D. Simeoni (Eds.), *Les Convergences culturelles in les sociétés pluriethniques* (pp. 147–58). Quebec City: Presses de l'Université du Québec.

Plourde, M. (Ed.). (2000). *Le Français au Québec: 400 ans d'histoire et de vie.* Quebec City/Montreal: Conseil de la langue française/Fides.

Poisson, M.-M. (2011). Arguments contre une propagande. In N. Baillargeon & J.-M. Piotte (Eds.), *Le Québec en quête de laïcité* (pp. 109–17). Montreal: Éditions Écosociété.

Poole, R. (1999). *Nation and Identity.* London: Routledge. http://dx.doi.org/10.4324/9780203209158.

Porcher, L. (1981). *The Education of the Children of Migrant Workers in Europe: Interculturalism and Teacher Training.* Strasbourg: Council for Cultural Co-operation, School Education Division, Council of Europe.

Potvin, M. (2004). Racisme et discrimination au Quebec City: Réflexion critique et prospective sur la recherche. In J. Renaud, A. Germain, & X. Leloup (Eds.), *Racisme et Discrimination: Permanence et résurgence d'un phénomène inavouable* (pp. 171–95). Quebec City: Presses de l'Université Laval.

Potvin, M. (2005). Discours publics et discriminations au Québec. *Les Cahiers du 27 juin, 2*(2), 47–52.

Proulx, J.-P. (1999). *Laïcité et Religions: Perspective nouvelle pour l'école québécoise.*
    Quebec City: Gouvernement du Québec, Ministre de l'Éducation.
Putnam, R.D. (2007). *E Pluribus Unum*: Diversity and Community in the Twenty-
    First Century (2006 Johan Skytte Prize Lecture). *Scandinavian Political Studies,*
    30(2), 137–74. http://dx.doi.org/10.1111/j.1467-9477.2007.00176.x.
Quebec. Institut de la statistique du québec (ISQ). (2008a). *État du marché*
    du travail au Québec: Le point en 2007. Quebec City: Gouvernement du '
    Québec.
Quebec. Institut de la statistique du québec (ISQ). (2008b). Projections dé-
    mographiques 2006–2031 pour le Grand Montréal. *Perspective Grand Montréal,*
    no. 13. Quebec City: Gouvernement du Québec.
Quebec. Ministère de l'Éducation, du Loisir et du Sport (MELS). (2009).
    Programme d'enseignement des langues d'origine (PELO). Quebec City:
    Gouvernement du Québec.
Quebec. Ministère des Communautés culturelles et de l'immigration (MCCI).
    (1981). *Quebecers Each and Every One: The Government of Québec's Plan of Action*
    for Cultural Communities. Quebec City: Gouvernement du Québec.
Quebec. Ministère des Communautés culturelles et de l'immigration (MCCI).
    (1990a). *Let's Build Québec Together: Vision, a Policy Statement on Immigration*
    and Integration. Direction des communications. Quebec City: Gouvernement
    du Québec.
Quebec. Ministère des Communautés culturelles et de l'immigration (MCCI).
    (1990b). *L'intégration des immigrants et des Québécois des communautés culturelles:*
    Document de réflexion et d'orientation. Direction des communications. Quebec
    City: Gouvernement du Québec.
Quebec. Ministère des Relations avec les citoyens et de l'Immigration (MRCI).
    (2000). *La Citoyenneté québécoise: Document de consultation pour le Forum national*
    sur la citoyenneté et l'intégration. Montreal: Direction des affaires publiques et
    des communications.
Quebec. Ministère des Relations avec les citoyens et de l'Immigration (MRCI).
    (2004). *Shared Values, Common Interests to Ensure the Full Participation of*
    Quebecers from Cultural Communities in the Development of Québec. Montreal:
    Direction des affaires publiques et des communications.
Quebec. Ministry of State for Cultural Development. (1978). *A Cultural*
    Development Policy for Quebec. Quebec City: Éditeur officiel du Québec.
Quérin, J. (2009). *Le Cours éthique et culture religieuse: Transmission de connaissances*
    ou endoctrinement? Montreal: Institut de recherche sur le Québec.
Quérin, J. (2011). Djemila Benhabib: Les soldats d'Allah à l'assaut de l'Occident.
    L'Action Nationale (Toulouse), 101(9–10), 245–9.
Raffestin, C., & Bresso, M. (1979). *Travail, espace, pouvoir.* Lausanne: Éditions
    L'Âge d'Homme.

Raffestin, C., & Bresso, M. (1982). Tradition, modernité, territorialité. *Cahiers de Geographie de Quebec, 26*(68), 185–98. http://dx.doi.org/10.7202/021557ar.

Rawls, J. (1971). *A Theory of Justice.* Cambridge, MA: Belknap.

Rawls, J. (1993). *Political Liberalism.* New York, Columbia University Press.

Raz, J. (1988). *The Morality of Freedom.* Oxford: Clarendon. http://dx.doi.org/10.1093/0198248075.001.0001.

Reichhold, S. (2011). Où en sommes-nous après 20 ans d'interculturalisme au Québec? In G. Bouchard, G. Battaini-Dragoni, C. Saint-Pierre, G. Nootens, & F. Fournier (Eds.), *L'Interculturalisme: Dialogue Québec-Europe.* Actes du Symposium international sur l'interculturalisme, Montreal, 25–27 May. http://www.symposium-interculturalisme.com.

Reitz, J.G., Breton, R., Dion, K.K., Dion, K.L., Phan, M.B., & Banerjee, R. (2009). *Multiculturalism and Social Cohesion: Potentials and Challenges of Diversity.* Dordrecht: Springer. http://dx.doi.org/10.1007/978-1-4020- 9958-8.

Renaud, J., Germain, A., & Leloup, X. (Eds.). (2004). *Racisme et Discrimination: Permanence et résurgence d'un phénomène inavouable.* Quebec City: Presses de l'Université Laval.

Rocher, F. (2008). Fédéralisme canadien et culture(s) publique(s) com-mune(s): Le casse-tête du pluralisme identitaire. In S. Gervais, D. Karmis, & D. Lamoureux (Eds.), *Du tricoté serré au métissé serré? La culture publique commune au Québec en débats* (pp. 141–63). Quebec City: Presses de l'Université Laval.

Rocher, F., & Labelle, M. (2010). L'interculturalisme comme modèle d'aménagement de la diversité: Compréhension et incompréhension in l'espace public québécois. In B. Gagnon (Ed.), *La Diversité québécoise en débat: Bouchard, Taylor et les autres* (pp. 179–203). Montreal: Québec Amérique.

Rocher, F., Labelle, M., Field, A.-M., & Icart, J.-C. (2007). *Le Concept d'interculturalisme en contexte québécois: Généalogie d'un néologisme.* Research report no. 3, Consultation Commission on Accommodation Practices Related to Cultural Differences. http://www.accommodements-quebec.ca/ documentation/rapports/rapport-3-rocher-francois.pdf.

Rocher, F., Rocher, G., & Labelle, M. (1995). Pluriethnicité, citoyenneté et inté-gration: De la souveraineté pour lever les obstacles et les ambiguïtés. *Cahiers de Recherche Sociologique, 25,* 213–45.

Rocher, G. (1973). Les conditions d'une francophonie nord-américaine originale. In Rocher, *Le Québec en mutation* (pp. 89–108). Montreal: Éditions Hurtubise HMH.

Rocher, G. (2000). Droits fondamentaux, citoyens minoritaires, citoyens majori-taires. In M. Coutu, P. Bosset, C. Gendreau, & D. Villeneuve (Eds.), *Droits fondamentaux et citoyenneté: Une citoyenneté fragmentée, limitée, illusoire?* (pp. 23–42). Montreal: Éditions Thémis.

Rocher, G. (2006). Les origines et les raisons de la Charte de la langue française. In M. Venne & M. Fahmy (Eds.), *L'Annuaire du Québec 2007: Le Québec, en panne ou en marche?* (pp. 217–22). Montreal: Fides.

Rose, M. (2009). *Our Shared Europe: Swapping Treasures, Sharing Losses, Celebrating Futures.* London: British Council.

Rousseau, G. (2006). *La Nation à l'épreuve de l'immigration: Le cas du Canada, du Québec et de la France.* Quebec City: Éditions du Québécois.

Rousseau, L. (2011). Le cours Éthique et culture religieuse: De sa pertinence in un État laïque. In N. Baillargeon & J.-M. Piotte (Eds.), *Le Québec en quête de laïcité* (pp. 99–108). Montreal: Éditions Écosociété.

Rousseau, L. (Ed.). (2012). *Le Québec après Bouchard-Taylor: Les identités religieuses de l'immigration.* Quebec City: Presses de l'Université du Québec.

Ruiz, R. (2010). English Language Planning and Transethnification in the USA. *Télescope, 16*(3), 96–112. Published in French as *L'aménagement linguistique de l'anglais et transethnification aux États-Unis.*

Rumbaut, R.G. (1997). Paradoxes (and Orthodoxies) of Assimilation. *Sociological Perspectives, 40*(3), 483–511. http://dx.doi.org/10.2307/1389453.

Said, E.W. (1994). *The Politics of Dispossession: The Struggle for Palestinian Self-Determination, 1969–1994.* New York: Pantheon.

Salée, D. (2001). De l'avenir de l'identité nationale québécoise. In J. Maclure & A.G. Gagnon (Eds.), *Repères en mutation: Identité et citoyenneté in le Québec contemporain* (pp. 133–64). Montreal: Québec Amérique.

Salée, D. (2007). "The Quebec State and the Management of Ethnocultural Diversity: Perspectives on an Ambiguous Record." In K. Banting, T. J. Courchene. & F. Leslie Seidle (Eds.), *Belonging? Diversity, Recognition and Shared Citizenship in Canada* (pp. 105–42). Montreal: Institut de recherche en politiques publiques.

Salée, D. (2010). Penser l'aménagement de la diversité ethnoculturelle au Québec: mythes, limites et possibles de l'interculturalisme. *Politique et Sociétés, 29*(1), 145–180. http://dx.doi.org/10.7202/039959ar

Sandel, M.J. (2010). *Justice: What's the Right Thing to Do?* New York: Farrar, Straus and Giroux.

Savidan, P. (2009). *Le Multiculturalisme.* 1st ed. Paris: Presses universitaires de France.

Schnapper, D. (2003). *La Communauté des citoyens: Sur l'idée moderne de nation.* Paris: Gallimard.

Schnapper, D. (2007). *Qu'est-ce que l'intégration?* Paris: Gallimard.

Segalen, M. (Ed.). (1989). *L'Autre et le Semblable: Regards sur l'ethnologie des sociétés contemporaines.* Paris: Presses du CNRS.

Sercia, P. (2009). Modèles d'intégration sociale d'élèves fréquentant les écoles ethnoreligieuses au Québec. In P. Eid, P. Bosset, M. Milot, & S. Lebel-Grenier

(Eds.), *Appartenances religieuses, appartenance citoyenne: Un équilibre en tension* (pp. 261–81). Quebec City: Presses de l'Université Laval.

Sewell, W.H., Jr., (1985). Ideologies and Social Revolutions: Reflections on the French Case. *Journal of Modern History, 57*(1), 57–85. http://dx.doi.org/10.1086/242777.

Seymour, M. (1999). *La Nation en question.* Montreal: L'Hexagone.

Seymour, M. (2001). *Le Pari de la démesure: L'intransigeance canadienne face au Québec.* Montreal: L'Hexagone.

Seymour, M. (2008). *De la tolérance à la reconnaissance: Une théorie libérale des droits collectifs.* Montreal: Boréal.

Seymour, M., & Laforest, G. (Eds.). (2011). *Le Fédéralisme multinational: Un modèle viable?* Brussels: P.I.E.-Peter Lang, coll. "Diversitas."

Shachar, A. (2001). *Multicultural Jurisdictions: Cultural Differences and Women's Rights.* Cambridge: Cambridge University Press. http://dx.doi.org/10.1017/CBO9780511490330.

Shiose, Y., & Fontaine, L. (1995). La Construction des figures de l'"Autre": Les communautés culturelles au Québec. *Canadian Review of Sociology and Anthropology/La Revue Canadienne de Sociologie et d'Anthropologie, 32*(1), 91–110. http://dx.doi.org/10.1111/j.1755-618X.1995.tb00836.x.

Sides, J., & Citrin, J. (2007). European Opinion about Immigration: The Role of Identities, Interests and Information. *British Journal of Political Science, 37*(03), 477–504. http://dx.doi.org/10.1017/S0007123407000257.

Silver, A.I. (1997). *The French-Canadian Idea of Confederation, 1864–1900.* 2nd ed. Toronto: University of Toronto Press.

Singh, P. (2011). We-ness and Welfare: A Longitudinal Analysis of Social Development in Kerala, India. *World Development, 39*(2), 282–93. http://dx.doi.org/10.1016/j.worlddev.2009.11.025.

Smith, A.D. (1991). *National Identity.* Reno: University of Nevada Press.

Spencer, V. (2008). Language, History and the Nation: An Historical Approach to Evaluating Language and Cultural Claims. *Nations and Nationalism, 14*(2), 241–59. http://dx.doi.org/10.1111/j.1469-8129.2008.00334.x.

Stoeckel, F. (2012). The Effect of Transnational Interactions on Attachment to Europe: New Evidence from a Panel Survey. Paper presented at the Council for European Studies (CES) Meeting, Boston, 22–24 March.

Subramanian, N. (2013). Myths of the Nation, Cultural Recognition and Personal Law in India. In G. Bouchard (Ed.), *National Myths: Constructed Pasts, Contested Presents* (pp. 259–75). New York: Routledge.

Symons, G. (2002). The State and Ethnic Diversity: Structural and Discursive Change in Quebec's Ministère de l'Immigration. *Canadian Ethnic Studies, 34*(3), 28–46.

Tamir, Y. (1993). *Liberal Nationalism*. Princeton: Princeton University Press.

Taylor, C. (1988). Le juste et le bien. *Revue de Metaphysique et de Morale, 93*(1), 33–56.

Taylor, C. (1989). Cross-Purpose: The Liberal-Communitarian Debate. In N.L. Rosenblum (Ed.), *Liberalism and the Moral Life* (pp. 159–82). Cambridge, MA: Harvard University Press.

Taylor, C. (1992). The Politics of Recognition. In A. Gutmann (Ed.), *Multiculturalism* (pp. 25–73). Princeton: Princeton University Press.

Taylor, C. (2003). Dialogue avec Charles Taylor. *Les Cahiers du 27 juin, 1*(1), 8–11.

Taylor, C. (2012). Interculturalism or multiculturalism? *Philosophy & Social Criticism, 38*(4-5), 413–23. http://dx.doi.org/10.1177/0191453711435656.

Tevanian, P. (2007). *La République du mépris: Les métamorphoses du racisme in la France des années Sarkozy*. Paris: La Découverte.

Thériault, J.-Y. (2010). Entre républicanisme et multiculturalisme: La commission Bouchard-Taylor, une synthèse ratée. In B. Gagnon (Ed.), *La Diversité québécoise en débat: Bouchard, Taylor et les autres* (pp. 143–55). Montreal: Québec Amérique.

Thomas, P. (2011). *Youth, Multiculturalism and Community Cohesion*. New York: Palgrave Macmillan. http://dx.doi.org/10.1057/9780230302242.

Todorov, T. (2008). *La Peur des barbares: Au-delà du choc des civilisations*. Paris: Robert Laffont.

Tolley, E. (2004). National Identity and the "Canadian Way": Values, Connections and Culture. *Canadian Diversity, 3*(2), 11–15.

Toussaint, P. (Ed.). (2010). *La Diversité ethnoculturelle en éducation: Enjeux et défis pour l'école québécoise*. Quebec City: Presses de l'Université du Québec.

Trevor-Roper, H. (1992). The Invention of Tradition: The Highland Tradition of Scotland. In E. Hobsbawm & T. Ranger (Eds.), *The Invention of Tradition* (pp. 15–42). Cambridge: Cambridge University Press.

Tully, J. (1995). *Strange Multiplicity: Constitutionalism in an Age of Diversity*. Cambridge: Cambridge University Press. http://dx.doi.org/10.1017/CBO9781139170888.

Turp, D. (2005). *Nous, peuple du Québec: Un projet de Constitution du Québec*. Quebec City: Éditions du Québécois.

Vachon, R. (1986). Les grandes lignes de notre Institut. *Interculture, 19*(2), 3–32.

Vachon, R. (1997). Le mythe émergent du pluralisme et de l'interculturalisme de la réalité. Address to Séminaire I: Pluralisme et Société, Discours alternatifs à la culture dominante, Institut Interculturel de Montréal, Montreal, 15 February.

Vatz-Laaroussi, M. (2009). *Mobilité, réseaux et résilience: Le cas des familles immigrantes et réfugiées au Québec*. Quebec City: Presses de l'Université du Québec.

Waters, M.C. (1990). *Ethnic Options: Choosing Identities in America.* Berkeley: University of California Press.

Waters, M.C. (2000). *Black Identities: West Indian Immigrant Dreams and American Realities.* Cambridge, MA: Harvard University Press.

Weinfeld, M., & Eaton, W.W. (1979). *The Jewish Community of Montreal: Survey Report.* Montreal: Canadian Jewish Congress and Allied Jewish Community Services.

Weinstock, D. (1995). Le nationalisme civique et le concept de la culture politique commune. In F. Blais, G. Laforest, & D. Lamoureux (Eds.), *Libéralismes et Nationalismes: Philosophie et politique* (pp. 95–115). Quebec City: Presses de l'Université Laval.

Weinstock, D. (2003). La neutralité de l'État en matière culturelle est-elle possible? In R. Le Coadic (Ed.), *Identités et Démocratie. Diversité culturelle et mondialisation. Repenser la démocratie* (pp. 365–80). Rennes: Presses universitaires de Rennes.

Weinstock, D. (2009). Frayed Federation: Challenges to Canadian Unity in the Wake of Trudeau's Failed Nation-Building Project. In J. E. Fossom, J. Poirier, & P. Magnette (Eds.), *The Ties That Bind: Accommodating Diversity in Canada and the European Union* (pp. 279–99). Brussels: P.I.E.-Peter Lang.

Weinstock, D. (2011). Laïcité ouverte ou laïcité stricte? Une critique de la Déclaration pour un Québec laïque et pluraliste. In N. Baillargeon & J.-M. Piotte (Eds.), *Le Québec en quête de laïcité* (pp. 32–42). Montreal: Éditions Écosociété.

Wieviorka, M. (2005). *La Différence. Identités culturelles. Enjeux, débats et politiques.* La Tour-d'Aigues. France: Éditions de l'Aube.

Wimmer, A. (2002). *Nationalist Exclusion and Ethnic Conflict: Shadows of Modernity.* Cambridge: Cambridge University Press. http://dx.doi.org/10.1017/CBO9780511490415.

Wimmer, A. (2013). *Ethnic Boundary Making: Institutions, Power, Networks.* New York: Oxford University Press.

Winter, E. (2010). Ni communauté, ni société: Penser la société pluraliste au-delà des binaires. *Swiss Journal of Sociology, 36*(3), 451–69.

Winter, E. (2011). *Us, Them, and Others: Pluralism and National Identity in Diverse Societies.* Toronto: University of Toronto Press.

Wirth, L. (1945). The Problem of Minority Groups. In R. Linton (Ed.), *The Science of Man in the World Crisis* (pp. 347–72). New York: Columbia University Press.

Yiftachel, O. (1999). Ethnocracy: The Politics of Judaizing Israel/Palestine. *Constellations (Oxford, England), 6*(3), 364–90. http://dx.doi.org/10.1111/1467-8675.00151.

Young, I.M. (1990). *Justice and the Politics of Difference.* Princeton: Princeton University Press.

Index